SCREEN ACTING

While not everyone would agree with Alfred Hitchcock's notorious remark that 'actors are cattle', there is little understanding of the work film actors do. Yet audiences' enthusiasm for, or dislike of, actors and their style of performance is a crucial part of the film-going experience. *Screen Acting* discusses the development of film acting, from the stylisation of the silent era, through the naturalism of Lee Strasberg's 'Method', to Mike Leigh's use of improvisation.

The contributors to this innovative volume explore the philosophies which have influenced acting in the movies and analyse the styles and techniques of individual filmmakers and performers, including Bette Davis, James Mason, Susan Sarandon and Morgan Freeman. There are also interviews with working actors: Ian Richardson discusses the relationship between theatre, film and television acting; Claire Rushbrook and Ron Cook discuss their work with Mike Leigh, and Helen Shaver discusses her work with the critic Susan Knobloch.

Exploring the relationship between script and performance, and drawing out the individual elements of performance, such as the awareness of the frame, and the use of voice and physique to embody a character, *Screen Acting* reveals the centrality of the actor's performance to a film's impact and offers new directions for the study of performance on film.

Alan Lovell is Senior Lecturer in Media Studies at Staffordshire University. **Peter Krämer** lectures in Film Studies at the University of East Anglia.

SCREEN ACTING

Edited by Alan Lovell and Peter Krämer

London and New York

First published 1999
by Routledge
11 New Fetter Lane, London EC4P 4EE

Simultaneously published in the USA and Canada
by Routledge
29 West 35th Street, New York, NY 10001

Routledge is an imprint of the Taylor & Francis Group

Typeset in Garamond by Keystroke, Jacaranda Lodge, Wolverhampton
Printed and bound in Great Britain by T.J. International Ltd, Padstow, Cornwall

British Library Cataloguing in Publication Data
A catalogue record for this book is available from the British Library

Library of Congress Cataloging in Publication Data
Screen acting / edited by Alan Lovell and Peter Krämer.
p.   cm.
Includes bibliographical references and index.
1. Motion picture acting. I. Lovell, Alan. II. Krämer, Peter,
1961– .
PN1995.9.A26S36 1999
791.43′028—dc21   99-24317

ISBN 0-415-18293-X (hbk)
ISBN 0-415-18294-8 (pbk)

CONTENTS

Figures   vii
Contributors   viii

1 Introduction   1
   PETER KRÄMER AND ALAN LOVELL

2 Acting in silent film: Which legacy of the theatre?   10
   DAVID MAYER

3 Crafting film performances: Acting in the Hollywood
   studio era   31
   CYNTHIA BARON

4 Bette Davis: Malevolence in motion   46
   MARTIN SHINGLER

5 A star performs: Mr March, Mr Mason and Mr Maine   59
   ROBERTA E. PEARSON

6 Lee Strasberg's paradox of the actor   75
   SHARON MARIE CARNICKE

7 Susan Sarandon: In praise of older women   88
   ALAN LOVELL

8 Helen Shaver: Resistance through artistry   106
   SUSAN KNOBLOCH

9 Actors and the sound gang   126
   GIANLUCA SERGI

CONTENTS

10 *Secrets and Lies*: Acting for Mike Leigh   138
    PAUL McDONALD

11 An interview with Ian Richardson: Making friends with
    the camera   152
    CAROLE ZUCKER

12 Bibliographical notes   165
    PETER KRÄMER

    Bibliography   171
    Index   180

FIGURES

4.1   The framing and mirroring of Bette Davis in *Of Human
         Bondage* (1934)   51
5.1a, b Two Norman Maines: Fredric March in the 1937 version
         of *A Star Is Born* and James Mason in the 1954 remake   60
7.1   A defining image: Susan Sarandon in *Atlantic City* (1980)   90
7.2   Using the body for comic effect: Susan Sarandon with
         Tim Robbins in *Bull Durham* (1988)   97
8.1a–c   Helen Shaver moves on a bodily axis made prominent in
         the frame   111
8.2a–d   Shaver physicalizes dialogue within a frame's tight limits   112
8.3a, b Shaver's movements stress a background character
         otherwise unemphasized in a shot   116
8.4a, b Shaver reprises a gesture in consecutive shots of different
         lengths, feeding the editing   118
8.5   Shaver and Fairuza Balk's props play up their characters'
         incendiary mother–daughter bond   120
8.6   Shaver celebrates an all girls paradise with Neve
         Campbell, Rachel True, and a Connie Francis-only
         jukebox   121
10.1a, b Claire Rushbrook with Phyllis Logan and Lee Ross; and
         with Marianne Jean Baptiste, both from *Secrets and Lies*
         (1996)   145
11.1   Acting cruel: Ian Richardson as Francis Urquhart in
         House of Cards (1990)   160

CONTRIBUTORS

Cynthia Baron is Assistant Professor in the Film Studies Program at Bowling Green State University. She is currently working on a study of the institutions and approaches that helped shape performances in the studio era and is preparing an introductory text on analysing acting in film and television.

Sharon Marie Carnicke is Associate Professor and Associate Dean of the School of Theatre, University of Southern California. She has published numerous articles on Stanislavsky in *Theatre Journal*, *The Drama Review*, and *Theatre Three*. She was keynote speaker for the Moscow Art Theatre's international symposium in 1990. Her work with Lee Strasberg began in the late 1970s when she served as assistant director and interpreter for a Russian director at the Actors' Studio in New York. She has directed plays in New York, Los Angeles, and Moscow. She is the author of *The Theatrical Instinct* (Peter Lang 1989), a study of the director and playwright, Nicolai Evreinov, and *Stanislavsky in Focus* (Harwood Academic Press 1998), which examines the complex impact of Stanislavsky's System on actor training in the United States and in Russia.

Susan Knobloch received her PhD in Film and Television Critical Studies from the University of California, Los Angeles in 1998. Her dissertation is a study of the formal and ideological intersections between rock music and film. She is currently researching acting, gender, and sexuality in post-1970s Hollywood.

Peter Krämer lectures in Film Studies at the University of East Anglia. He has written essays on Buster Keaton, Audrey Hepburn, and the popular appeal of Hollywood cinema for a variety of books and publications including *The Oxford Guide to Film Studies* (Oxford University Press 1998) and *Contemporary Hollywood Cinema* (Routledge 1998).

Alan Lovell lectures in Media Studies at Staffordshire University. He is the author of *Anarchist Cinema* (Peace News 1962); *Don Siegel: American Cinema* (British Film Institute 1975); and co-author of *Studies in Documentary*

(Secker & Warburg 1972). He has also written and directed short films and television documentaries including *Star*, *Traces Left* and *The Black and White Pirate Show*.

Paul McDonald is Senior Lecturer in Film and Television, in the Department of Drama, Roehampton Institute. He has published on screen performance in *The Oxford Guide to Film Studies* (Oxford University Press 1998); *Semiotics of the Media: State of the Art, Projects and Perspectives* (Mouton de Gruyter 1994); and *Sexing the Groove: Popular Music and Gender* (Routledge 1997). He recently contributed a supplementary chapter to the second edition of Richard Dyer's *Stars* (British Film Institute 1998). He previously trained as a professional actor at the Royal Academy of Dramatic Art.

David Mayer is Emeritus Professor of Drama Research at the University of Manchester. His books include *Harlequin in His Element: English Pantomime, 1806–1836* (Harvard University Press 1969); *Western Popular Theatre* (with Kenneth Richards; Methuen 1977) *Henry Irving and 'The Bells', Henry Irving's Personal Text and Score* (University of Manchester Press 1980), *Four Bars of 'Agit', Music for Victorian and Edwardian Melodrama* (The Theatre Museum and Samuel French 1983); *Playing out the Empire: Ben Hur and Other Toga Plays and Films* (Oxford University Press 1994). His essays on nineteenth- and early twentieth-century popular stage entertainments and their links with early film have appeared in a variety of books and journals.

Roberta E. Pearson is Senior Lecturer in the School of Journalism, Media and Cultural Studies at Cardiff University. She is the author of *Eloquent Gestures: The Transformation of Performance Style in the Griffith Biograph Films* (University of California Press 1992) as well as the author, co-author, and co-editor of numerous books, edited collections, and articles about the cinema.

Gianluca Sergi teaches Media Studies at Staffordshire University. His main research interest is film sound and he has published several articles on this subject. He is currently working on a PhD thesis on the development of sound in Hollywood since the arrival of Dolby.

Martin Shingler teaches Media Studies at Staffordshire University where he covers both film and radio. His PhD was a study of Bette Davis. He is the co-author of the recently published introduction to radio entitled *On Air* (Edward Arnold 1998).

Carole Zucker is a Professor in the Department of Cinema at Concordia University in Montreal. She studied acting at The HB Studios and The Neighborhood Playhouse in New York City. She is the author of *The Idea of the Image: Josef Sternberg's Dietrich Films* (Fairleigh Dickson University Press 1988); *Making Visible the Invisible: an Anthology of Original Essays on Film*

Acting (Scarecrow 1990); and *Figures of Light: Actors and Directors Illuminate the Art of Film Acting* (Plenum 1995). She has contributed to journals such as *Film Quarterly*, *Literature/Film Quarterly*, *Cinetracts*, and *Postscript*. Her book of interviews with British and Irish actors will be published in 1999.

1

INTRODUCTION

Peter Krämer and Alan Lovell

Recently there has been a revival of interest in film acting. Books like James Naremore's *Acting in the Cinema* have provided thoughtful and detailed analyses of actors' performances. Collections of interviews, such as Carole Zucker's *Figures of Light* have encouraged film actors to discuss their work in an illuminating way.[1] However, it's still a limited and relatively undeveloped area of film scholarship. Our collection of essays is designed to support development of the area.[2]

The starting point for our work is a concern with the basics of film acting. What do actors do to create a performance? What are their specific skills? What are the general ideas which inform the use of those skills? We have organized the book so that the concern is expressed at two different levels. At one level there are studies of, or interviews with, individual actors like Bette Davis, Fredric March, James Mason, Ian Richardson, Susan Sarandon, and Helen Shaver. At the other level, there are accounts of the general context within which actors have worked. These accounts include discussions of the relationship between early film and theatre acting, the work of studio drama coaches, the adaptability of 'the Method' for cinema acting, the importance of the voice, and the distinctive ways in which directors use actors.

Taking advantage of the range and depth of recent scholarship on American cinema, this collection focuses primarily on Hollywood acting. Although the essays do not constitute a systematic history of Hollywood film acting, they do cover the major developments within it, from the very beginnings up to the present day. In doing so our contributors establish links with traditions in British acting, in particular its influence on early American cinema and with acting in other media like theatre and television. In fact a strong theme running through this collection is the intimate relationship between theatre and film acting with performers, teachers, and ideas moving freely between the two media. Not coincidentally, several of our contributors have a background in Theatre Studies, where acting has been a much more central preoccupation than it has been in Film Studies.

Why has acting been neglected by academic film scholarship? After all, it was an important concern for early theorists of the cinema like Vsevolod

1

Pudovkin, Sergei Eisenstein, Lev Kuleshov, Bela Balazs, and Rudolf Arnheim. The main reason for its more recent neglect was the way Film Studies as an academic discipline grew out of the second wave of theorizing about the cinema. That theorizing was powerfully stimulated by writings of the *Cahiers du Cinéma* critics in the 1950s and 1960s. From these writings, Film Studies took authorship as a central concern.[3] Authorship made the director the key figure in film making. As a consequence, the creation of a film became increasingly regarded as an individual rather than a collective process. The contributions of actors, along with cinematographers, editors, sound recordists, production designers, etc. was, if acknowledged at all, subordinated to the director's genius.

As part of the discussion of authorship, *mise-en-scène* came to be accepted as a basic tool for the analysis of films. It's a tool which isn't particularly amenable to a discussion of film acting. In so far as actors play a part in it, they are one of the elements, along with setting, lighting and costume, which are 'put into the scene'. This encourages actors to be regarded as visual objects. This can easily lead to their being regarded as puppets of the director. However Hitchcock meant it, his remark that 'actors are cattle' captures this view exactly. The work of actors is further neglected because of the way the notion of *mise-en-scène* either excludes or downplays sound. By principally regarding actors as visual objects, the use of the voice – a key part of acting – is neglected.

Mise-en-scène isn't a precisely defined analytical tool. It has a looseness which comes from its place in the development of film criticism since the term was appropriated from the theatre by French critics in the 1950s. It emerged out of the important struggle to free film from literature, to direct serious attention to a film's visual quality. In the struggle to demonstrate how important the visuals are in a film, *mise-en-scène* was often equated with the 'writing' of a film. It is through the deployment of *mise-en-scène* that a film is created. The enemy, of course, in this struggle was the script because it was equated with literature. Put crudely, a film wasn't written with words but with images.

The struggle to free film from literature needed to be fought but it had some unfortunate consequences for film criticism. The primary one was the neglect of the script. Sporadic efforts have been made to direct attention to the work of screenwriters but there has been no serious analysis of scripts in terms of their narrative construction, the way characters are created, or the kind of dialogue that has been written.[4] One result of this is that the discussion of scripts has come to be dominated by the simplistic accounts offered by Sid Field, Robert McKee, and other scriptwriting gurus.

This neglect of the script has impoverished film scholarship generally and has had a particularly important effect on explorations of acting. A number of contributions in this book deal with the relationship between actor and script. It's clear from these that there are different kinds of relationship, depending on such factors as acting philosophies or the approaches of particular directors and writers. Actors trained by studio drama coaches of the 1930s and 1940s were likely to be more respectful of the script than Method actors: the intimate contribution to the work of creating a script encourages the actors in Mike Leigh's films to have a greater involvement with it than is the case in films by other directors. But however different the relationship is, *there always is one*. To understand acting properly, you need to know not only about the way actors work but also about the nature of the materials they are working with.

A proper understanding of the nature of scripts is important at another, more general, level. Acting doesn't develop in a self-enclosed way. It develops in a close relationship with the way scripts are written. Stanislavsky's approach was very much a response to the new naturalistic plays of writers like Chekhov. 'The Method' was a response to the social psychological drama which was written for the American theatre and cinema in the 1930s and 1940s. The relationship isn't, of course, one way: writers are also encouraged to develop their writing by the possibilities opened up by new approaches to acting.[5]

The preoccupation with authorship and *mise-en-scène* in Film Studies undoubtedly limited the interest in acting. But from the mid-1970s, this preoccupation was subsumed into a broader semiological/psychoanalytic position. This development encouraged some interest in acting but its principal themes never made the interest anything but marginal.

Those themes might be broadly characterized as the specificity of the cinema and its ideological effects. Discussion of the specificity of the cinema proceeded from the modernist assumption that all art forms have their specificities. The cinema was taken to be essentially a visual medium. If it was close to any of the other arts, it was painting. Inevitably acting is of limited importance when such a comparison is made. If the assumption of art forms having distinct identities hadn't been accepted, if the cinema had been regarded as a hybrid form, as much a dramatic medium as a visual one, with relations to theatre as well as painting, acting would have assumed a more important place.

The problems this creates can be seen in Laura Mulvey's extremely influential article, 'Visual Pleasure and Narrative Cinema'.[6] For Mulvey, the cinema is a visual medium, so voyeurism becomes a key concept. The psychic mechanisms of mainstream cinema make actresses objects to look at. Mulvey doesn't recognize that they have to use their faces, bodies, and voices expressively and that to do this demands intelligence and perception. The unintended consequence of this approach is that the considerable skills and abilities of a wide range of actresses, from Bette Davis to Susan Sarandon, go ignored. To take one example from our collection, Susan Knobloch's discussion with Helen Shaver indicates the varied skills and sophisticated technical awareness a good actress employs in her work.

Ideology was a central concept for the semiological/psychoanalytic position. A fundamental critical operation has been the close analysis of films to identify their ideological meanings. This operation rather confused discussion of the cinema's specificity. It encouraged a view of films as 'texts to be read'. As such, the obvious analogy is with literature. The result is no more favourable to an interest in acting: if a film is like a novel, the dimension of performance is lost.

More broadly, any position which makes ideology central is likely to have a bias against forms of make-believe, like fictional narratives, which invent stories and use human beings to represent other human beings. In the most radical form of this position, all forms of fiction in the cinema were regarded with great suspicion. Obviously, actors have no place in such a position. In a more moderate form, the attitude to fiction associated with the work of Bertolt Brecht was valued; as a consequence, Brecht's ideas about acting aroused interest.[7] Since these ideas had little impact on the cinema – no school of Brechtian actors developed to match the impact of the Method – they didn't stimulate a sustained interest in problems of film acting.

Not all the responsibility for the neglect of acting by Film Studies can be put on the semiological/psychoanalytic approach. Ever since Richard Dyer's book[8] was published in 1979, there has been a considerable interest in stars amongst film scholars of varying intellectual positions. Such an interest might reasonably be expected to generate a strong concern with acting. It hasn't done so for two main reasons.

1 The discussion has never properly freed itself from the belief that stars are a special category, differentiated from other actors by some ineffable 'star quality'. Nor has it freed itself from a residual acceptance of the popular belief that 'stars can't act'. The consequence of this has been that stars have been separated off from the general run of film actors. They haven't been seen as facing most of the same problems, or of having similar skills for dealing with those problems, as other actors.
2 The study of stars has been powerfully affected by the concern with identifying ideological effects. Individual stars are regarded as texts to be analysed. The analysis then integrates the star into the film's ideological meanings or connects him/her with more general ideological systems. So a great deal of interest has been shown in other textual areas like those created by publicity and advertising. Whatever the merit of these analyses, they direct interest away from performance.

As well as unfavourable theoretical paradigms, there are practical problems which hinder the development of the study of film acting. Discussion of theatrical acting is greatly helped by the fact that there are many productions of a central core of plays. It then becomes possible to compare actors' performances, to distinguish what an individual actor brings to the role and to make judgements about this. The comparison is given weight by the easy availability of definitive versions of the play scripts. The nearest film comes to this is with occasional remakes. In her essay on the two versions of *A Star Is Born*, Roberta Pearson takes advantage of one of these remakes to compare the performances. But as her discussion makes clear, the differences between the two versions are considerable. The relationship between a film and its remake is much looser than the relationship between different productions of the same play, even when allowances are made for the script alterations which are common in the theatre.

Both in theatre and cinema, acting is an elusive art. A performance is made out of a large number of actions, gestures, facial and vocal expressions. It's made all the more elusive when the dominant acting convention is a naturalistic one.[9] Viewing a naturalistic performance, it's easy to assume that the gestures, actions, and expressions are the only appropriate ones – anybody would have lit a cigarette at a moment like that! The decisions the actor has made are invisible. Given this, it becomes almost inevitable that the actor disappears into the character or, vice versa, the character disappears into the actor: it is assumed that Humphrey Bogart was brave, had a strong personal code of honour and a nice line in wit! Many analyses of film acting are in fact discussions of a fictional character (whose creation is the work of a writer) rather than analyses of how that character is embodied (the work of an actor).

To add to all these practical problems, the way technology mediates acting in the cinema is a disincentive to taking it seriously. The effect of camerawork and picture editing, sound recording and editing have to be taken into account in the discussion of film acting. In such a context, it is all too easy for the work of the individual actor to be discounted.

As we've indicated, our collection hasn't been designed as a systematic or comprehensive collection. However, the connections the authors make at various points do suggest how a more substantial account of film acting might be developed. In their respective essays, David Mayer, Cynthia Baron, and Sharon Carnicke deal with key periods in the history of film acting. Taken together, they constitute the basis for a serious history of American film acting.

Understanding how acting developed in the early cinema is obviously crucial to constituting a proper history. David Mayer questions existing accounts which have opposed an excessive melodramatic style of acting to a more restrained, 'naturalistic' one. He also questions an account that sees the more restrained style beginning to become dominant from around 1910. Against this, he points to a variety of theatrical traditions which informed silent film acting and the persistence of extended gesturing into the 1910s and possibly throughout the whole of the silent period.

The studio era of film making in the 1930s and 1940s is often seen as a bleak period for film acting, only warmed by individual genius. Through her discussion of acting coaches, Cynthia Baron's account demonstrates this to be a limited view. Generally, there was a conscious concern with the demands of film acting. The driving force for much of this concern was people formed by the Stanislavsky-influenced American theatre of the period. Many of the ideas, still dominant in contemporary film acting, were first put into practice then. Given this account of studio era acting, the break with the Method seems much less dramatic than is presented in established accounts.

Any history of American film acting obviously has to engage with the impact of the Method. Sharon Carnicke outlines the ways in which it was a particular reading and appropriation of Stanislavsky's ideas by Lee Strasberg. She suggests this reading encouraged a downgrading of the importance of the script, an emphasis on emotional memory and sense recall, and an upgrading of the role of the director, working closely with and on the actor. Carnicke goes on to suggest reasons why this approach became influential in Hollywood cinema, despite Strasberg's attempts to distance himself and his actors from Hollywood.

Clearly the Method did have an important influence on Hollywood film acting. However, if some of the other essays are read in the context of Baron and Carnicke's essays, it seems likely that this influence has been exaggerated. The ideas which underpin Helen Shaver's and Susan Sarandon's approaches to acting owe more to the basic Stanislavskian ideas established in the studio era than to Strasberg's variant of them.

Apart from these general ones, most of the other essays are concerned with detailed studies. Between them they indicate the range of ideas, skills, and difficulties which make up the craft of film acting. Some of the issues that they highlight are common to acting in all media. Martin Shingler's discussion of the way Bette Davis 'physicalized' her roles is perhaps the best example of such a broad concern. Other issues are specific to film (and, to a certain extent, television). Gianluca Sergi's discussion of the actor's use of the voice highlights the particular importance of sound in the cinema for actors. Susan Knobloch shows how an awareness of the frame is an important consideration for an actor like Helen Shaver.

As we've indicated, the principal concern of this collection is with the kind of acting that is and has been dominant in American cinema. Two essays reach beyond this area. Carole Zucker's interview with Ian Richardson opens up the relationship between British and American acting and between film and television acting. And Paul McDonald's exploration of the way a director like Mike Leigh works with actors points towards other traditions of acting and film making.

Overall, we think our collection of essays has a wide-ranging perspective. We are also conscious of its limitations. There are two areas in particular which are touched on in the book which need more substantial discussion.

Physical attractiveness is an area of acting which has hardly been discussed by film scholars. Indeed, there's great uncertainty as to whether it should be considered as part of acting. A residual Puritanism encourages the view that it's an illegitimate quality; it seems more like a gift from God rather than a skill or ability which has been developed through work. In a society where physical attractiveness is such a common media currency, it's easy to assume that it is a counterfeit currency. But from the very early days of the cinema, it has always been closely associated with acting, just as it has in the theatre. And there is no doubt that it forms an important part of an audience's response to an actor, both in the cinema and the theatre.

Even if the importance of physical attractiveness in acting is recognized, there are great difficulties in the way of intelligent discussion. It's an elusive concept. There are a range of terms that are used to express attractiveness – beautiful, lovely, handsome, sexy. All of these overlap but have different connotations. In areas like art history or social psychology where there has been some study of the concept, the answer to central questions are still unclear. How much are judgements about physical attractiveness time bound? How much are they culture specific? Is any kind of objective discussion possible in this area?

The importance of feminism in film scholarship has also made the discussion a difficult one. Actresses are most likely to be discussed in terms of their physical attractiveness; often it seems that it is the only quality they are expected to have. Feminists have quite rightly objected to the limitations of such a perspective and have argued that it turns actresses into objects. The strength of these arguments has made the area a sensitive one for discussion. Because it is a sensitive area, the discussion shouldn't be avoided. If it is to develop properly, it needs to be reoriented to focus just as strongly on male as well as female actors. And the words that are traditionally used need to be closely examined to see what their gender implications are.

As well as physical appearance, we would have liked to provide more discussion of acting as a profession, especially the way actors' careers develop. In what terms should this development be discussed? The focal point of the discussion can't be conscious choices on the part of actors. Apart from the most powerful stars, their positions have been weak in terms of choosing which films they will appear in and what roles they will play. In the studio era, contract actors were at the mercy of producers and other people with power in a studio. Since the end of that era, they have been freelances in a very competitive situation. Few actors have anything unique to offer potential employers. For most roles, they can easily be substituted by other actors. In such a situation the power clearly lies with the employers – studio heads; producers, directors, and, to a lesser extent, casting directors.

The focal point of any discussion therefore has to be how the decisions are made by the employers. Unfortunately, while there's well-known folklore about how actresses are chosen – the casting couch – there's not much systematic knowledge. So far as the studio era is concerned, the various discussions of the Classical Hollywood Cinema provide a broad understanding of the way power functioned in a studio while some accounts of actors' careers are also illuminating.[10]

The sources for understanding the contemporary situation are limited. In their discussion of the casting director's role,[11] Janet Hirshenson and Jane Jenkins identify the director as the key figure in the process, the person they need to satisfy. They describe the process by which they make their initial choices as 'instinctual'. Steven Bach's and Julie Salamon's respective accounts of the making of *Heaven's Gate* and *The Bonfire of the Vanities*[12] provide helpful information about the way those films were cast (though mainly at the level of the more substantial roles). They describe a complicated interaction between studio heads, producers, directors, and casting directors over casting choices. Although there is a level of subjectivity and personal favouritism in the discussions, the process isn't an entirely arbitrary one. Certain issues are highlighted: overall appropriateness for the role, technical skills, physical attractiveness, commercial viability, and financial demands.[13]

Although their position may not be a powerful one, actors are not completely at the mercy of the system in which they work. They do exercise minimal control – at the very least, they can say no. Furthermore, few actors work as isolated individuals, nearly all have agents who have some power and knowledge of how to play the game.[14]

If we, as editors, had any theoretical ambitions in putting the collection together, it came from a conviction that much contemporary film theory and criticism is too abstract. This conviction doesn't spring from a simple-minded rejection of abstraction, rather it comes from a belief that if we are to make a proper use of abstraction, we need to capture the concrete and practical character of the work we are considering. Too much writing in Film Studies works on a high level of abstraction without paying sufficient attention to the concrete and practical dimensions of film making. It then becomes an easy target for philistines.

Actors, like all other contributors to the film making process, face a variety of challenges; in their case, a complicated mixture of technological, physical, intellectual, and emotional ones. We have tried to investigate what those challenges are and how actors meet them. A fuller understanding of this process will put us in a better position to understand both film making and how it connects with the larger social and political world.

And finally! We wanted this book to be a tribute to all the women and men whose acting abilities help make us laugh, cry, be excited, thrilled, scared, unsettled, or reflective in the movies.

Notes

1 James Naremore, *Acting in the Cinema*, Berkeley, University of California Press, 1988; Carole Zucker (ed.) *Figures of Light*, New York, Plenum, 1995.

2 Generally, 'actor' is used in this book as a gender-neutral word. Occasionally, where gender differences are important in the discussion, 'actor' and 'actress' are used.

3 It would be illuminating to explore how the idea that there are great individual artists in the cinema eased the way for Film Studies to become established in universities.

4 The concept of Classical Hollywood Cinema has had an important effect here in the way it has encouraged a view that there is only one kind of script.

5 As well as the blocks imposed by theoretical positions, analyses of scripts have been discouraged by more practical considerations. For a long period, few scripts were available for analysis. Obviously that situation has now dramatically changed. Even now, however, there are difficulties. Too many publications aren't scripts but descriptions of the finished film. From the point of view of the study of acting, this has important consequences. The actor's work is subsumed into the script; an action or a gesture which an actor has invented is made to look as if it were invented by the writer. Given the number of times scripts are rewritten both before and when a film is being made, it is not easy to establish a definitive version of a script. But if you want to study acting, the best version is, undoubtedly, the shooting script.

6 The article was originally published in *Screen*, vol. 16, no. 3, Autumn 1975, but its influence can be measured by the number of collections in which it has been reprinted.

7 The Channel 4 documentary, *The Acting Tapes* plus Lez Cooke's, *Notes on the Acting Tapes*, London, British Film Institute, 1986, provide a good account of this interest.

8 Richard Dyer, *Stars*, London, British Film Institute, 1979. A new edition with a supplementary chapter by Paul McDonald was published in 1998.

9 David Mayer rightly points out in his essay that naturalism was a coherent artistic philosophy which embodied a general view of the world. In much modern theatre, films, and television drama, its basic artistic method of observing ordinary life and reproducing it in detail has loosened itself from the general philosophy and often has almost no relationship with it.

10 David Bordwell, Janet Staiger, Kristin Thompson, *The Classical Hollywood Cinema*, London, Routledge, 1985. Robert Sklar, *City Boys*, Princeton, Princeton University Press, 1992.

11 In Alexandra Brouwer and Thomas Lee Wright, *Working in Hollywood*, New York, Avon, 1990.

12 Steven Bach, *Final Cut*, London, Faber & Faber, 1986 and Julie Salamon, *The Devil's Candy*, London, Picador, 1993.

13 Although John Sayle's account of the casting of *Matewan* is from the perspective of an independent film-maker, it generally reveals similar concerns. John Sayles, *Thinking in Pictures*, Boston, Houghton Mifflin, 1987.

14 Chance and accident seem to be just as important in casting as conscious choice. Ron Base's discussion of a variety of stars' roles is a sobering reminder of this. Ron Base, *Starring Roles*, London, Little Brown, 1994.

2

ACTING IN SILENT FILM

Which legacy of the theatre?

David Mayer

Problems begin with our first viewing of silent film. Expectations and prior experiences of spectatorship stand in our way. Conditioned as we are to performance through our late-twentieth-century experience of what we view as more-or-less realistic acting within a more-or-less realistic *mise-en-scène*, we are unable or unwilling to accept early actors' work as an effective means of explicating narrative, clarifying character relationships, expressing appropriate or valid emotion, or providing aesthetic pleasure. We are conditioned to the camera as an instrument for recording truth and the actor's performance as a means of validating that truth. From personal experience of American and Western European cinema, we expect that a cinema actor, with facial nuances, small suggestive gestures, and vocal modulations such as those we might use in our daily lives, will try to confirm the corporeality and actuality of the environment that he or she inhabits. The actor makes fiction into reality.

The silent film actor, particularly the film actor working before 1915,[1] cannot be depended upon to fulfil the same function. Rather, even as the camera ventures out-of-doors to a 'location' and places the actor in an actual townscape or countryside, or the camera finds the actor placed before a setting displaying – as much as pre-orthochromatic film will allow – the late-Victorian scenic artist's skill in representing realistic interiors, the actor is viewed gesticulating and posing in a manner recognizably discrepant to what, at worst, is perceived as scenic backdrop or, at best, as environment. Against this would-be realistic background, the actor explicates prior conditions or events, current narrative, and changing emotional states through bodily stance, broad and numerous gestures and – to the extent that these are visible to a camera lens which keeps at some distance from the performer – large facial expressions.

This disjunction is troubling. To us at this end of the century, particularly those who live in Western societies where Protestant inhibition and self-restraint have long been equated with decorum, the actor does too much

– perhaps because audiences demand too much of him or her. Full gesture is used alike for intimate domestic moments and emotionally fraught situations, even to convey abstract or conceptual information (e.g. deity, sanctity, wickedness, ethnicity) with what sometimes appears to be equal frequency and intensity – and, by our modern standards, inappropriateness. Such elaborations and variation of stance and gesture are read by us as florid, over-emotional, excessive, particularly to the degree and distance gesture is carried away from the body, elaborated, or, as often, a series of random gesticulations which, while suggesting extremes of passion and emotion, either fail to clarify or overstate their case.

How do we reconcile ourselves to these performances? How do we explain the nature of the film actor's performance and why it happens as it does? Can we discern in apparent excess and, in what some modern observers describe as a lack or loss of control, a method and an aesthetic – or, to be more exact, methods and aesthetics? Are realism (or naturalism) and movement-to-realism the only valid criteria for measuring and assessing early silent film performance? Are there generalities which cover the considerable expanse of film acting which apply equally to particular instances?

Explanations for what some may perceive as extravagant and excessive acting have been forthcoming in studies that link broad gesture and 'over-stated' performance to Victorian theatrical praxis.[2] Such studies focus upon an approach to acting and gestural vocabulary developed first in France in the 1830s by François Delsarte,[3] then selectively promulgated in North America and later finding its way into early film. Other film historians inaccurately describe Victorian stage acting as a sequence of 'poses' which convey dramatic situations.[4] These studies, teleologically anticipating 'realistic' film acting, describe changes – 'transformations' – from what is claimed to be the excessively gesticulatory 'histrionic code' of a debased popular stage to a more restrained technique, the 'verisimilar code', and thus, as a consequence, film acting begins to align with the realistic *mise-en-scène*.[5] This apparent development towards realism is the argument of Nicholas Vardac, whose *Stage to Screen*[6] stood as the dominant model of the derivation of narrative film: from exhausted popular stage to the new medium of the realistic motion picture.[7] What therefore marks a development in these later studies is that actors progress from the 'histrionic' and the 'pose' and move towards the 'verisimilar', i.e. towards realism, with the actor's face and body expressing a more intimate inner truth, the camera moving ever closer to the actor to assist in this endeavour. Within two decades, this code shift is complete.

The purpose of this essay is neither to contradict altogether nor to diminish these recent studies, but to place alongside their conclusions a number of contemporary theatrical phenomena which take into account performances in narrative films on both sides of the Atlantic. I intend, in addition to vitiating the idea of a simple transformation or evolution – stage acting into film acting – to provide a more complex picture of complementary sources, influences, and possibilities. My approach is twofold: a re-examination of the variegated theatrical scene and an identification of the specifically gestural modes that may have influenced film actors' work. I shall argue that the theatrical milieu these actors inhabited was varied, rich, cosmopolitain, aesthetically aware – certainly neither 'cheap'[8] nor inferior. Although I consider in this essay chiefly American films, I am concerned equally with American and British and other European stage performers – actors and dancers – and their performances because film acting derives not from a single source, but is influenced by numerous techniques and aesthetics. In particular, I shall insist that gestural alphabets available to actors are informed by several contiguous aesthetics other than those of realism or naturalism. Only late in the nineteenth century is *real* used as a term of critical approval. But a taste for realism is not universally shared, and so to speak approvingly of *the real*, to depict it in painting or in sculpture, or to attempt to emulate it in performance, is only one of several aesthetic choices.

There are in play at the century's end a range of gestural systems or partial systems, some used in stage plays, some in various approaches to narrative or interpretive dance, some American in origin, some on the American stage arriving with British and European performers. These uses of gesture-in-performance are concurrent, not sequential, and thus my approach makes no attempt – unnecessary in my view – to establish a chronology. I am not replacing earlier direct cause-and-effect trajectories with a pick 'n mix assortment of choices, but suggesting both that theatrical influences on early screen acting – a wide range of actors' performances, a wide range of dramatic *genres* – may be multiple and that audiences for early film may have viewed these entertainments with a range of critical and aesthetic expectations.

A necessary starting point is contesting the master narrative which theatre and film historians have embraced and embedded in their historiographic practice for nearly seven decades describing the last quarter of the nineteenth century and the first four decades of this century as the period in which naturalism challenged and overcame the exhausted, mindless popular genres of the late-Victorian stage.[9] Nicholas Vardac, whose *Stage to Screen* is still read by film and theatre historians, is the heir to such historiographic thinking. But by adding his own twist, realistic – or naturalistic – film drives out exhausted popular melodrama and laboured stage spectacle, and replaces them with a pictorial medium which accurately reproduces the material world and offers unrivalled spectacle. And Vardac, in turn, has transmitted this paradigm to numerous offspring over several generations.

Whether such a development was in the minds of those associated with either theatre or film much before the 1920s is now in doubt.[10] We are free to question to what extent the lens through which we examine acting in the three decades from 1896–1925 should focus on the evolution and triumph of naturalism (or its less theorized popular counterpart: pictorial and environ-mental realism).[11] We are at liberty to consider additional theatrical influences.

As critical responses to early film actors' performances turn on questions of stance and gesture, it may be helpful to review briefly historical understandings of how the actor was to use his or her body as a means of emotional and intellectual expression. In the theatre of the Age of Reason, the era in which European acting was first theorized, the actor's task began with depicting the ideal individual, one admirable in the context of the play and who – without uttering a word – might be immediately recognized by audiences as an admirable being. To convey such an individual, the actor's stance is the prescribed *crux scenica*: the relaxed body upright, arms similarly relaxed to gesture easily, knees slightly flexed, heels together, toes apart at a ninety-degree angle. This posture, which coincides with the development of ballet positions, we recognize as First Position. In any departure from a posture in which the body is always seen in control, denying or subduing all unruly and anti-social impulses, the actor begins to define character. Should the actor assume another stance, the audience, reading these signs, may make inferences about the character depicted. The *crux scenica* identified the man or woman of intellect and self-discipline. Self-control – a few key gestures and a virtual absence of multiple histrionic gestures – allowed an admirable person to survive intrigues without needing to reach for his sword or break her fan.[12]

Some of these practices and dicta survive into the Enlightenment, but what had been a part of the former era's vocabulary of acting was now expanded by a language of stance and gesture. The Enlightenment's interest in gesture arises because physical signs were thought to be associated with the innocent behaviour of 'primitive' societies. Thinkers such as Henri Rousseau held that before such societies were corrupted and separated by the numerous spoken languages of Europe, Asia, and Africa, all people communicated through a universal 'language of action' alone. In the lexicon of this graphic pre-language, there was assumed to be a gesture – universally practised and universally recognized – for everything. Actors of the Enlightenment were therefore encouraged to acquire a gestural vocabulary which might render speech unnecessary, and choreographers and artists across Europe vied to describe visual alphabets which transcended language and dialect.[13] By the late eighteenth century, ideas of a gestural vocabulary, now linked to the emotions and inner psychological states, were underpinned by scientific observation[14] and by the first manuals addressed to the English-speaking actor and orator,[15] and this expansion of gestural acting continued for a further half-century. However, by the later decades of the nineteenth century, the consensus between actor and audience about the meaning and necessity for gesture has begun to break up. George Taylor's study of the Victorian actor indicates a variety of aesthetic or intellectual systems for actors' work as well as various physical regimes for the actor to follow. Consequently, resultant variations in approaching gesture arose from differences of national temperament and the kinds of tasks assigned the actor (e.g. comic or serious roles).[16] That dissolving consensus is affirmed by scientific publications.

13

Charles Darwin used photographs of simians and humans to argue that gesture and facial expression are innate and universal,[17] whilst anthropologists, even in attempting to uphold Darwin's thesis of greater and less-evolved human species, began to declare that gesture and facial expression are culturally and racially determined and thus far from universal.[18]

Americans noted these European developments. By the 1870s the United States had produced not only effective home-grown performers, but also performers whose work was seen and appreciated abroad. Traffic in actors and in touring productions, however, flowed chiefly towards the American shore, and, as a consequence, towards the American stage; the plays seen and those acting on it were often international in origin.[19] There was, in consequence, divergence and variation in acting styles, but there was also, inevitably, convergence as some foreign influences predominated and influenced American actors and audiences alike. Despite loud and frequent calls to Americanize the stage and to exclude foreign actors,[20] foreign actors – English actors especially – regularly crossed the Atlantic to perform in American theatres.[21] None of these vistors performed within the verisimilar code, but all were known as truthful actors. All would have assented to a proposition to the effect that acting is always a conspiracy to tell the truth – but truth told in a selective, pre-agreed manner.

Although some actors made only a single journey to America, others, either on favourable terms of engagement from American promoters or enjoying remunerative tours, made repeated visits. Some of these actors[22] were known as detailed, subtle actors. Some[23] were known for overt, visibly mannered or extravagant, 'tuppence coloured' performances. Some actors of each school brought their performances into film.[24] There were actors from Continental Europe, but they were outnumbered by British actors, and – as Seymour Hicks notes – right up until the end of the century, the American theatre was in thrall to the British stage:

> Theatrical America twenty years ago was not what it is now. The interchange of actors with Great Britain had not commenced then. For every one American actor in England, there were a hundred English ones in New York.[25]

Nowhere is the influence of English acting more evident than in a 1909 Biograph film which has been identified as a crossing point between the excessively gestural acting of the stage and a more contained domestic style appropriate to the approaching 'verisimilar' code.[26] This film is the Griffith-directed drama *A Drunkard's Reformation*. In this film we see a drunkard (Arthur Johnson) – a husband and a father – turning away from alcoholism when, at his wife's (Linda Arvidson) anguished behest, he accompanies his small daughter (Adele DeGarde) to a temperance play and is repelled by the example of drunkenness and alcoholic death he sees upon the stage. Pearson sees restraint and verisimilar acting in the framing domestic action, meanwhile insisting that the theatrical episodes are relentlessly over-performed and recognizably so. The framing performances are characterized as good acting, the stage performances as bad acting.

This is a substantial misreading of Griffith's film. Pearson and other film historians, taking their lead from the *Biograph Bulletin*, assert that the play is Émile Zola's *L'Assommoir*. In fact, it is not. The play to which Arthur Johnson is taken is not Zola's *L'Assommoir* but the British dramatist Charles Reade's 1879 adaptation *Drink*, a dramatic version widely performed in Britain and America by the English actor Charles Warner.

Differences between the French original and the English adaptation are significant. We know that this inner play is *Drink*, not *L'Assommoir* because Gervaise (Florence Lawrence) is courted by Coupeau (David Miles) in Phoebe's presence; because their daughter Nana remains a child throughout the drama; because Coupeau resists Virginie's (Marion Leonard) advances; and because Virginie tricks Coupeau into drinking the brandy that kills him.[27] Above all, we know that this play is *Drink* because David Miles has been costumed and made up – in precise replica make-up[28] – in imitation of Charles Warner's Coupeau and has been deliberately coached to reproduce Charles Warner's known and remembered mannerisms in this role. Warner created the role of Coupeau in the play's first success in London and thereafter performed the play on three separate tours to the US. From his first performance in 1879, Warner was famed for the 'truthful and impressive . . . appalling and necessarily repellent'[29] moment when Coupeau finds the lethal brandy. Jessie Millward, who took the role of Gervaise in a London revival of *Drink* in 1891 and who accompanied Warner to New York to perform this play, said of this alarming episode:

> The simulated delirium tremens was horrifying; never had a stage drunkard been more realistically played, and medical men asserted that all the ghastly symptoms were reproduced with absolute faithfulness . . . the vacant, staring eyes, the lolling, protruding tongue, the hideous clutching at the imaginary snakes, and the last ghastly caressing of the last bottle of brandy before the horrible death.[30]

Griffith and members of the Biograph Company are almost certain to have seen one or more performances of *Drink* and thus become well aware of Warner's approach to this role. They had frequent opportunity to do so. Warner played Coupeau in New York in 1891, again in 1895–96, and once again in 1903–4. His performances continued to be well received by critics and audiences, and he returned to America in early 1909 to arrange a further tour. He was, however, suffering from depression and, on 11 February 1909, committed suicide in a New York hotel room. His death and his funeral on

13 February were fully reported in American and British newspapers and in the theatrical and film trade press of both countries, with obituary writers observing that 'His most striking part was Coupeau in *Drink*, produced at the Princess's, which he played over a thousand times in different parts of the world.'[31] Only a fortnight later, on 25 February, Griffith began filming *A Drunkard's Reformation*. The film was completed and copyrighted within a month of Warner's death.[32]

What are we to make of *A Drunkard's Reformation*? Has Griffith intentionally opposed Arthur Johnson's restrained performance with an excessively animated performance by David Miles because the director has intended to contrast the quiet despair of real-life alcoholism with the artificialities of the stage drunk? Or could it be that Johnson's reformation is actually caused by the strong, intense, and moving performance of an admired actor in a major role on an up-market – not cheap – stage? Warner's playing may not meet later criteria of realism or naturalism, but, a mere two weeks after his death, his performance is remembered and deliberately reproduced. It is, if not 'real' or 'verisimilar', none the less truthful, disturbing, and intended to be received as a strong – aesthetically valid – warning of the perils of drink. Biograph's and Griffith's expectation of this performance cannot be overlooked. The intense gestural acting which Miles-as-Warner displays is neither, in 1909, altogether outmoded nor aesthetically disjoined from theatre and film tastes.

At the turn of the century, British and American acting shared similar characteristics and conditions.[33] Both were similarly gestural. Training for performers on both sides of the Atlantic was haphazard. Most actors learned their craft through apprenticeships, beginning on small rural circuits where, observing and playing against more experienced actors, they acquired skills sufficient to seek engagements with larger companies. Few attended professional schools. Some, like Henry Irving, made their start in weekend and evening 'spouting academies' – *ad hoc* schools run by out-of-work actors for city clerks and tradesmen where roles were distributed, not by ability but according to the amateur actor's ability to pay.[34] Actors were taught, amongst other skills, to use their voices effectively; to scan metre and inflect poetic lines; to stand still and yet be significant; to stand without over-balancing; to place their weight so as to step off without swaying; to 'round' their crossing of the stage; to develop telling and economic gestures; and to maintain a readable profile or silhouette whilst changing stance and gesture.[35] Just as theatrical professionals such as Steele MacKaye and Dion Boucicault opened schools of acting in New York, well-known actors such as the acclaimed Henry Neville operated schools in London from the early 1880s. In advertisements in the professional press, Neville described the intention and focus of the training offered his pupils and promised an entrée to the stage: 'Thorough Practical Instruction for the Stage, Voice Production, Elocution, Gesture, and Performances. Lessons in Studio Theatre. Introduction to Profession.'[36]

Boucicault and MacKaye offer versions of the Delsarte system; Neville a gestural technique similar to Delsarte. Neville's system – eventually, in 1895, explicated in a text aimed alike at platform reciters, amateurs, and professional actors[37] – implies, however, a distinctly *fin-de-siècle* aesthetic. The once upright spine – the inflexible *crux scenica* of the early eighteenth-century actor – now bends in sinuous curves, and gestures are encouraged to follow ovals and arcs. Gestures, even conventionally domestic – those which Neville describes as 'colloquial' and drawn from everyday gesticulations – are still large and away from the body. But these too describe circles, parabolas, and arcs, and stand at some distance to the verisimilar. What aesthetic, if indeed there is one, is at play?

One of our ways of answering this question and that of the larger question of gestural performance is to consider an element of the dramatic event which theatre and film historians have almost equally neglected.[38] This element is the almost continual presence of incidental music in stage plays, at silent film showings, and during much filming itself. Victorian and Edwardian stage performances and their reception, as theatre historians are beginning to accept, depend upon the close lamination of many discrete and, separately, frail theatrical elements: script, *mise-en-scène*, acting, spectators. The unifying bonding element, above all others, for these multi-tiered aggregates is music. Music reaches into the auditorium to underline dramatic action and enclose the audience within an aura of sound. Often intertextual, quoting bars of familiar airs, hinting at musical styles or genres, or signalling through key and modal changes, incidental music teaches the spectator – now an auditor as well – how, in moral and emotional terms, to read the play, to interpret character and behaviour.[39] Imparting an external dynamic to the action, it quickens or slows the spectator's pulse. Further, music supports the physical and emotional work of the actor. Gestures which seem large, excessive, vacuous, or grafted-on as an afterthought in total silence or against the dry clicking of a film-projector's sprockets, are – when fully supported by musical accompaniment – sustained by the actor and altogether plausible to the audience.

When we examine acting manuals such as Henry Neville's or that of his contemporary Gustave Garcia[40] and include in our research the pictorial evidence of plays and motion picture frame-enlargements, we see actors caught in extreme poses – 'attitudes' – at the full extent of a gesture. We see these same attitudes in Victorian sculpture and in much narrative painting of the period[41] and are properly encouraged to consult this anecdotal material to gain a clearer understanding of how telling gesture defined the key moment of these frozen narratives.[42] A gesture, however, is far more than these discrete extremes of attitude.[43]

A gesture is not an isolated moment, unless the end of a scene or a key moment in that scene has been intentionally selected to form a momentary 'picture'. Rather, within and around any gesture there are innumerable permutations of movement – all at the discretion of the actor, the demands of the role, and dozens of other variables on the way. As several actors may be sharing a scene, gestures constitute a part of the exchanges between them and, like visual conversations with give and take, express the unspoken subtext of the theatrical moment. Part of these difficulties lie in what these manuals and pictorial resources less successfully tell us – if at all: *how* the actor negotiates the intermediate stages of the gesture to reach its limits or *how* the actor makes effective transition from one gesture to another or *how* these gestures work with music.[44] Yet it is these very negotiations which are vital to gauging the dramatic power and fluency of performed gesture and which film historians have failed to recognize.

Here again, music assists the transitional process, not only sustaining gesture as it travels from the actor's trunk into limbs, joints, wrists, hands, and extending or curling fingers, but also hinting at a shifting or intensifying emotional climate between gestures and, concurrently, setting the groundwork for the gesture to follow. As when music conveying one emotional climate may segue into altogether different music, so gesture can segue into gestures that elaborate or contradict. Sometimes music initiates the gesture; sometimes dialogue or thought or emotional impulse drives the gesture, and music follows; sometimes gesture initiates further thought, and again music follows. At other times gesture, impulse, and music appear to begin together. There is no fixed running order. And, all the while, the audience usually remains unaware that music has served the drama and its performance so well. Although plays and some films have been accompanied by substantial pit orchestras,[45] the presence of music may be overlooked by audiences. In fact, if the spectator is too aware of music, the illusion is less than perfect. The dramatist Charles Reade, eulogizing a recently deceased theatre musician, remarked of his work:

> I suppose two million people have seen Shaun the Post[46] escape from his prison . . . how many are aware that they saw with the ear as well as the eye, and that much of their emotion was caused by a mighty melody . . . being played all the time on the great principle of climax, swelling higher and higher, as the hero of the scene mounted and surmounted? Not six in the two million spectators, I believe.[47]

Thus, music is to the stage or silent film actor what water is to the swimmer. Music, emotionally and imaginatively drawing in the audience, buoys up and physically supports the actor. In this way, although thought – particularly the verbs that shape the intellectual and emotional content of the spoken text – provides the impulse for gestures, music acts as the medium for gesture, furnishing tempo, orchestral colouring, tonality, rhythm, direction, and force. Music, like water, is the medium of support, propulsion, and resistance; the actor or swimmer continually moving with and against its currents and density.

Music is inseparable from melodrama. When, at the end of the third act of Lottie Blair Parker's 1898 *'Way Down East*, the following exchanges take place, they are heavily informed by forceful, pertinent gesture, and words and gestures alike are bound closely together by continual orchestral music:

SQUIRE: . . . I tell ye! I want no supper of *her* gettin'! (ANNA *stops arranging the dishes and . . . staggers backward up stage*) And the sooner she goes the better . . . My son marry this . . . beggar without a home or a name? (ANNA *stretches out her hands towards him*) . . . You've . . . struck me in the heart! . . . Go! Out o' thet door, and never let me see your face again! (*Turns away R.*)

DAVID: Take care – father! . . . You are insulting the woman I want for my wife! (*Takes* ANNA *in his arms*)

SQUIRE: (*drawing back*) The woman ye want fer yer wife 'n what is she? . . . Ask her about the child, 'bout the child that's buried in Beldin church-yard (ANNA *totters towards* SQUIRE, *imploringly; sinks at the feet, back to audience.*) . . .

ANNA: You found out so much! . . . Did you find out also that I had believed myself to be an honorable wife? That the father of that child was a wretch who betrayed an ignorant girl through a mock marriage . . . (*impatient gesture*) You have been hunting down the defenseless girl who only asked to earn her bread in your house. There is a man, an honored guest at your table – why don't you find out what his life has been? For he (*pointing to* SANDERSON) is the father of my child – he is the man who betrayed me![48]

Here, as was typical for plays of the period, is an exchange rich in specified action, in stage effect, in movement and gesture. Evidence from numerous theatrical promptbooks and actors' manuals suggests that music works with and through these elements, supporting, allowing searing, expansive gestures – the Squire's dropped head, upstage arm pointing. Music supports Anna's stretching hands and the Squire's shuddering withdrawal as his son clasps the woman his father would drive from home. And again music underlines Anna's question – 'There is a man . . . why don't you find out what his life has been? For he (the questioning upturned wrist and palm now turning to stage floor and *pointing to* Sanderson) is the father of my child – he is the man who betrayed me!' Music enables, indeed encourages, gesture to be checked, to work with or against the tempo of speech, to be elaborated, modified, turned, 'stretched', supported. When this scene, the words still spoken but now repeated in intertitles, is filmed by Griffith in 1919, the confrontations, passions, and gestures of Burr McIntosh as Squire[49] and Lillian Gish as Anna remain as emotionally charged and physically large – and, fortunately, as dramatic as ever. Close-up shots, the intensity of gesture now transferred to the face, reduce the frequency of such big moments, but intense emotions are not constrained nor all large gestures fettered, and neither seem out-of-place in a realistic New Hampshire farm kitchen. Music again sees to that.

We know that many silent film directors used accompanying music to assist their actors performing before the camera. Photographs of Alice Guy filming on an interior set show a string trio providing music which, inaudible to the cinema audience, nevertheless allowed her actors to find and hold and build appropriate emotive gesture. It was essential, not alien, to performance. Even as the period of silent film was ending, Chili Bouchier recalls:

> There was a rather seedy little musical trio to play our 'mood' music, and we were allowed to choose our own. I had 'Sweet Sue' for the jolly scenes and 'The Songs my Mother Taught Me' for the sad ones.[50]

Musical accompaniment was again added by the house orchestra or piano when her films were shown to cinema audiences. For the spectator, as well as the actor, music remained an interpreter of the dramatic event.

Once music has been linked to gesture, we may identify other *fin-de-siècle* theatrical genres which depended upon this link. There are several such genres. Perhaps, arising from our concern to identify stage entertainments which may share gestural languages with early film, the most significant are the dance entertainments on offer in the variety houses of Western metropoli from the mid-1880s until the start of the First World War. What is pertinent to our concerns about these entertainments is that they share programmes of miscellaneous variety turns with singers, comics, sapient animals, jugglers and acrobats, sketches, and, most significantly, motion pictures. What is equally notable is that these dances are narrative in content, each with its own plot and cast of dramatic characters, and each deploying choreographed narrative gesture as a means of developing plot and explicating character. These ballets have been carefully studied by dance historians, especially by Ivor Guest,[51] and the brief – initially 18-minute – narrative dramatic sketch's proximity to film has been described and queried,[52] but there has been no overarching examination of the conditions and complementary entertainments which accompanied the screening of early film and which may have conditioned audience expectations of performance style in narrative cinema.

Guest has described variety-house ballet, often drawing on the gestural languages developed in Russian ballet and carried westward by relays of ballet-masters, as brief dramatic playlets, few exceeding 30 minutes' duration, which use a developing narrative as the pretext for presenting a sequence of dances. These dances – solos, duets, trios, and chorus pieces, much as the fully musical numbers in opera – are to be enjoyed for their beauty and brilliance. Linking them are the narrative sections, much like recitative in opera, in which the plot, accompanied by instrumental *continuo*, moves forward and in which characters act out the dynamics of their relationships in carefully determined pantomime. We see such pantomime gesture in such surviving *fin-de-siècle* ballets as Marius Petipa's 1894–95 *Swan Lake*. It is far more economical and far less spontaneous than either theatrical or film gesture, but it is as fluid and as large.

Guest also describes a moment when, at the Alhambra Music Hall in London, ballet and film are integrated:

> [Alfredo] Curti produced his next ballet[53] . . . on the dangers of gambling. To play the hero, Julia Seale returned to the Alhambra after an absence in France and Italy . . . having . . . studied under . . . mime teachers who practised in those two countries . . . Her part was that of a young sculptor, who . . . falls under the spell of a Parisian dancer, and . . . gambles disastrously . . . To drown his misery he drinks himself into a stupor, at which point the services of the cinematograph . . . were called upon . . . for the first time in a ballet. In flickering black and white, the moving picture depicted his dream of . . . shooting his rival. When the picture faded, the screen was raised.[54]

Here, in a single theatrical event for an English audience, we have Russian-influenced choreography staged by an Italian choreographer for an English dancer who has learned mime gestures in Italy and France in concert with gestures – probably in the same mime language – read from film. Gestural languages are intersecting, but they are not homogenizing. No one, moreover, has expressed concern that there might be a clash of styles or that any of these styles or their sum was discordant to a setting.[55] That, in turn, is also how we may view the abutting domestic episodes and the theatrical scenes of *A Drunkard's Reformation*.

Dance shared the variety and legitimate stages with other gestural performances. Unhampered by linguistic frontiers, mime dramas, largely French, Italian, English, or Spanish in origin, enjoyed success in Europe, then frequently crossed to North America. Mime plays, often spectacular in effect, were performed by troupes of acrobats and dancers. Many were wholly silent, although some were interspersed with songs. Although these largely silent pieces are recorded from the late eighteenth century, they begin to receive more international attention from the 1820s, as a series of 'Jocko' or 'sagacious ape' plays captivate European audiences.[56] These pieces gave way to even more energetic mime pieces, best exemplified by the English Hanlon-Lee acrobatic pantomime troupe, whose work and influence on silent film comedy has been described by Laurence Senelick[57] and Joseph Sokalski.[58]

If we seek an aesthetic other than realism to explain gestural acting in early Biograph film and directorial attitudes to what we might regard as oversized performance, we might look to the work of another performer, the American actress-dancer Loïe Fuller. Film scholars, if otherwise unfamiliar with Loïe Fuller, will know her work through her simulacrum Annabel Whitford and her 'Serpentine' and 'Butterfly' dances, which Edison frequently filmed for the kinetoscope between 1894–97. These brief films of a young woman, dancing as she swirls large pieces of drapery – often, in surviving prints, tinted with changing bursts of colour – reproduce highlights of dances which Fuller performed to unusual acclaim in Europe and America from the early 1890s into the 1920s. Although Fuller choreographed and appeared in narrative ballets which bear similarities to Alhambra ballets and dramatic sketches, it was for her solo speciality dances and her innovative lighting effects that she was renowned. Fuller devised her dance effects to be used with fluctuating tinted electric back-lighting, which shone through diaphanous muslin skirts and sleeves extended by slender wands well beyond arm and leg-length. In her performances sleeves and skirts spiralled, extended, and wrapped, folding and unfolding in irregular pleats, onto her body as shifting light cast opalescent colours. She was the inspiration to the poster artists Toulouse-Lautrec and Chéret, to numerous jewellers, to the glass-makers Lalique and Tiffany, to countless *fin de siècle* sculptors and painters. All translated her movements into the pliant, sinuous, tangled-root lines of *art nouveau*, and her recent biographers have said of her, 'Loïe's dancing was the *Art Nouveau* of choreography.'[59] Fuller herself described an *art nouveau* aesthetic and its fusion of sensation, movement, colour, and music in an autobiography published in 1913.[60]

It would substantially overstate my argument to suggest that, whilst many scene designers and theatrical producers and, in time, film-makers were concerned with transferring a species of pictorial realism to their dramatic products, their efforts at creating this realism were unintentionally and unconsciously subverted by actors performing in a gestural code derived from or related to the non-realistic aesthetic of *art nouveau*. Nevertheless, I find that the sinuous curving lines of *art nouveau* are echoed in Henry Neville's gestural instructions, and I note that George Taylor has drawn a connection between the gestural theories of Delsarte and the Aesthetic Movement.[61] But these gestural patterns are only some of the numerous possibilities for late-Victorian and Edwardian actors living and working in the vicinity of the New York and New Jersey film factories to observe and aspire to. There may be a further claim for the influence of *art nouveau* as a graphic and typographic – if not an acting – style on film-makers in Biograph's recognizable 'AB' trademark, visible in the backgrounds of many film scenes and in Biograph's and Griffith's intertitles, where text is wrapped in *art nouveau* vines, leaves, and adventurous curlicues.

A final factor affects our reading of gesture in early film. Here the factor is not aesthetic but technical. If we examine films made before 1909 and, in particular, note performances in indoor settings, we may observe that the actors perform in settings where perspective has been foreshortened and where almost all gesture is lateral or vertical – that is, parallel to the picture-plane. Gestures made in these planes – away from the body – will invariably appear large, particularly if actors are standing in some proximity to one another in circumstances where large gestures appear superfluous. In contrast, stage gestures and stage movements, unrestricted by a less limited acting space and performed before audiences who perceive stage depth, are usually more multi-dimensional than these performances: actors gesticulate upstage and – especially – downstage or on downstage diagonals. Yet in film such gestures and movements appear out of bounds. What explains these gestural differences?

What we may be viewing is an artistic response to two constraints: the restricted focal depth of early lenses and 'slow' emulsion speed on current film. Both factors together severely limit the zone in which actors may perform and remain in focus. In various Biograph films of 1908 we see directors working out how to fool the spectator's eye into believing in the existence of ample interior space, when, in fact there is little working depth.[62] In one episode of *The King's Messenger*, actors are seated downstage, with their backs to the camera, whilst the action happens immediately upstage. The resultant illusion is of a deep room. In *Old Isaacs, the Pawnbroker* a pawnshop counter is awkwardly upstage and parallel to the picture-plane, but in Griffith's *The Romance of a Jewess* the counter has been placed on a diagonal which neither compromises focal depth nor obliges the actors to turn continually downstage to perform to the camera.

Out-of-doors, where there is more light and therefore greater focal depth, the actor is not so restricted and may move and gesture towards and away from the camera, or may actually break the picture-plane and move towards and pass behind the camera. With the freedom to use state-of-the-art equipment openly, which comes with the formation of the Motion Picture Patents Company in 1908, lenses, emulsions, and indoor lighting improve. Gestures can be made in all directions; the actor is less obliged to perform directly to the camera and may develop more subtle stances which no longer oblige such obvious lateral movement and gesture.

Many questions remain about early film acting. We know the names of only a handful of the actors; we have scant biographical information about most of these. We cannot identify what enabled some actors to develop their performing skills as they gained experience, nor have we yet learned how some promising actors learned from their peers, whilst others had performances sabotaged by clumsy newcomers or lazy professionals. We want to know how film actors were taught and trained. What really is the relationship of most of these early film actors to live stage performance? We know from Arvidson and other contemporary sources that lack of regular theatrical work induced some stage actors to take roles in early films but that some did so condescendingly whilst others enthusiastically took to the new medium and eventually forsook the theatre for film work. Others returned to the stage at the first job offer. Can we always tell the difference between the experienced stage actor and the untrained film actor? It is likely that what we criticize as excessively theatrical acting is by novice film actors, their performances shaped by technical limitations of lens, film stock, and lighting – imitating what they imagine is acting, as in 'stage-acting' – rather than badly trained stage actors moonlighting in a film studio.

What we do know is that acting is a learned craft which improves with effort and experience but also requires a measure of innate talent. Actors had to work in plays and films to build up the experience necessary to their development, and employment in either medium was not easy to find. We know that inspired and dedicated film actors worked intelligently and diligently at perfecting their craft:

> The acting has to be as forceful and natural as on the legitimate stage ...and, indeed, repeated rehearsals[63] have to be called before a picture can be worthy of being taken.[64]

It takes practice to know what is 'forceful'. It takes even more practice and experience to know and to agree upon what is 'natural' and how to act naturally. Early screen actors, I contend, had numerous theatrical models of the forceful and the natural from which to choose to guide their own developing performances. Audiences, likewise, had numerous and varied examples of theatrical performance styles from which to shape their preferences. There was no overarching mode, no overriding aesthetic because both styles and aesthetics were emerging in variegated national cultures. A range of professional, critical, and aesthetic practices were at play in determining a range of entertainments for spectators whose expectations were equally various and equally in flux. Our response to experiencing early screen acting might be to marvel at how effectively the various possibilities have come together, sometimes to fuse into vivid works of imagination and virtuosity.

Notes

1 1910 is usually cited as the date at which standardized technologies and common industrial and commercial practices create a world cinema. Nearly an additional five years are needed before there is some agreed uniformity in acting technique.

2 Cooper C. Graham, 'Unmasking Feelings, The Portrayal of Emotions in the Biograph Studios Films of 1908–1910', *Library of Congress Performing Arts Annual, 1988*, ed. Iris Newsome, Washington, Library of Congress, 1989, pp. 96–131. Graham notes that the New York theatrical innovator, producer, and dramatist Steele MacKaye studied with Delsarte and brought his approach to America where, opening an acting school, he subsequently introduced Delsarte's technique to a succession of American actors. Graham reproduces gestures from Delsartian acting manuals and compares these to frame enlargements taken from Biograph films. He finds some useful correspondences but does not claim that any Biograph actors were trained in Delsarte technique. Rather, he suggests, 'the Delsarte system [is] only a paradigm of nineteenth century gesture, a system of

expression that was in the air, and that was especially useful to the new film industry.' Graham's compelling study is followed by Roberta Pearson, *Eloquent Gestures: The Transformation of Performance Style in the Griffith Biograph Films*, Berkeley and Los Angeles, University of California Press, 1992.

3 Although Delsarte himself wrote no account of his approach, his work was described in various manuals or guides for the platform orator, singer, and actor. His work has been described by Genevieve Stebbins, *Delsarte's System of Expression*, New York, Dance Horizons, 1977 (reprint from 1885) and, more recently, by George Taylor, *Players and Performances in the Victorian Theatre*, Manchester, Manchester University Press, 1989, and George Taylor, 'François Delsarte: a Codification of Nineteenth Century Acting', *Theatre Research International*, forthcoming, 1999.

4 Ben Brewster and Lea Jacobs, *Theatre to Cinema: Stage Pictorialism and the Early Feature Film*, Oxford, Oxford University Press, 1997, pp. 79–110.

5 Pearson, echoing Graham, but reliant on a lesser understanding of Victorian and Edwardian theatrical practice, argues that early film acting derives from a non-specific but none the less theatrical 'histrionic code' (i.e., stage acting) as practised in 'cheap stage melodrama' in a debased popular theatre. Whereas Graham describes artistry, definition, and clarity in the Delsarte system, Pearson finds clumsiness and distortion. She also notes D.W. Griffith's experience in Nance O'Neill's touring company and the reviews which emphasize this leading actress's heavy-handed outdated acting and especially O'Neill's – whom she describes as a 'theatrical atavism' – limited success in performing such new authors as Ibsen (pp. 78–79).

6 A.N. Vardac, *Stage to Screen: Theatrical Method from Garrick to Griffith*, Cambridge, Mass., Harvard University Press, 1949.

7 In contrast, there is Russell Merritt, 'Rescued from a Perilous Nest: D.W. Griffith's Escape from Theatre into Film', *Cinema Journal*, vol. 21, no. 1, 1981, pp. 2–30, who locates D.W. Griffith as an actor and identifies his lengthy ties with the stage. For an opposing view to Vardac, see David Mayer, 'Learning to See in the Dark', *Nineteenth Century Theatre*, vol. 25 no. 2, Winter 1997, pp. 92–114.

8 In Pearson's study, *melodrama* is used pejoratively. I categorically reject the proposition that melodrama is, by definition or practice, a 'cheap' or low genre. Neither its popularity nor ubiquity was indicative of the quality of individual dramas. As the prevailing expressive mode of the era, melodrama could be – equally and unpredictably – perceptive and revelatory, profound, acutely analytical, or – alternatively – reductively trivial, formulaic, and banal.

9 This challenge allegedly led to the creation of a new stage and the 'New Drama' identified with Ibsen, Hauptmann, Strindberg, and their British, Continental, and American successors. The New Drama had its theorists and historians as well as its playwrights, and these represented the creation, development, and triumph of naturalism in deterministic, moral, and evangelical terms. Thus, melodrama and spectacle are retrograde, inferior, vacuous, demeaning, and doomed to expire as these debased *genres* consume themselves catering to an ever-insatiable public; naturalism, by contrast, is innovative, superior, enlightening, uplifting, and destined to be the predominant aesthetic. American theatre historians particularly favour this rhetoric. Typically, George Freedley and John Reeves,

A History of the Theatre, New York, Crown Publishers, 1968 (3rd edn) in a chapter entitled 'America takes its place, 1906–40 – A real drama is born' heralds the 'realistic phase of the American renaissance' offering 'honest, clear-cut realism' against the sort of earlier dramatist who produced 'a hundred melodramas of no importance' (pp. 584–89).

10 Thomas Postlewait, 'From Melodrama to Realism: The Suspect History of American Drama', *Melodrama: The Cultural Emergence of a Genre*, Michael Hays and Anastasia Nikolopoulou (eds), New York, St Martin's Press, 1996, pp. 39–60. Postlewait usefully questions the historiographic orthodoxies gathered around the impact of naturalism in America and points to their sources. He identifies a constellation of dramatists and theorists and, later, historians who, writing for and about the stage in the closing years of the last century and in the early years of this, propagated a series of oppositional binaries: spectacle/ realism, trivial/significant, crude and popular/significant, melodrama/new drama, bad/good, destined-to-fail/destined-to-succeed. These binaries and this self-fulfilling narrative – which tends to exclude alternate and discrepant accounts – actually distorts more accurate understandings and histories of the stage.

11 I am making an intentional distinction between 'realism' and naturalism. Realism, for the purposes of this essay, is concerned with a faithful reproduction of the material world and its inhabitants. Thus characters (or actors) are judged to the extent that their actions faithfully reproduce the behaviour of persons who live in that world. No action is required of the spectator apart from admiring the accuracy of the rendering. Naturalism, by contrast, is a comprehensive scientific, philosophical, and socio-political system in which human behaviour and environment are inextricably linked.

12 Joseph Roach, *The Player's Passion: Studies in the Science of Acting*, Newark, University of Delaware Press, 1985.

13 Marian Hannah Winter, *The Pre-Romantic Ballet*, London, Pitman Publishing, 1974. See, especially, numerous references to Gregorio Lambranzi, and Susanne K. Langer, 'Virtual Powers' and 'The Magic Circle', *Feeling and Form*, London, Routledge & Kegan Paul, 1953, pp. 169–207.

14 Roach, *The Player's Passion*.

15 Aaron Hill, *The Art of Acting*, London, 1746: Sir John Hill, *The Actor*, London, 1750: Henry Siddons, *Practical Illustrations and Rhetorical Gestures and Action Adapted to the English Drama (taken from a work on the same subject by M. Engel, member of the Royal Academy of Berlin)*, London, 1807.

16 George Taylor, *Players and Performances in the Victorian Theatre*.

17 Charles Darwin, *The Expression of the Emotions in Man and Animals*, London, 1872.

18 Paolo Mantegazza, *Physiognamy and Expression*, London, c. 1880.

19 The influence of foreign acting companies and leading performers is evident in the listings of foreign actors performing in New York and on American circuits. See George C.D. Odell, *Annals of the New York Stage*, 15 vols, New York, Columbia University Press, 1949, and reviews of visiting actors and companies reported weekly in the English language trade press: *New York Clipper* (US) and *The Era* (UK).

20 Bruce A. McConachie, *Melodramatic Formations, American Theatre and Society, 1820–1870*, Iowa City, University of Iowa Press, 1992, pp. 147–50.

21 George Arliss, Dorothea Baird, Wilson Barrett, Sarah Bernhardt, John Brougham, Charles Calvert, Mrs Patrick Campbell, Constant Coquelin, Eleonora Duse, Charles Fechter, Johnston Forbes-Robertson, John Hare, Henry Irving, John Lawson, John Martin-Harvey, Jessie Millward, Helena Modjeska, Mary Moore, Alla Nazimova, Carlotta Nillson, Gabriele Réjane, George Rignold, Tommaso Salvini, E.H. Sothern, Elizabeth von Stamwitz, Conway and Osmond Tearle, Ellaline Terriss, Ellen Terry, Herbert Beerbohm Tree, E.S. Willard, Mrs John Wood, and Charles Wyndham were regular visitors as motion pictures began.

22 Willard, Duse, Modjeska, Forbes-Robertson.

23 Barrett, Salvini, Lawson.

24 Tree, Lawson, Forbes-Robertson, Arliss, Bernhardt.

25 Seymour Hicks, *Twenty-four Years of an Actor's Life*, London, Alston Rivers, Ltd., 1910, pp. 74–88.

26 Pearson, *Eloquent Gestures*, pp. 95–96,140–43.

27 In the stage version of *Drink*, Virginie substitutes a bottle of brandy for 'medicinal' wine which a doctor has prescribed for the convalescent Coupeau.

28 Illustrations of Charles Warner in street-dress and in two stages of his stage make-up for the role of Coupeau may be seen in Charles Harrison, *Theatricals and Tableaux Vivants for Amateurs*, London, 1885–86, p. 26. Warner was the father of the actor H.B. Warner, perhaps best known for his portrayal of Jesus in De Mille's *The King of Kings* (1927).

29 Richard Eyre Pascoe (ed.), *Dramatic Notes, an Illustrated Handbook of the London Theatres, 1879*, London, 1879, p. 30.

30 Jessie Millward (in collaboration with J.B. Booth), *Myself and Others*, London, Hutchinson & Co., 1923, p. 147.

31 *The Era*, 13 February, 1909, p. 17.

32 Griffith was not the only person to mount a replica of *Drink*. August 1909 editions of *The Era* advertised 'DRINK, A Free Adaptation of Zola's Novel in Four Acts by J. PITT HARDACRE, who appears as Coupeau supported by a Company of Melodramatic Artists who know their business . . .'

33 Acting manuals and other English language theatrical how-to-do-it publications in this period are predominately British. Residual American puritanism and lingering attitudes towards stage people in the aftermath of President Lincoln's assasination by an actor in 1865 substantially reduced publications for the aspirant American actor until *c.* 1914.

34 'Spouting academies' were patronized only by males; they were too indecorous for respectable females to attend. When these academies gave public performances, female roles were undertaken by professional actresses engaged for the occasion.

35 The idea was for the actor to maintain a distinctive silhouette by creating a series of imaginary triangles with his or her body. Overall body shape created one triangle, the visible space between the trunk and the extended arms was another, the space between the legs another.

36 This advertisement appears regularly in *The Era* and *The Era Almanack* from the 1880s until about 1912.

37 Hugh Campbell, M.D., R.F. Brewer, B.A., and Henry Neville (eds), *Voice, Speech, and Gesture: A Practical Handbook to the Elocutionary Art including Essays on Reciting*

and Recitative by Clifford Harrison, and On Recitation with Musical Accompaniment by Frederick Corder, R.A.M., with upwards of a hundred illustrations by Dargavel and Ramsey, comprising also selections in prose and verse adapted for recitation, reading, and dramatic recital, edited, with an introduction, by Robert D. Blackman, London, 1895, reprinted in 1897 and 1904. See also David Mayer, 'Parlour and Platform Melodrama', *Refigured Worlds: Melodrama as Cultural Mediator*, Michael Hays and Anastasia Nicolopoulou (eds), New York, St Martin's Press, 1996, pp. 211–34.

38 As exceptions to this neglect, see Martin M. Marks, *Music and the Silent Film, Contexts and Case Studies*, New York and Oxford, Oxford University Press, 1997; David Robinson, *Music of the Shadows: The Use of Musical Accompaniment with Silent Films, 1896–1936*, Pordenone, Le Giornate del Cinema Muto, 1990; David Robinson, *Musique et Cinéma Muet, Les Dossiers du Musée D'Orsay No. 56*, Paris, Réunion des Musées Nationaux, 1995; David Mayer and Matthew Scott, *Four Bars of 'Agit': Music for Victorian and Edwardian Melodrama*, London, The Theatre Museum and Samuel French, Ltd., 1983.

39 Earlier in the nineteenth century, characters were identified by musical signatures which heralded or accompanied each character's entrance. By the 1880s this practice was largely abandoned.

40 Gustave Garcia was a teacher of acting to opera students. His *The Actor's Art: a Practical Treatise of Stage Declamation, Public Speaking, and Deportment, for the Use of Artists, Students, and Amateurs*, London, 1880, takes as self-evident the presence of music in stage performance.

41 The very best of these sources is Martin Meisel, *Realizations: Narrative, Pictorial, and Theatrical Arts in Nineteenth Century England*, Princeton, Princeton University Press, 1983.

42 Some histories of nineteenth century acting tend to describe acting as a mere sequence of fixed attitudes or gestural units. Michael R. Booth, *Theatre in the Victorian Age*, Cambridge, Cambridge University Press, 1991, pp. 120–25. See also Brewster and Jacobs, *Theatre to Cinema*, pp. 79–137. Brewster and Jacobs, in stressing the static nature of the poses, invite comparison with those puzzles in which the solver is invited to connect numbered dots. As these authors describe acting, meaning lies solely in the dots. As I describe it, meaning and effect lie both in the quality, i.e. visible intent, force, grace, direction, subtlety, timing, etc. of the through-line of an actor's movements between these pivotal points, as in the points themselves, as well as the various readings audiences assign such movement.

43 This section on gesture and music is indebted to Helen Day-Mayer's thinking and work on *'Way Down East*.

44 Throughout the nineteenth century, actors are praised for the fluency and eloquence, or otherwise criticized for the shortcomings of their 'transitions'.

45 The composition of such cinema orchestras is illustrated by an advertisement in the 'Musicians Wanted' column of *The Era*: 'JOHN CODMAN'S PICTURE PALACE. Wanted, for above, Small Family Band; also Violin, Cornet, Drums, Double Bass, Trombone. Particulars. JOHN CODMAN, Coliseum, Aberystwyth' (10 July 1909). In contrast, Linda Arvidson describes first seeing Florence Lawrence on film in 'a little motion picture place [with] a rough wooden floor, common kitchen chairs, [where] the reels unwound to the tin-panny shriek of

28

a pianola'. Linda Arvidson (Mrs D.W. Griffith), *When the Movies Were Young*, Reprint, New York, Dover Publications, 1969, p. 58.

46 In Dion Boucicault's melodrama *The Shaughraun*.

47 Charles Reade, *Readiana: Comments on Current Events*, London, 1881, pp. 28–31. Reprinted from *The Era*, 2 November 1878.

48 Lottie Blair Parker, *'Way Down East*, elaborated by Joseph R. Grismer, Manhattan Theatre, New York, 1898.

49 In casting Burr McIntosh as Squire Bartlett, Griffith engaged the actor who performed this role in the original 1898 stage production.

50 Chili Bouchier, *Shooting Star: The Last of the Silent Film Stars*, London, Atlantis, 1996, p.53.

51 See especially, Ivor Guest, *Adeline Genée, A Lifetime of Ballet under Six Reigns*, London, Adam & Charles Black, 1958; Ivor Guest, *The Empire Ballet*, London, Society for Theatre Research, 1962; Ivor Guest, *Ballet in Leicester Square*, London, Dance Books, 1992.

52 Mayer, 'Learning to See in the Dark'.

53 *Queen of Spades*, 25 February 1907.

54 Guest, *Ballet in Leicester Square*, p. 71.

55 George Taylor writes: 'Eisenstein's first essay in film was a similar insert into his vaudeville-style production of Ostrovsky's *Wise Man* (1922). The filmed insert, like a typical comedy short, created a trick illusion of a man leaping from a clock tower into a moving car. Eisenstein described the whole production as a "Montage of Attractions", and his subsequent theory of cinematic montage suggests that he was consciously using "aesthetic contradiction" to provoke a consciously critical response from his audience to the drama.' Personal letter to the author.

56 Prefiguring *King Kong* by nearly a century, the 'Jocko' plays featured an athletic acrobat-dancer costumed in the skin of an ape. Although details of such pieces are scant, there is evidence that they were invariably narrative in character and that narrative content was largely communicated through gesture. Interpreters of Jocko, such as the French acrobat-dancer Mazurier, were famed for their expressive subtlety.

57 Laurence Senelick, *The Age and Stage of George L. Fox, 1825–1877*, Hanover and London, University Presses of New England, 1988, p. 220.

58 Joseph Sokalski, 'From Screen to Stage: A Case Study of the Paper Print Collection', *Nineteenth Century Theatre*, vol. 25, no. 2., Winter 1997, pp. 115–36.

59 Richard Nelson Current and Maria Ewing Current, *Loïe Fuller, Goddess of Light*, Boston, Northeastern University Press, 1997, p. 128.

60 Loïe Fuller, *Fifteen Years of a Dancer's Life, with Some Account of her Distinguished Friends*, London, Herbert Jenkins, Ltd., 1913, pp. 62–72.

61 Taylor, 'François Delsarte: a Codification of Nineteenth Century Acting'.

62 Arvidson remarks on this limited playing space, noting that 'a [Biograph Studio] "scene" was set back center, just allowing passage room' (p. 56) and she explains how the area in focus was laid out for the performers: 'Johnny Mahr with his five-foot board would get the focus and mark little chalk crosses on the floor, usually four, two for the foreground and two for the background. Then Johnny would hammer a nail in each cross and with his ball of twine, tying it from nail to nail, enclose the set' (p. 94), Arvidson, *When the Movies Were Young*. By 1910,

as Brewster and Jacobs, confirm, developments in lens technology permitted actors to perform and remain in focus in deeper settings (*Stage to Cinema*, pp. 169–71).

63 Rehearsals pose another problem. Not all directors rehearsed their casts. Griffith was unusual because he did so.

64 Unsigned article, possibly by L. Carson (ed.), 'The Triumph of the Animated Picture', *The Stage Year Book, 1908*, London, Carson & Comerford, 1908, p. 48.

3

CRAFTING FILM PERFORMANCES

Acting in the Hollywood studio era

Cynthia Baron

In the 1930s and 1940s, studio publicity focused the public's attention on stars' personalities rather than their craftsmanship. In promotional campaigns for specific pictures and behind-the-scene bios of individual stars, audiences were told that Hollywood actors were natural actors whose unique qualities were captured by the camera. That image – of Hollywood actors playing themselves – might in some circumstances be entirely accurate. Clearly there was little craftsmanship involved in cases where inexperienced actors simply memorized their lines and hit their marks, or, to portray emotional intensity, worked themselves into agitated states by remembering traumatic experiences. Similarly, it makes no sense to discuss stars' agency and expertise in cases where established, experienced actors chose not to prepare for parts, and instead relied on habit, guidance from directors, and support from fellow actors.

Cases such as these, however, need not be taken as representative. In marked contrast to the view that film performances were produced with no effort expended by actors themselves, practitioners of the period consistently argue that training, labour, and practical craft experience allowed actors and their collaborators to create performances and respond to the specific challenges of Hollywood studio productions in the 1930s and 1940s. Put most broadly, professionals working in Hollywood during this period seem to have found ways to integrate methods developed in American silent film with principles formulated by individuals working in American theatre. Hollywood workers whose focus was dramatic performance appear to have derived strategies based on their understanding of Moscow Art Theatre productions and Stanislavsky's System, or to have found similar solutions to shared problems of 'modern' performance.

Throughout the period, the disparate demands of specific characters, narratives, and genres required actors and their collaborators to use an eclectic collection of methods borrowed from dance, modelling, vaudeville, and the legit stage. Rather than there being a single method, or even style of acting, actors' methods and performance styles reflected the demands of each screenplay. For example, a Marx brothers' comedy like *A Night at the Opera* (1935) required methods of preparation and performance styles that were very different from those built into John Ford's expressionistic drama *The Informer* (1935). Similarly, the screwball comedy *Bringing Up Baby* (1938) would necessarily lead an actor like Cary Grant to acting methods and performance styles quite different from those called for by Clifford Odet's low-life melodrama *None but the Lonely Heart* (1944).

Recognizing that descriptions of methods and styles of acting cannot and need not apply to any and all film performances of the period, in the discussion that follows I shall consider points of contact that do exist in accounts that address the basic demands of film performance, for there is a remarkable consistency in acting professionals' views on relationships between stage and screen acting. I shall also examine repeated patterns in practitioners' observations on methods for approaching and executing performances in character-driven narratives, for in material concerning dramatic performances or character-based comedic performances a few central points consistently emerge. Professionals of the period believed that actors' minds and bodies formed a unified, organic whole, and from that position continually argue for the value of training body and voice. Practitioners assumed that the actor (not the director) was responsible for studying the script to create a character with a complete life history, and they consistently argue that the script must serve as the blueprint for building characters. Professionals believed that only after exhaustive preparation could an actor integrate direction and accommodate the unique demands of film production, and they repeatedly discuss the need for dispassionate execution of performance. In short, rather than presenting a single method or theory of acting, practitioners describe a collection of assumptions, beliefs, strategies, and pragmatic guidelines for training the actor's instrument, developing characterizations, representing characters, and accommodating the demands of sound cinema.

Production context and the transition to sound

While methods for creating film performances became increasingly formalized and well articulated in the years following the transition to sound, the mystery or perhaps confusion about what was actually involved in producing film performances seems to have been heightened by production conventions that accompanied that transition. No longer were actors and directors rehearsing on stages next to productions in progress. No longer were directors guiding actors through performances with verbal instructions and/ or the support of musical accompaniment to set the mood. As a consequence of production demands that developed in the years between 1926 and 1934, film performances were the result of ever-increasing levels of division of labour. Most pointedly, the people who developed acting talent and worked with actors during rehearsals were often not the same people who worked with actors on the set. Beginning in the 1930s, the studios hired *dialogue coaches* or *dialogue directors* to work with actors on specific parts and dialogue scenes. The studios also brought in *drama coaches* to train young contract players and prepare even experienced actors for screen tests and actual performances. In the years following the transition to sound, these acting experts became an integral – but consistently hidden – part of the process of producing film performances.

The transition to sound not only led to changes in actual production processes and the creation of new positions. Sound cinema also provided work for actors and directors who would draw on their sometimes extensive experience in theatrical stock companies and Broadway productions. Industry observers of the period saw the migration of acting talent from Broadway to Hollywood as highly significant. One finds that by 1929, articles in the *New York Times* are often discussing the central role theatre actors had played in the casts of 'audible pictures'. In an article entitled 'Acting for the Sound Film', *New York Times* critic Otis Skinner perhaps summarizes the received wisdom of the day in arguing that the 'traditional actor', the stage actor 'schooled in the method of bringing life, emotions, and humor directly to the audience' looked to be the dominant type of actor in theatre and the Hollywood sound film.[1]

The transition to sound made stage experience a valuable commodity, and opened the floodgates to scores of theatrically trained actors. It also indirectly and incrementally led to new venues and methods for actor training, for Hollywood's transition to sound not only made stage training increasingly important, it also made securing that experience increasingly difficult. In the teens and twenties, actors had learned their craft through apprenticeships in film and/or theatre, but the arrival of sound reduced actors' opportunities for on-the-job training, and in particular training in theatrical venues. Participating in a process shaped by multiple economic and industrial forces, Hollywood sound cinema contributed to the decline of vaudeville, Broadway, and theatrical stock companies by cutting into stage productions' already reduced audiences. Exemplifying the trend of all American theatre, the number of productions mounted on Broadway dropped from 300 in the 1928/1929 season to 80 productions ten years later.

As the 1930s progressed, film executives openly discussed the fact that traditional training grounds for Hollywood actors had been raided to breaking point. The steady decline in the number of stage productions forced the studios to search for other ways of developing and maintaining acting talent. They began to hire acting experts and establish actor training programmes on the lots. The first dialogue directors and drama coaches were brought into the system in 1933, when Paramount hired veteran stage producer/director Lillian Albertson as a dialogue coach, and, as head of the talent department, Phyllis Loughton, who had stage managed for Norman Bel Geddes and the Jesse Bonstelle stock company. In 1935, Florence Enright, a founding member of the prestigious Theatre Guild in New York, became a drama coach at Universal, and the next year moved to Twentieth Century Fox. In 1936, Lillian Burns, an actress who learned her craft with the Belasco Company and had been a member of the Dallas Little Theatre, was put in charge of MGM's drama department. In 1938, Warner Bros hired Sophie Rosenstein to design their actor training programme. Rosenstein came to Warner Bros with ten years of experience as a drama teacher at the University of Washington. As a child she had studied with Josephine Dillon, yet another figure who in the studio years joined the ranks of film acting teachers. In the mid to late 1930s, drama schools were established throughout Hollywood and by 1939 all of the major studios had actor training programmes.

In addition to opening drama schools on the lots, the studios developed an increasingly close relationship with established institutions such as the American Academy of Dramatic Art and the Pasadena Playhouse, as well as drama schools set up by Moscow Art Theatre expatriate Maria Ouspenskaya and theatre companies such as the Actors' Laboratory. The Academy of Dramatic Art, founded in 1884, was the oldest acting school in America, and from its inception had been guided by the philosophy that 'imitative methods' of coaching must be replaced by what Academy directors such as Charles Jehlinger believed were 'methods of scientific training'. Courses in acting were first offered by the Pasadena Playhouse in 1928. The two-year programme that emerged from those first classes provided training in what Playhouse founder Gilmor Brown and his colleagues believed were the principles of 'modern stagecraft' that guided developments at the Moscow Art Theatre and the 'little theatre' movement in America. An interest in providing scientific, modern, and systematic methods for developing acting skills and specific performances also informed the actor training programs at the other noteworthy drama schools in Hollywood. Maria Ouspenskaya's School of Dramatic Art, founded in New York in 1929 and moved to Holly-wood in 1940, offered a two-year programme which, like other programmes of the period, required actors to spend the first year working almost entirely on developing the actor's instrument. The Actors' Laboratory – established in 1941 by former members of the Group Theatre such as Morris Carnovsky, Roman Bohnen, J. Edward Bromberg, and Phoebe Brand – provided actor training for a collection of contract players from RKO, Twentieth Century Fox, and Universal throughout the 1940s. The two-year programme they developed integrated courses in diction, body movement, improvisation, and life study, and was shaped by a philosophy Lab members referred to as a 'conscious approach to acting'.

The emerging importance of formal training for film actors was accompanied by increasingly systematic methods for developing skills and specific performances. Acting teachers working in Hollywood seem to have played a significant role in articulating and formalizing the period's methods of acting, for there is a collection of manuals authored by individuals who were integral to the network of actor training programmes in Hollywood. For example, *Modern Acting: A Manual* (1936), co-authored by Sophie Rosenstein, became a basic primer for Rosenstein's students in the drama school at Warner Bros, and also for contract players at Universal-International after Rosenstein became head of their talent development programme in 1949. *General Principles of Play Direction* (1936) by Gilmor Brown was a primary text for actors and directors at the Pasadena Playhouse, which for two decades served as a training ground and showcase for scores of film actors, and stage actors making the transition to film. In 1940, freelance acting teacher Josephine Dillon, who was Clark Gable's first acting teacher and later his first wife, published *Modern Acting: A Guide for Stage, Screen and Radio*. One finds Dillon's exhaustively detailed textbook consistently listed as a reference for courses offered at the Pasadena Playhouse and the Actors' Laboratory. In 1947, Lillian Albertson summarized the methods she had been presenting to contract players at Paramount and later at RKO in a manual entitled *Motion Picture Acting*, which opens with endorsements from actors Rosalind Russell and Cary Grant, journalist Adela Rogers St Johns, RKO casting director Ben Piazza, director Leo McCarey, and producer Jesse Lasky.

At this stage of research, it is not possible to determine how widely these manuals were studied. There is evidence, however, that following the transition to sound, acting experts became a recognized part of the Hollywood system. Trade papers of the period refer to the Actors' Lab as the best independent drama school in the country. Files from the Pasadena Playhouse show that a collection of film executives consistently secured casting advice from Playhouse directors, and openly admitted to using the Playhouse as a feeder school. Newspapers and archival records reveal that in 1940 Hedda Hopper asked drama coach Maria Ouspenskaya to write a guest column in which Ouspenskaya described the two-year programme offered by her drama school. A year later, the recognized role of acting experts, and of Ouspenskaya's unique contributions, is suggested in a Louella Parsons' column where Parsons describes Ouspenskaya as 'one of the finest coaches in the business'.

Stage and screen: quantitative adjustments

The transition to sound brought new acting experts to Hollywood and led to reconfigured working relations between actors and directors. It also brought with it a reassessment of stage and screen acting. In film acting manuals from the early 1920s, practitioners consistently argue that 'screen acting had become an art in itself [and that] it is not acting as we understand the word from what we see on the stage'.[2] Yet professionals working in Hollywood after the coming of sound no longer saw acting on stage as fundamentally different from acting on screen. Finding quantitative rather than qualitative distinctions in this later period, they discuss the need to adjust gestures and vocal delivery when moving from one venue to the other, and the fact that film acting required more training, experience, and concentration.

The period's changed perspective on screen acting is suggested by the fact that while practitioners in the early 1920s held conflicting views about the value of training in drama schools and theatrical productions, by the mid to late 1930s Hollywood professionals seem to have developed a definite consensus that training in dramatic schools and on the stage was not only valuable, but essential training for film actors. Training in tone production and diction were seen as important for work on both stage and screen. Training to create and maintain a body flexible enough to represent different types of characters was seen as a basic requirement of both stage and screen acting. Doing exercises to develop one's sensibilities, emotional recall ability, and skill in observation and concentration were considered part of any actor's work. The labour of building a character by analysing the script as a whole, creating a backstory for the character, and breaking down each scene to discover its purpose and the character's task, was seen as central to an actor's preparation for performances on both stage and screen.

In an article in *Theatre Arts*, American Academy of Dramatic Art graduate Hume Cronyn argues that 'the difference between acting for the screen and acting for the stage is negligible and the latter is, despite the exceptions, the best possible training for the former'.[3] He explains that the difference is negligible because in film, the actor's 'business, as in theatre, remains with the character he is to play and this will require his full powers of concentration'.[4] In another article in *Theatre Arts*, Bette Davis demystifies the stage/screen opposition by explaining that acting in theatre and film does not require actors to approach their characters differently, but that in preparation and performance certain adjustments need to be made. She writes that while 'it is axiomatic that a screen actor works in a medium that has its own, its special technical demands . . . this is not a qualitative distinction; it is merely quantitative'.[5] Davis explains the difference is merely quantitative because 'the art itself is not different . . . there does not exist one kind of acting for the stage, another for the films'.[6] Instead, stage and screen actors all 'work with the same tools. Our craft requires slight modification in them, that is all'.[7]

Practitioners of the period emphasize the fundamental bond between acting on stage and screen, and at the same time acknowledge that film practice in the studio era had its own technical demands. One finds actors consistently discussing the adjustments actors made when moving from one venue to another. They explain that 'acting in the movies [is] the same as acting anywhere [and that while they use] different projection, [they use] the same energy [because the transition is] like going from a big to a small theatre'.[8] Actors who came to film from theatre had to unlearn the practice of presenting large gestures on the stage, and discovered instead that 'shades of feeling could be made intimately visible by minute contractions of a muscle'.[9]

Many theatre actors came to enjoy working in film precisely because it allowed them to use small pieces of business to convey meaning. As Bette Davis explains, 'while the process of acting is basically the same [on stage and screen], the screen is a fantastic medium for the reality of little things'.[10] Cronyn echoes that point in saying that

> it may take a little time and some guidance for the stage actor to become accustomed to the degree of projection which will be most effective on the screen, but the technique of film acting is no unique or mystic formula.[11]

He explains that in film

> a whole new range of expression is opened to the actor. He can register with a whisper, a glance, a contraction of a muscle, in a manner that would be lost on stage. The camera will often reflect what a man thinks, without the degree of demonstration required in the theatre.[12]

These observations are repeated throughout materials from the period, for practitioners found that a film actor's new range of expression did not appear 'naturally' by virtue of being photographed, but instead had to emerge under his or her conscious control.

Working in a medium that magnified everything, actors and their collaborators clearly articulated the specific demands of acting in film. One finds acting experts explicitly stating that 'the fundamental difference between acting on the stage and the screen [was] the size of the actor from the viewpoint of the audience'.[13] Acting teacher Josephine Dillon explains that because images projected on the screen were sometimes 30 feet high, gestures and expressions would be 'huge and ridiculous if exaggerated . . . even if they [were performed only] as large as sometimes used in real life'.[14] Discussing the effect of performances being framed in close-up and projected on large screens, MGM drama coach Lillian Burns explains that actors coming to film from theatre had

> [to learn] projection from the *eyes* instead of just the voice [for] in motion pictures there is a camera, what I have termed a 'truth machine'. You cannot say 'dog' and think 'cat' because 'meow' will come out if you do.[15]

The magnification of actors' expressions and gestures led acting experts to formalize methods for creating film performances devoid of exaggerated, distracting, meaningless, and confusing movement. In her analysis of 'thought conversation', Josephine Dillon clarifies Burns's observation that the camera is a truth machine. Dillon explains that

> the expressions of the eyes . . . represent the emotions of the part played [and so] the actor should, in studying the part, improvise the probable mental conversations of the person portrayed, and memorize them as carefully as the written dialogue.[16]

Even more specifically, Dillon points out that

> the dialogue ascribed to the persons in the play conveys what the other people in the play are to believe [while] the expressions in the eyes and the body show to the audience what the character in the play is actually feeling and thinking.[17]

Dillon's advice to use internal dialogue to colour expression in actors' eyes suggests the integral points of contact between stage and screen acting in this period, for the method is in fact an extension of practices developed for performances in 'modern' theatre. As Rosenstein and her colleagues explain in *Modern Acting: A Manual*, actors should give themselves 'positive silent lines [that are] as true and absorbing as any lines' spoken on stage.[18] The authors point out that it will be easier for the actor 'to guarantee his attention in [a] particular scene if he works out a suitable thought pattern of definite reactions which he undergoes as religiously as he adheres to the written dialogue the author has given him.'[19] Rosenstein and her colleagues refer to the thought pattern developed for each and every scene as 'silent thinking'.[20]

Echoing observations about *quantitative adjustments* made for performing on camera, practitioners of the period consistently discuss shooting out of sequence, and having little or no rehearsal on the set in terms of adjustments to established (theatrical) methods. That is, even given the logistics of Hollywood film production, the transition to sound seems to have led professionals to minimize distinctions between methods for approaching stage and screen performance. With the addition of filmed 'dialogue scenes', at least some practitioners seem to have considered various methods of preparation for film performances as modifications of processes involved in theatrical rehearsals. Actor Hume Cronyn explains that when he worked in his first film 'it became obvious that in theatre terms there was to be practically no rehearsal'.[21] Understanding that, Cronyn responded like other experienced actors working in Hollywood and took the task of preparation on himself. He studied his script, chose his wardrobe, studied his character's relationship to other characters in the screenplay, developed 'some detailed ideas on [his] own character's background and his action throughout the story'.[22] He used an extension of theatre's dress rehearsal routine by choosing his character's house in the neighbourhood they were shooting, his character's place of work, and so on. He kept a notebook that gave him 'a point of reference . . . to return to, and recheck, character fundamentals'.[23] Cronyn explains that a film actor's individual preparation makes it possible to 'step before the camera with a clear and logical plan of what you would like to do and how you would like to do it'.[24]

Repeating points made by theatrically trained actors like Cronyn, MGM drama coach Lillian Burns describes the work of film professionals who came to the set fully prepared, able to incorporate directors' suggestions precisely because they had done their homework and could create characters on their own. In an interview with columnist Gladys Hall, Burns explains that little rehearsal time on the set meant more, not less, labour for film actors. Burns argues that while 'they say it's so easy [to act in film] you don't go over and over it [on the set] as you do on stage'.[25] Burns sees overcoming the problem of working without rehearsal and shooting out of sequence as one that required skill, rather than reliance on a larger-than-life personality. Noting that she gets 'angry when people say [film acting] isn't as difficult as the stage', Burns points to the example of Greer Garson, who in playing a scene in *Madame Curie* 'sat absolutely quiet, didn't talk for ten minutes, then walked to a drape and broke down and sobbed'. Burns remarks, 'to walk into that on a cold morning, that takes doing'.[26]

Coming from Burns, the insight and the compliment is worth noting, for before Burns came to MGM in 1936, there had been classes in diction, body movement, and so on, but 'working through production [helping to cast and rehearse actors] had never been done quite the way [she] did it'.[27] Burns not only worked with executives on hiring and casting, she also worked with, and sometimes around, studio directors. She would work privately with leading actors because, as MGM executive Al Trescony explains, she could 'get performances out of actors that even surprised them'.[28] Trescony notes that Burns not only prepared 'most of our stars for their specific roles . . . often she would be asked by the heads of the other studios to work with their stars'.[29] 'Respected because of her talent and feared because she leveled with everyone',[30] like other dialogue directors and drama coaches of the period, Lillian Burns played a pivotal role in the production of film performances in the 1930s and 1940s.

Building a dramatic character

For the people whose job it was to produce performances, the script served as a blueprint that was studied to ensure that actors arrived on the set prepared to deliver their performances. Bette Davis explains that 'without scripts none of us can work. It's the beginning of the work.'[31] Hume Cronyn points out that the actor's first task is to establish the facts, and he remarks, 'it's surprising how much information is contained in the text, how many questions are answered by careful re-reading.'[32] He argues that 'your own creative work should be based on the fact and suggestion supplied by the author, rather than on independent fancy.'[33]

Echoing the actors' observations, Lillian Burns explains: 'the writer – that's the seed'.[34] Working with Burns, one learned that after studying the script, actors begin to give their characters life by 'establishing a complete person, a complete life', for example, where the character went to school, what he or she liked to wear, what that character would do in a certain circumstance because of his or her relationships with parents, brothers, and sisters, and so on.[35] Janet Leigh recalls Burns taught her that

> you give that person a real entity, so that wherever you happen to start the story you are coming from somewhere; you know where this person's been, why this person reacts the way she does. Because it may not be your way of reacting, but it would be the character's.[36]

Cronyn echoes her point. He explains that an actor's own responses are immaterial, and that actors must always ask, 'If I were *this kind of person* in this situation, what would I do? How would I feel, think, behave, react, etc.?'[37]

In her 1947 acting manual, drama coach Lillian Albertson also presents the script as the starting point for the production of film performances. Albertson argues, in no uncertain terms, that '*before performance comes interpretation*. By that, I mean the strictly intellectual analysis of a role.'[38] In a strictly intellectual analysis, actors use the script to determine the character's background, asking 'what made this person feel the way he or she does, and do the things they do?'[39] Albertson points out that 'if there is not enough in the dialogue to provide you with all the motives animating them, *make up stories about them* so that they seem alive to you.'[40] For actors in the studio era, the practice of filling in characters' backgrounds was part of the process of slowly and methodically entering into the world of the characters. That process required actors to be touched by the characters emotionally. Actors' Laboratory member Morris Carnovsky explains that great parts 'give us "thoughts beyond the reaches of our souls" . . . they are great images [that actors] learn to use and to be shaken [by].'[41]

Like other professionals of the period, Albertson acknowledges that acting was not simply a matter of transcribing what one found in the script. She argues that an actor is a kind of prism through which the character is refracted, and explains that '*the author supplies the material which {actors} cut and fit to their own personalities and physical appearances*'.[42] Here Albertson is not suggesting that actors play themselves. Instead, she is articulating the era's dominant view that an actor's instrument necessarily colours a performance, and that as a consequence an actor must take conscious control of it. Echoing Albertson's point, the Actors' Laboratory teaching staff describe the art of acting as one that incorporates in *sensible* terms and by means of the actor's personal equipment an impression or image previously indicated by the author. Acting experts of the period saw the process of acting as one in which actors take in an impression of the character from the script, and in the process of representing the character necessarily colour it with their own expression. Underscoring the period's holistic or organic view of this process, Morris Carnovsky explains that acting is never a passive experience because, as he puts it, 'there's no taking in [of the character] without giving out – no reaction without action. All is in process of becoming.'[43]

Representing a dramatic character on screen

Materials from the period suggest that in the 1930s and 1940s, actors and their collaborators believed that actors should work to produce convincing performances without recourse to 'living the part'. Lillian Albertson explains that 'mental pictures', which an actor develops in the course of studying the script, make the events of the scene *alive in {the actor's} memory*.[44] Consequently they can be used by the actor to make his or her performance convincing, vivid, lifelike. Albertson exhorts actors to

> make all the mental pictures you can in *preparation of the scene* – and the more graphic the better . . . make your mental pictures as real as you possibly can in *studying* the part, then *play from memory – the synthetic memories you have invented*.[45]

An interview with Jessica Tandy provides a gloss on Albertson's statement. When asked how she prepared for and then enacted her portrayal in the Actors' Laboratory stage production of *Portrait of a Madonna*, Tandy explained that she worked through the process she always had, first reading and re-reading the script, then looking for points of contact with her own experience she could draw on, then developing a background for the character. For the performance she explains that she never recalled an emotion, but instead that the feelings which coloured her performance were always the result of seeing the pictures she had created in her study, and that each speech led to another through a series of mental pictures.

Manuals from the period explain that actors could and should use their mental pictures once they developed their ability to concentrate on them. Albertson explains that 'through *concentration* you learn to *use* the creative acting imagination, and concentration is something that *can be developed*'.[46] She argues that actors must develop their ability to concentrate on the character during performances because it is only 'concentration [that] enables you to shut out every thought but the scene and the character you are portraying'.[47] By using concentration to connect to the mental pictures one creates in studying the character in his or her given situations, 'you develop the *mood* that must "color" every action and every word you speak'.[48] Albertson argues that it is not enough to move gracefully and naturally and to read lines intelligently. Instead, actors need to understand that 'to get every ounce of meaning out of your lines . . . your MOOD [must] be what it should be [because] *spoken words mean practically nothing unless mood colors them.*'[49]

For experienced practitioners of the period, moods that colour actions and lines of dialogue were established by actors making decisions about how a character would feel in a certain circumstance. Those decisions would become 'scripted' into a series of mental pictures, which actors would then recall during performance. Because they were 'synthetic memories' invented by actors during their study of the script, they could be activated by opening one's 'mental notebook', and let go of immediately after the scene or take was over. Albertson explains that 'as your powers of concentration increase, you will be able *to turn mood on and off* as readily and as surely as you turn on a faucet and get water, and turn it off to stop the flow!'[50]

Rosenstein's *Modern Acting: A Manual* anticipates Albertson's observations, and is especially clear that actors must learn to transfer emotions to the circumstances of the scene. Describing the role imagination plays in the process of preparing a part, Rosenstein and her colleagues explain that 'once we recall a former emotion we must sustain it long enough to transpose it to the new situation', and that while it may not be easy to dispense with recollected details, 'by constant drill . . . we can learn to drop them at will and preserve only the emotion they served to revive'.[51] In other words, for acting experts of the period, developing the ability to concentrate did not just keep actors from being distracted – it was seen as the basis of convincing performance.

For practitioners in the 1930s and 1940s, concentration, not feeling, was the key to great acting. Like other acting professionals of the period, Morris Carnovsky articulates the logic of striving to maintain emotional distance from the feelings portrayed. He explains that actors cannot get lost in emotional moments because they need to keep up with and anticipate the sequence of actions in the narrative. He writes: 'I always think of the actor as not only doing, but standing aside and watching what he is doing, so as to be able to propel himself to the next thing and the next thing and the next.'[52] Josephine Dillon also makes the point that actors need to be able to think about what they are doing, and she argues that acting in film makes emotional distance an especially high priority. Dillon explains that 'to submerge one's self into the emotion of the part being played would be to put the actor at the mercy of his emotions and make him incapable of using the skillful technique that the camera demands.'[53]

Drama coach Lillian Albertson continually contrasts the methods she describes with positions that encouraged actors to use their own feelings to generate convincing performances. Albertson notes that she had seen 'young actors in motion pictures try to lash themselves into a pathetic mood [by trying] to think of something *real* that [would] harrow their souls'.[54] She explains that in the process, actors would find themselves in an 'agonizing attempt to *feel* something' that was easily and invariably disturbed by the concrete reality of the performance and production context.[55] Albertson argues that the strategy of drawing on mood patterns and voice patterns that have been embedded into the mental pictures actors construct in their study of the part was a technique for generating lifelike performances that was 'much surer and far less wearing on the nervous system'.[56]

The ability to 'divorce outward gestures and expressions from their ordinary affective content',[57] prized by practitioners in the 1930s and 1940s, is precisely what proponents of Method acting in the 1950s would reject, for they saw that 'ability' as the source of inauthentic performance, and argued that dispassionate execution of performance, along with extensive preparation and an investment in training the actor's physical instrument, necessarily led to performances and performance styles that were 'unrealistic' and unimaginative. Yet the methods described by Albertson, Carnovsky, Davis, Cronyn, and others who articulated the views of the 1930s and 1940s are not necessarily recipes for conventional performances. Instead, they represent a definable position in a long history of debates within the acting profession.

As stated by Denis Diderot in the eighteenth century, the paradox of acting is that one cannot act without feeling, yet if one feels one cannot act. For practitioners in the 1930s and 1940s, the solution to the paradox was to use synthetic memories to fuel controlled emotional experience during performance. Like Stanislavsky, they believed that actors should welcome personal and primary experience for the insights it could offer in the process of studying a script and building a character, but that during performance, actors needed to summon feelings that they had connected to the mental pictures they themselves had crafted after close study of the script. Like Stanislavsky, they argued that training, preparation, and cool-headed acting provided the secure basis for performances and performance styles that emerged from the unique demands of each script. And prosaic as it may sound, acting professionals of the period seem to have found that Hollywood's assembly-line mode of production, with its intense division of labor, developed within it rather efficient ways for actors and their collaborators to craft performances.

Notes

1 O. Skinner, 'Acting for the Sound Film', *New York Times*, 25 January 1931.
2 I. Klump and H. Klumph, *Screen Acting*, New York, Falk Publishing, 1921, p. 104.
3 H. Cronyn, 'Notes on Film Acting', *Theatre Arts* 35, June 1949, p. 46.
4 Ibid.
5 B. Davis, 'On Acting in Films', *Theatre Arts* 25, September 1946, p. 634.
6 Ibid.
7 Ibid.

8 L. Penn, 'Stanislavski and a Ten Day Shooting', *Actors' Laboratory Newsletter*, Actors' Laboratory Collection, University of California, Los Angeles, *c.* 1946.

9 D. Powell, 'Acting for Motion Pictures', *Theatre Today*, Actors' Laboratory Collection, University of California, Los Angeles, *c.* 1947.

10 B. Davis, interview, *Filmmakers on Filmmaking: The American Film Institute Seminars on Motion Pictures and Television Vol. 2*, Los Angeles, Tarcher, 1983, p. 106.

11 Cronyn, 'Notes on Film Acting', p. 46.

12 Ibid.

13 J. Dillon, *Modern Screen, and Radio, Acting: A Guide for Stage*, New York, Prentice Hall, 1940, p. 3.

14 Ibid., p. 4.

15 L. Burns, interview, Performing Arts Oral History Collection, Southern Methodist University, 17 August 1986.

16 Dillon, *Modern Screen, and Radio, Acting*, p. 9.

17 Ibid.

18 S. Rosenstein, L.A. Haydon, and W. Sparrow, *Modern Acting: A Manual*, New York, Samuel French, 1936, p. 61.

19 Ibid., p. 62.

20 Ibid., p. 110.

21 Cronyn, 'Notes on Film Acting', p. 45.

22 Ibid.

23 Ibid., p. 46.

24 Ibid., p. 47.

25 L. Burns and G. Sidney, interview, Gladys Hall Collection, Margaret Herrick Library of the Motion Picture Academy of Arts and Sciences, *c.* 1945.

26 Ibid.

27 Burns, interview, Performing Arts Oral History Collection, 1986.

28 A. Trescony, interview, Performing Arts Oral History Collection, Southern Methodist University, 20 August 1986.

29 Ibid.

30 Ibid.

31 Davis, interview, *Filmmakers on Filmmaking*, p. 107.

32 Cronyn, 'Notes on Film Acting', p. 48.

33 Ibid.

34 Burns, interview, Performing Arts Oral History Collection, 1986.

35 J. Leigh, interview, Performing Arts Oral History Collection, Southern Methodist University, 25 July 1984.

36 Ibid.

37 Cronyn, 'Notes on Film Acting', p. 48.

38 L. Albertson, *Motion Picture Acting*, New York, Funk & Wagnalls, 1947, p. 65.

39 Ibid.

40 Ibid.

41 M. Carnovsky, 'Let's Talk', *Workshop Craftsmen*, Actors' Laboratory Collection, University of California, Los Angeles, January 1948.

42 Albertson, *Motion Picture Acting*, p. 66.

43 Carnovsky, 'Let's Talk'.

44 Albertson, *Motion Picture Acting*, p. 63.

45 Ibid.
46 Ibid., p. 55.
47 Ibid.
48 Ibid.
49 Ibid., pp. 55–56.
50 Ibid., p. 57.
51 Rosenstein, Haydon, and Sparrow, *Modern Acting: A Manual*, p. 29.
52 M. Carnovsky, 'The Actor's Eye', *Performing Arts Journal*, 1984, p. 23.
53 Dillon, *Modern Acting*, p. 7.
54 Albertson, *Motion Picture Acting*, p. 61.
55 Ibid., p. 62.
56 Ibid.
57 J. Roach, *The Player's Passion*, Ann Arbor, University of Michigan Press, 1996, p. 135.

4

BETTE DAVIS
Malevolence in motion

Martin Shingler

Bette Davis's attempt to seduce Leslie Howard has failed. Suddenly she seems pathetic, vulnerable and, for a brief moment, almost angelic. But when Howard tells her she disgusts him, a dramatic transformation occurs. In close shot, her face registers the shock of his words, her shoulders drawn up to her chin, her eyes wide and staring. Her jaw moves very slightly forward and her eyes glare with hostility as her first words spew from her mouth. 'Me!' In a medium-close shot, her shoulders twitch with tension as she proceeds, 'I disgust you!' She takes a short step backwards and repeats the word 'You!', pronounced 'yew' with an emphasis on the 'w'. Her shoulders drop slightly as she takes another short step back and once more utters her own version of the word 'you', this time louder and more emphatic. Now her shoulders drop further revealing a long neck and she launches herself into a hysterical tirade, gathering speed and volume with every word, her eyes flaring open and her arms jerking in spasms at her sides (largely below the frame of the camera). She turns around abruptly as if to walk away but immediately spins back round.

As she returns to the attack, she unleashes a torrent of abuse. A medium-shot reveals the upper half of her body writhing with tension. Her mouth bites viciously on every word, getting faster and louder all the time. Her eyes narrow, her brow contracts, and she gazes hard at Howard's (off-screen) feet, then his face, then his feet again. The initial outpouring is succeeded by a sudden release of tension, a dissipation of energy as she shifts her weight, repositioning her feet (out of shot, below the frame). Her head tilts back brazenly and with a grimace she tells him to his face that she never cared for him. Her eyes flick back and forth from his face to his feet, her voice lifting to a higher register. The higher pitch imposes more strain on the voice as she tells him she was always making a fool of him, of how he bored her and how she hated him: 'It made me sick when I had to let you kiss me.' The word 'sick' is vomited out of her mouth following a surge of energy running up through her body. 'I only did it because you begged me. You hounded me, you

46

drove me crazy.' Now her arms have broken free from her sides and with her fists tightly clenched they jab out in front of her, beating the air.

Another very slight pause follows as she turns around and walks away but, once again, instantly spins round and thrusts herself forward, hands still clenched and jabbing the air. 'And after you kissed me, I always used to wipe my mouth.' Her eyes flare, at his feet, at his face. 'Wipe my mouth', she repeats, literally wiping her mouth with her forearm and violently throwing the offending kiss to the floor with a repulsive gesture. 'But I made up for it – for every kiss I had to laugh, we laughed at you!' She screams these words, her in-takes of breath clearly audible, and then laughs like a maniac. 'Miller and me and Griffith and me, we laughed at you because you were such a mug.' She backs away repeating the words 'a mug', backing up further and casting about her, searching for something. 'A mug!', she shouts, grabbing a plate and flinging it down to the floor at his feet. 'D'you know what you are, you gimpy-legged monster? You're a cripple, a cripple, a cripple!' She screams these last words. They are so high-pitched that her voice breaks, producing a shrill sound, both piercing and fragile. With the last word out of her mouth she gazes around her for an instant, then dashes from the room, slamming the door behind her. Her tirade has taken just over a minute. It is powerful, shocking, and intense: a bravura display of hysteria, fury, and bitterness, edged with vulnerability.

This is not Davis in a rage but an actress in motion, presenting fury through her shoulders, neck, torso, her arms and hands, her eyes and her mouth, through her voice and her breathing. Fury is the result of a systematic orchestration of all of these elements, developed through the use of muscles, movements, and sounds. The scene reveals an actress in full command of her body, face, and voice, whose movements are used to convey in a most vivid way the thoughts and emotions of her character. The character is Mildred Rogers and the film is *Of Human Bondage* (John Cromwell, Radio Pictures, 1934). It marks Bette Davis's most dramatic and accomplished performance in that film, even of her career up to that point in time. It reveals techniques she had developed as a student of dance and drama and as a professional actor of stage and screen. It reveals qualities that she would later perfect and refine. It is a defining moment, when Bette Davis revealed what she was truly capable of as an actor.

In due course, Bette Davis became one of Hollywood's most celebrated actors. During the late 1930s and early 1940s she enjoyed tremendous success both at the box office and with the critics. After receiving an Academy Award for her performance in *Jezebel* (William Wyler, 1938), she was subsequently nominated over the next four consecutive years for her performances in the films *Dark Victory* (Edmund Goulding, 1939), *The Letter* (William Wyler, 1940), *The Little Foxes* (William Wyler, 1941) and *Now, Voyager* (Irving Rapper, 1942). In short, from 1938 to 1942, Bette Davis was the most successful, most popular, and most acclaimed film actress in the United States. This was in stark contrast to the early to mid-1930s, when her performances in individual films were very largely ignored in favour of her more famous co-stars (e.g. George Arliss, Ruth Chatterton, and Spencer Tracy). However, in 1934 this changed when Davis appeared opposite Leslie Howard in *Of Human Bondage*. Her performance as the vile waitress Mildred Rogers impressed many critics as not only her best work but also as one of the finest achievements of any actress in an American movie. From this time on, critics paid increasing attention to Davis's work, scrutinizing her performances, judging her strengths and weaknesses. By the late 1930s, she was widely held to be one of the most accomplished actresses in Hollywood, even respected as an authority on film acting with her opinions published regularly. This began in 1937 when she was chosen to contribute a chapter for a book entitled *We Make the Movies*.[1] Davis was invited to provide an account of her role as a film actress, speaking on behalf of her female colleagues in Hollywood. From this time on she would continue to publish her opinions on film acting in motion picture journals and magazines, and much of her autobiography was devoted to establishing her approach as an actress.[2]

Over the years, Bette Davis held firm and consistent views on just what constituted good film acting and maintained her opinions despite significant changes in the philosophy and practices of acting in the American film industry. Although her published statements are both interesting and insightful, it is not my intention to explore these in this essay. Whilst I will be drawing on a number of Davis's remarks about her approach to film acting, I am more concerned here to investigate how she developed as a screen performer by analysing the characteristics of her technique as revealed in a number of films from the first stage of her film career. For this essay, I concentrate primarily on two films which reveal most clearly the major developments of her acting technique during her formative period: *Of Human Bondage* and *Dangerous* (Alfred E. Green, 1935). It is my belief that these represent a pivotal moment in Bette Davis's development as a screen actress and that while in both she produces fine and compelling performances, the latter marks a significant advance, a consolidation and refinement of the method she had evolved.

Despite more than a year and a half in Hollywood and appearances in ten motion pictures, Bette Davis had yet to receive any praise for her acting until the end of September 1932, when Warner Bros released *Cabin in the Cotton* directed by Michael Curtiz. This film, starring Richard Barthelmess, featured Davis amongst the cast and, despite limited screen time, she made a striking impression. Charles Higham wrote that, 'As Madge, the dizzy, selfish, peroxided Southern belle, she created a fully rounded character, at once ruthless, bold, and pathetic.'[3] Madge was a new kind of character for Davis, no longer the nice girl, the girl-next-door, or the good sister type she had been used to playing up until this point but a temptress, a 'sex-bomb', a tramp. Gone was the need for her to just gaze doe-eyed at her male lead, all dreamy and wistful. Now she could entice, toy with, and dominate her victim. Where before her characters had been either simpering or sentimental, now she could be sexual, scheming, and sinful, all of which called for more in terms of her performance. The part itself might still be as small as her previous roles but the scope was considerably greater.

One particular scene captured the interest of both the public and the critics. It is described here by Charles Higham:

> There is one marvelous scene, daring for its time, that succeeds in conveying a surprising degree of eroticism. . . . Though played entirely at shoulder level, the scene conveys great power: Bette undressing in a closet, undoing the bow of her dress, and emerging, it is clearly implied, brazenly naked.[4]

This scene has also been described by another of Davis's biographers, Barbara Leaming. She writes that,

> Unremarkable in itself, the shot is of special interest on account of the peculiar expressiveness Bette imparts to her shoulder movements. Her background in interpretative dance has taught her to communicate depth of feeling by animating the shoulders . . . as her dancer's physical training has allowed her to engage the eye with subtle articulations of muscle and collarbone, made visible beneath the skin.[5]

Back in October 1927, as a full-time student at the John Murray Anderson and Robert Milton School of Theatre and Dance in New York City, Bette Davis had attended the classes of Martha Graham, pioneer and leading exponent of modern dance. One of Graham's foremost principles was that to dance was to act, alerting her pupils to the expressive potential of the body. Her technique centred primarily on achieving control of the back and the pelvis. Having developed a remarkably expressive use of her spine, neck, and shoulders as well as her arms, Graham developed these in her pupils by having them begin their training seated on the floor. Working only with their arms and torsos, her students concentrated on strengthening and refining the movements of their bodies from shoulders to hips.[6]

Throughout her film career, Bette Davis was to draw repeatedly on many of the expressive techniques she had acquired from her lessons in dance. This is most often to be seen in the way she concentrates her performance specifically on the movements and tensions of her shoulders, torso, hips, and arms. For instance, her tirade against Leslie Howard in *Of Human Bondage* involves her body registering a sequence of changes which entail her shoulders descending, her arms becoming increasingly animated, her hands becoming increasingly tense, her body hestitating between pulling away and thrusting forward, producing two full body spins. This is the product of an actress trained in the art of expressive movement and, more specifically, in the Graham technique. Another actress may have performed the whole scene with nothing more than her voice and her face, making her eyes and her lips register all the anger, hatred, and loathing felt by her character. But this is not Davis's approach. As she pointed out in her autobiography of 1962: 'I believed that there were emotions too great not to use full body. I believed – as onstage – that one acts with the complete body. One's back can describe an emotion.'[7]

For Davis, it is not enough to tell Leslie Howard she despises him so much that she always wiped her mouth after he kissed her. To express the full extent of her disgust, she has physically to wipe her mouth and violently fling the imagined kiss away from her. In this and other ways, every part of her must express the mounting hysteria unleashed by her words, creating what appear to be involuntary movements of the body, spasms running through her, which make her seem out of control. But, of course, this is a highly controlled performance: one that is deftly orchestrated, building steadily with repeated gestures, movements, muscle tension, and expressions. Each action is carefully deployed in relation to the other, gradually increasing the pace and the scale of each action as it is repeated until she reaches a climax on the words 'Cripple! Cripple! Cripple!'.

Of Human Bondage, shot in February and March 1934, was the actress's twenty-second picture and her most important role to date: a leading role, playing opposite the English actor Leslie Howard. Howard, as the greater star at this time, had greater screen time devoted to him; however in the scenes in which the two actors appear together, it is Davis who holds the attention of both the camera and the viewer. The camera follows her movements (even when she is doing no more than walking across the room to open a door) and mirrors are frequently used to emphasize and duplicate Davis's body. If the framing and mirroring of Davis directs our attention to her body, so does the actress's own unceasing movements. Where Howard is often static or, at most, slow moving, Davis is all restless motion. When she walks, it is not just her legs that move but also her shoulders, her hips, her arms, and her fingers.

Yet her performance was by no means restricted to her body. As Gavin Lambert put it in an article in *Sight & Sound* in 1951, 'miraculously, the face had "taken", the full range of mobility, expression, temperament, had broken through the earlier image'.[8] The most notable aspect of Davis's face was her eyes: large, liquid, and constantly moving. Her pupils rove restlessly from side to side and up and down in grand sweeping arches whilst her eyelashes have a very pronounced and emphatic motion. Close-ups of Davis's eyes are used frequently, shot slightly from above, enabling the viewer to peer right into them as she looks upward, her lids wide open and the lights strongly reflected, making them glossy. The liquidity of her eyes is particularly highlighted in a scene of her sipping champagne. Here Davis gazes wide-eyed

Figure 4.1 The framing and mirroring of Bette Davis in *Of Human Bondage* (1934) directs attention to her body, as do the actress's own unceasing movements. Throughout her career, Davis maintained her full-bodied technique, believing that 'One's back can describe an emotion'

Source: RKO Radio Pictures

directly into the camera, the champagne reflected in her eyes, lending them added sparkle and luminosity. This image forms a striking contrast with later shots of the actress's eyes, dimmed and vacant, following her descent into disease and destitution.

Whilst Davis's eyes are used throughout the film very self-consciously to chart the fate of her character, her voice plays a key role in her characterization. Davis was concerned to use every aspect of her voice to reveal the thoughts and feelings of her character. Occasionally, as in her furious tirade, this is used to tremendous effect: the rising volume, pace, and pitch of her voice combined with increasingly audible breaths produce an effective climax with the painful shrieks of the word 'cripple', at once violent and vulnerable. At other times, however, her voice seems too self-conscious and over-determined, primarily due to her cockney accent. Rather than simply make her character sound like a working-class woman from London's East End, Davis also injected into this voice a failed attempt to sound more refined. Whilst attempting to reflect the natural cadences of the dialect, Davis wanted Mildred's voice to betray her as a fake, even at the expense of making her cockney accent sound false. The result is a voice that is recognizably contrived, making her performance seem stagey. It is not that her cockney accent is a poor imitation of the real thing but that the noticeable care and attention going into producing it alerts us to the fact that it is a contrivance, that this is not the speaker's accustomed mode of speaking. Consequently, it is not the character that is speaking but the actress and, as such, it is not Mildred's comments that we judge but the success or otherwise of Davis's performance.

What can be said of Davis's voice in *Of Human Bondage* can also be said of her look. Much effort went into the creation of her make-up, costume, and hair – and it showed. Her appearance stands out as something almost unique in Hollywood film making of the period. For most of the film Davis strove to make Mildred cheap and vulgar, the only exception being when she appears as the hero's ideal woman in his dream sequence. Here – and only here – Davis receives the Hollywood treatment, beautifully coiffed, made-up and elegantly dressed (the lighting and soft focus enhancing the effect). But elsewhere, in stark contrast, Davis's hair, make-up, and clothes are anything but tasteful, expensive, or attractive. Whilst fellow actresses Francis Dee and Kay Johnson are stylish and fashionable by the standards of the day (corresponding closely with the images of fashion magazines), Davis's use of costume and make-up lends her a very different kind of image. Repeatedly throughout her career, she would willingly sacrifice glamour in favour of what she considered to be realism. *Of Human Bondage* marked the beginnings of such an approach which would be developed in films such as *Marked Woman* (Lloyd Bacon, 1936) and *The Private Lives of Elizabeth and Essex* (Michael Curtiz, 1939). Creating unglamorous looks for her characters would enable her to distinguish herself from the archetypal female movie star and promote herself as a serious actress prepared to sacrifice her own physical appeal for the sake of her characterization. It would not, however, always ensure that she seemed any less fake or fabricated than her female colleagues, given that often her determination to defy the unwritten Hollywood rule that all female actresses below a certain age be beautiful often led her to use wigs, costumes, and make-up more suited to the stage than the high street.

It is clear that, in many ways, Davis was taking chances with her characterization in *Of Human Bondage* and, like most gamblers, sometimes she won and sometimes she lost. She had produced some magnificent scenes, demonstrated a serious and uncompromising approach to her role as an actress, and demonstrated her own distinctive qualities as a performer. But she had also produced some moments of excessive and highly self-conscious acting which would widely be seen as over-acting when magnified through the camera and microphone and projected on to the cinema screen. Despite such moments, her performance was widely greeted with rave reviews. As Barbara Leaming has pointed out, 'Critics extolled her Mildred Rogers as "easily her finest performance" (*New York Times*) and "probably the best performance ever recorded on the screen by a US actress" (*Life*)'.[9] In fact, many believed that she deserved an Academy Award for her role in *Of Human Bondage*. When she failed to be nominated, so strong was the feeling that the actress had been undeservedly overlooked that a campaign was organized to persuade the Academy of Motion Picture Arts and Sciences to include her amongst the nominees.

Although the Academy was not persuaded to nominate Davis for Best Actress of 1934, her performance in *Of Human Bondage* did have a positive effect on the actress's career in that it transformed the way in which she was used and marketed by her studio. In 1935 Warner Bros promoted Davis to the status of 'star' and radically reconstructed her image. Whereas previous attempts to market Davis as a glamorous seductress had failed (most notably with the film *Ex-Lady*, directed by Robert Florey in 1933), in 1935 the studio discovered a more effective means of enhancing Davis's star status by highlighting in her publicity not her glamour or physical attractions but her acting abilities.[10] As part of its new approach to the marketing of Bette Davis, Warner Bros produced a star vehicle designed explicitly to promote her as an actor of talent and distinction.

In *Dangerous* Davis would play the part of a jinxed actress who has forsaken a highly successful stage career in favour of drink and destitution, only to be saved and restored to the theatre by Franchot Tone. The role would require her to employ the full range of her emotional register in order to chart the fall and rise of the Broadway star. Drunkenness, addiction, hysteria, tears, love, selfishness, and self-sacrifice were all demanded by the part – on top of which Davis would have to convince audiences that her character was also a brilliant and charismatic actress. As with any star vehicle, the film was carefully tailored to the actress's personality, public persona, and acting style, building upon the strengths of her performance in *Of Human Bondage* and avoiding the weaknesses.

There is a scene in *Dangerous* strikingly reminiscent of the one described earlier in *Of Human Bondage*. Joyce Heath (Bette Davis) visits her estranged husband to persuade him to give her a divorce so that she can marry Don Bellows (Franchot Tone). Initially she is business-like, cold, and aloof to the point of becoming visibly contemptuous when she discovers that her husband still loves her after all she has done to destroy his life and make him miserable. When he informs her that he will never give her a divorce because she is all he has left, she grows angry but, realizing that this will get her nowhere, she hesitates and (after a brief moment of calculation) changes her tactics. Instead she pleads, begging him to take pity on her and set her free. But when her supplication has no effect whatsoever, she finally explodes in fury, hatred, and loathing, denouncing her husband as pathetic and repulsive to her.

Joyce's outburst lasts a little less time than Mildred's, about 20 seconds, culminating in her slapping her husband across the face. It is shot in a single static, high-angled close-shot up to the point just before she slaps him. The close-shot reveals Davis's head and shoulders, her arms stretched out along the back of an armchair on which she has thrown herself down when her pleading failed. For a second, Davis bites her lip, eyes glaring up at her husband's face off-screen, the muscles tensing around her eyes, her shoulders flinch and she begins to speak in a strained, rather low and emphatic voice, her lower jaw thrust a little forward producing a scowl. Her first words are delivered through clenched teeth, the tension in her mouth creating a deadened (rather than resonant) sound, firm but muffled: 'Every time I think that those soft sticky hands of yours ever touched me it makes me sick.' At the word 'sick' her eyes narrow and her mouth tenses further, producing a visible shudder through her head and shoulders. Now her voice bursts forth – faster, higher, and louder. 'Sick, you hear?' She pushes herself up from the chair with her elbow but slips immediately back into position and delivers the following line in a lower, clearer, and more resonant voice (having unclenched her teeth), 'You're everything that's repulsive to me.' 'Your wife!' she exclaims, a faint sarcastic smile appearing briefly and speaking more slowly and in a lower voice with extra force. The brow contracts as she shouts at the top of her voice in a higher register and much faster, 'I've never been a wife to you.' Her eyes flash down to his hands (or his groin). Her brow releases and in a slower, lower voice she continues, 'you poor simpering fool'. The word 'fool' is prolonged, slowing the pace right down and dropping in pitch. She looks away from him, turning her head to the left (to gaze off-screen right) and takes a slight, hesitant breath before swinging her eyes back, darting her eyes at his hands/groin: 'If you had any pride' – on the word 'pride' her eyes flare open and simultaneously the fingers of her right hand flinch. She shouts the word 'pride' and, after it, gathers speed: 'If you were a man' – at the word 'man' her eyes flare open again, darting up to his face, and her fingers once more respond by flinching. Her eyes now fix him in a wide open and intense gaze (tense and contemptuous), 'instead of a drooling milksop' – her eyes narrow viciously whilst her hands go into an uncontrollable bout of clenching and unclenching in rhythm to her speech (which is getting louder, faster, and higher) – 'you'd throw me out and admit that you were ashamed you'd ever married me.' At this point she thrusts herself up from the chair and delivers a smack across his impassive face, the camera cutting to a low-angled medium shot of her husband just as she begins to spring forward (i.e. cutting on action).

In many ways this is a similar scene to Mildred's ugly tirade against Philip Carey (Leslie Howard) in *Of Human Bondage* and, as one might expect, Davis uses her body, eyes, mouth, hands, and voice in similar ways. Many of the techniques she used in the earlier film are repeated here but in miniature. There is certainly no grand throwing away of an imagined kiss, no miming of a memory or thought. There is simply not the scope for such gesturing. Throughout the tirade the actress's body is restricted, pinned to an armchair and framed entirely within a close-shot, allowing her no backward or forward movements and no full body spins. The relentless close-shot means that not only is her body out of shot (torso and hips especially) but also the movements of her head are required to be kept to a minimum. Unable to use her full body, she compensates with a more emphatic use of her eyes. Meanwhile, her brow, neck, and shoulders form a communicating link between her face and her fingers.

What is particularly striking about the tirade in *Dangerous* is the relationship Davis establishes between her eyes and her fingers as the speech progresses: that is, the flaring eyes produce a corresponding flinching of the fingers which, as her speech gathers speed and volume and reaches a higher pitch, become increasingly agitated, forewarning of the inevitable slap she is to deliver as her climax. This means that despite the whole thing being filmed in a static close-shot, there is nothing static about the actual performance. On the contrary, there is constant movement but this time the movements are restricted. Produced under restraint, Bette Davis was forced to concentrate upon nuances rather than grand gestures. Unable to step back from the camera and launch into a full-scale theatrical assault and with the camera's relentless scrutiny of every detail of her performance, she reduced each gesture and movement to the most telling, dispensing with anything that did not add new meaning.

Her tirade in *Dangerous* demonstrates Bette Davis's greater finesse, greater subtlety, and also her greater confidence in the technology of cinema. Here the camera's ability to register and project minute movements and expressions is used to maximum effect. What has gone most noticeably from her earlier performance is the attempt to project thoughts and feeling via elaborate physical actions. It is not that she ceases to use physical movement to express her character's every thought and feeling but rather that, aided and abetted by the camera, muscle tension or tiny movements of eyes and fingers are used to convey as much (indeed more than) an arm thrown out from the body or a writhing torso. Under restraint, Davis was able to produce a more effective performance on screen, whereas, given greater freedom in *Of Human Bondage*, she had become excessive, even hammy. This was proof that she could use her technique to create vivid screen performances when her talents were harnessed by forceful direction. Throughout her career it was her most severe directors who elicited her most effective work: directors such as William Wyler and Joseph L. Mankiewicz. Those directors (e.g. John Cromwell) who gave her licence to direct the course of her own performance, allowing her movements to dictate to the camera rather than vice versa, seldom recorded her finest screen performances.

There is no doubt that the members of the Academy of Motion Picture Arts and Sciences saw a marked improvement in Bette Davis's abilities as a screen performer in *Dangerous*. The result was that they needed no persuading to nominate her for Best Actress of 1935. When in March 1936 Bette Davis won her first Academy Award, she entered upon a new phase of her career, one characterized by many years of continuous critical and commercial success as a film actress. By the late 1930s, Davis personified great film acting. Her status as one of Hollywood's most celebrated actors was such that she later proved to be the perfect choice for the role of Broadway star Margo Channing in Joseph L. Mankiewicz's film *All About Eve* (1950). In many ways, Bette Davis's performance as the doyenne of the American theatre was a reprisal of the role which first brought her recognition as an actress within the film industry. Like Joyce Heath before her, Margo Channing schemed, screamed, got drunk, became hysterical, and ultimately (and inevitably) made a great personal sacrifice.

Producing the finest and most celebrated performance of her long career, Bette Davis not only won the prestigious New York Critics Award for her performance in *All About Eve* but, more importantly, she demonstrated that the cinema screen could be the place for grand displays of dramatic excess. Her full-bodied, full-blown dramatics proved immensely effective in this movie. Yet what made them seem so impressive was that they appeared alongside her intense monologues delivered in close-shot directly to camera. In these moments, the actress exchanged her excessive mannerisms for finer subtleties, for something altogether more restrained and nuanced, just as she had done in *Dangerous* in 1935. In *All About Eve* in 1950, Bette Davis's ability to combine both extended and restrained performances affirmed her status as one of the cinema's most expert and compelling actors, denoting not only the extent of her range but also her courage as a performer. Although she had long since learnt the advantages of restraint and nuance, Bette Davis did not see this as a reason to reject the full-bodied technique she had developed under the guidance of Martha Graham. On the contrary, despite the fact that her reputation as a great screen actress was frequently tarnished by accusations that she was also a great ham, Davis continued to produce her full-blown dramatics for the camera in picture after picture. Once more, this was one of the many risks she was prepared to take in order to establish her originality as a screen performer. In her autobiography of 1962, she wrote the following:

> Within the smaller frame we have in pictures, I have been more often than not accused of the heroic and the excessive. Once I learned that – unlike the theatre – the slightest purse of the lip, lowering of the lid, vibration of the wrist, could convey what I wished in the Memling canvases of the movies, I tried to open the hearts of the women I played. I had to feel my way carefully through the strangeness of the new medium. Then came my refusal, even under the microscope, to rob the public by being 'natural.' Natural! That isn't the point of acting.[11]

Notes

1 N. Naumberg (ed.), *We Make the Movies*, New York, W.W. Norton & Co. Inc., 1937.
2 B. Davis, *The Lonely Life*, New York, G.P. Putnam & Sons, 1962.
3 C. Higham, *Bette*, London, New English Library, 1981, p. 87.
4 Ibid., pp. 87–88.
5 B. Leaming, *Bette Davis*, London and New York, Weidenfeld & Nicolson, 1992, p. 81.
6 D. McDonagh, *Martha Graham*, New York, Popular Library, 1973, p. 54.
7 B. Davis, *The Lonely Life*, p. 240.
8 G. Lambert, 'Portrait of an Actress: Bette Davis', *Sight & Sound*, 1951, vol. 21, no. 1, p. 17.
9 B. Leaming, *Bette Davis*, p. 89.
10 See C. Klaprat, 'The Star as Market Strategy: Bette Davis in Another Light', in T. Balio (ed.), *The American Film Industry*, Madison, University of Wisconsin Press, pp. 351–76.
11 B. Davis, *The Lonely Life*, p. 141.

References

Davis, Bette, (1962) *The Lonely Life*, New York, G.P. Putnam & Sons.
Higham, Charles, (1981) *Bette*, London, New English Library.
Klaprat, Cathy, (1985) 'The Star as Market Strategy: Bette Davis in Another Light', in *The American Film Industry*, Tino Balio (ed.), Madison, University of Wisconsin Press, pp. 351–76.
Lambert, Gavin, (1951) 'Portrait of an Actress: Bette Davis', *Sight & Sound* vol. 21, no. 1, August–September, pp. 2–19.

Leaming, Barbara, (1992) *Bette Davis*, London and New York, Weidenfeld & Nicolson.

McDonagh, Don, (1973) *Martha Graham*, New York, Popular Library.

Naumberg, Nancy (ed.) (1937) *We Make the Movies*, New York, W.W. Norton & Co. Inc.

5

A STAR PERFORMS

Mr March, Mr Mason and Mr Maine

Roberta E. Pearson

The climax of the Hollywood year – the Academy Award ceremonies. Vikki Lester, the bright new star in the motion picture firmament, has just won the award for best performance by an actress and is making her acceptance speech. From the back of the hall the sound of a single man clapping breaks the audience's attentive silence. The camera cuts to reveal Vikki's husband, the alcoholic fallen star Norman Maine, who makes his way to the stage and addresses the assembled Hollywood dignitaries. In the 1937 *A Star Is Born* Fredric March interrupts Janet Gaynor and in the 1954 *A Star Is Born* James Mason interrupts Judy Garland. Two Norman Maines, two Academy Award ceremonies, two stars are born, two stars have fallen, yet the scripts and performances create significant differences between the March/Maine and the Mason/Maine that resonate throughout the two versions, even when, in several scenes towards the end of the 1954 version, the Mason/Maine repeats the March/Maine's dialogue almost verbatim.[1]

The March/Maine's first words in the 1937 scene are 'Hey, that's fine. That's a very pretty speech, my dear, very pretty.' The loud, assertive delivery of the sarcastic lines sets the tone for the rest of the scene. The March/Maine strides to the stage to stand in front of his wife and shakes her hand. 'I want to be the very first to congratulate you on that valuable piece of bric-à-brac. Now I want to make a speech.' He puts his hands in his pockets, striking a confident pose and says, 'Gentlemen of the academy and fellow suckers. I got one of those once for best performance. They don't mean a thing. People get them every year.' He waves his hand dismissively. 'Well, I want a special award. Something nobody else can get. I want a statue for the worst performance of the year. In fact, I want three statues for the three worst performances of the year because I've earned them'. He points at his chest with his thumb. 'And every single one of you that saw those last masterpieces of mine knows that I've earned them. Well, I'm here to find out, do I get them or do I get them?' Vikki Lester walks towards her husband, as, in a yet louder voice, he continues, 'Now answer yes or no'. He swings his arm in a wide gesture and

Figures 5.1a & b 'Two Norman Maines, two Academy Award ceremonies, two stars are born, two stars have fallen': Fredric March in the 1937 version of *A Star is Born* (top; 5.1a) and James Mason in the 1954 remake (bottom; 5.1b)

Source: Courtesy of the Kobal Collection

accidentally hits his wife in the face. A cut to a medium close-up registers his change of mood. Now much less certain of himself, he permits Vikki to lead him to her table, kissing her on the cheek as they walk. Studio boss Oliver Niles helps him into his seat and the March/Maine manages to exchange an uncertain hello with a friend before saying, 'Somebody give me a drink'. He looks straight ahead, the more subdued delivery of this line conveying the character's dawning realization of the humiliation he has brought upon his wife and himself.

The Mason/Maine interrupts the ceremony with his clapping, but says nothing until he gets to the stage. He walks up the steps to his wife, kisses her, and congratulates her. 'May I borrow the end of your speech to make a speech of my own?' he asks, his tone more polite than his predecessor's, the words almost deferential. As he talks, he holds on to his wife's arm as if to steady himself. 'My method for gaining your attention might seem a little uncon-, unconventional, but hard times call for harsh measures'. His gestures are as uncertain as his speech; vague, loose hand movements rather than the forceful gestures employed by March. 'It's silly to be so formal, isn't it?' He sits on the stairs, stopping himself from falling backwards with his hands. 'I know most of you sitting out there by your first names, don't I? I made a lot of money for you gentlemen in my time, haven't I? Well, I need a job. Yeah, that's it, that's the speech, that's the . . . I need a job.' His voice rises, emphasizing the last phrase as if it really has just come to him. 'It's as simple as that. I need a job.' He gets up and paces along a step, looking down as he walks, as if to make sure that he places his feet properly. 'My talents, I may say, are not confined to dramatic roles. I can play comedy as well.' He begins to realize that he is causing a scene. 'Well, well play something somebody.' He flings out his arm in a wide gesture and, as did his predecessor, hits his wife in the face. But he reacts more extremely, gasping in shock, then holding, or rather holding onto, his wife. The camera cuts to a reverse-shot and he lowers his head to her shoulder, stunned disbelief and agony on his face, seeming on the verge of tears as he fully realizes the import of what he has just done. Vikki leads him back to his table, his arm around her shoulder, hers around his waist. The studio publicist, Libby, steadies him as he sits, but this Norman is not capable of exchanging pleasantries. He struggles to contain his emotions, his folded hands to his mouth. 'Get me a drink somebody', he asks weakly, lowering his head and shielding his face with his hands.

The two relatively similar scenes feature relatively dissimilar interpretations of the Norman Maine character. March portrays Maine as a loud, aggressive drunk, confronting the audience. His lost stardom distresses him, but the pain manifests itself as sarcasm in his demand for an Oscar for worst performance. He seems almost to have prepared his speech beforehand, to have known from the moment of his entrance what he wished to say. This scene makes clear that Maine has a drinking problem, but he still seems to retain a degree of dignity and even an actor's flamboyance, reflected in his cynicism and his forceful gestures. He represses whatever other emotions he may feel even at the end of the scene. The March/Maine confronts the audience; the Mason/Maine pleads with it, portraying the character as pathetic, a confirmed drunkard and a sick man. He moves unsteadily and seems not quite to know where he is or what he is doing. By contrast with the March/Maine, he clings to a belief in his acting abilities, asserting that he can play comedy as well as drama. At the moment he hits his wife, full realization of his public humiliation overwhelms him. By the end of the scene, his anguish manifests itself in his face and gestures.

Although the producers of the 1954 film drew quite heavily upon its seventeen year old progenitor, the differences apparent between the March/Maine and the Mason/Maine in the Academy Award scene resonate throughout the two versions of *A Star Is Born*. Eleven scenes (defined rather loosely as exhibiting a certain unity of time and place) in the 1954 version that centre upon Norman Maine follow the original action quite closely, much of the dialogue from the earlier script reappearing. Towards the end of the 1954 version, as Norman's decline proceeds, the similarities with the earlier version grow stronger.[2] The overlaps between the two films, coupled with the disjunctions between the two Norman Maines, provide an approach to that most vexed of all cinematic signifiers, performance. This essay compares scenes from the 1937 version with those of the 1954 version that repeat the original dialogue almost verbatim in order to investigate the ways in which the scripts, the editing, and the *mise-en-scène* combine with the performances of Fredric March and James Mason to create two very different renditions of a character called Norman Maine. This close textual analysis will reveal that the construction of a character may depend more upon the interaction of cinematic signifiers with performance than upon the script.[3]

But extratextual factors also enter into the interpretation of a character, in the minds of both the actors and the audience. The essay goes beyond formal analysis in an attempt to ground an inherently subjective, presentist approach in historical intertexuality.[4] How did March and Mason conceive of the Maine character? How might their previous roles have effected March and Mason's approach to the Norman Maine character? And how might March and Mason's star images have factored into the audience's responses to that character?

As the score provides the basis for a musician's performance, so does the script for an actor's. The words and actions that the script gives a character provide the first point of illumination into an actor's interpretation. In keeping with the differences apparent in the Academy Award scenes, aspects of the 1937 script create a stronger, less vulnerable Norman than does the 1954 script. The 1937 Norman seems almost to revel in his alcoholism, while Oliver Niles in the 1954 films speaks about the 'twenty years of steady and quiet drinking' that has destroyed the Mason/Maine. The March/Maine makes jokes about his drinking, consumes monstrous highballs and engages in extravagant peccadilloes such as stealing an ambulance and racing down Wilshire Boulevard. The backstage-at-the-benefit scene which introduces the 1954 Norman makes him more of a playful than a threatening drunk, showing him jumping on a horse and stumbling on stage to be incorporated in Garland's act. While the 1954 Norman talks ruefully about a woman hitting him with a plate, the 1937 version actually shows a girlfriend breaking a plate over Norman's head. While the March/Maine rather gratuitously attacks a photographer attempting to take his picture at the Hollywood Bowl, the Mason/Maine attacks photographers when he suspects that his press agent has set up a photo session to forestall his appearance on stage at the benefit.

The March/Maine, even when sober, is an altogether tougher character, who unabashedly tries to seduce Esther Blodgett (his soon-to-be wife and soon-to-be Vikki Lester) on first meeting her and goes to the fights – this is an ordinary fellow who has become a Hollywood star. Although the Mason/Maine first seeks to seduce Esther, he quickly becomes genuinely excited by her talent rather than the possibility of a romantic conquest. This is because the Mason/Maine is an actor who has become a Hollywood star: he quotes Shakespeare twice, refers to Ellen Terry, and knows how to apply make-up. Although neither script clearly motivates the character's self-destructiveness, the loss of star status seems to precipitate the March/Maine's decline, while it is the loss of his profession that seems profoundly to disturb the Mason/Maine. The Mason/Maine seems to have a much higher degree of self-awareness. Even when very drunk, he can still comment, 'I know myself extremely well and I'm just at the fighting stage. If I don't get what I want I begin to break up people and things.' When told of the termination of his contract, he laments, 'I have a genius, a positive genius, for doing things at the wrong time.' The script couples this self-awareness with a child-like vulnerability, which, as we have seen, Mason picked up on. At the benefit, other performers handle Norman like a child – two stage hands hold him up after he almost collapses, members of another act pull off the pearly jacket he has appropriated, and Garland incorporates him into her dance as if manipulating a rag-doll. The scene that follows shows Maine being put to bed by his valet who comments, 'Soon he'll smile in his sleep like a child.' After bringing him home from a four-day binge and a night court appearance, Garland puts him to bed. She echoes the valet, saying, 'He looks so helpless lying there, smiling in his sleep just like a child.'[5]

Just as musicians interpret the score to create an individual performance, so do actors interpret the script to create their character. Information concerning the performer's conception of the character he embodies is invaluable in analysing cinematic acting. In Ron Haver's book on the 1954 *Star*, James Mason is quoted as saying, 'I thought that Norman was very childlike'.[6] Mason's autobiography reveals a little more. The actor thought of the role of Maine as 'exactly my cup of tea' and hoped to get it, knowing that both Humphrey Bogart and Cary Grant had turned it down.[7] George Cukor, the 'actors' director', spent the first few days on the set 'talking at me, talking, talking' about his conception of the role:

> I was trying to assemble myself in the pattern that I had prepared and at the same time to incorporate the drift of his suggestions . . . I fancied that the Norman Maine whom Cukor had in mind had all the colours of John Barrymore, whereas I was putting together an actor who resembled much more closely some of my own drunken friends . . . Stylistically a Barrymore figure might have been preferable but I had never liked what I saw of Barrymore.[8]

I have not been able to find any comments by Fredric March on his conception of Norman Maine, but Mason's reference to Barrymore calls to mind the fact that March had won his first Academy Award nomination by lampooning John Barrymore in the 1930 film, *The Royal Family of Broadway*. Perhaps it was precisely the characteristics of the 1920 matinee idol – that Mason, by all accounts the consummate professional, 'had never liked' – that the 1937 scriptwriters (Dorothy Parker, Alan Campbell, and Robert Carson) and March drew upon in constructing their Norman Maine. Barrymore, like the March/Maine, revelled in his stardom but lacked commitment to his profession, indulging in amorous adventures and drunkenness at the expense of his acting and finally succumbing to cirrhosis of the liver in 1942 at the age of 60. Said one historian, 'John realized that his heart was never particularly with the theater and that he never took his profession seriously.'[9] Although he starred in several films now regarded as 'classics' (*Grand Hotel*, *Dinner at Eight* and *Twentieth Century* among them), Barrymore took up cinema acting to avoid the eight performances a week rigours of the live theatre, and he appeared in many pictures simply for the money. A passage in his autobiography expressing a certain disdain for Hollywood may have served as the template for the March/Maine's Academy Award speech:

> I was myself connected with what was probably the worst picture ever made. Not only did I play a part in this, but I had a great deal to do with the making of it. Come to think of it, it is quite a distinction that in all this great industry of the screen which has turned out so many bad pictures, I was largely responsible for about the worst picture I ever saw.[10]

A brief recount of the pre-Maine careers of the two actors may provide further hints as to their interpretations of the script by determining the kinds of roles to which they were accustomed. March came to Hollywood in 1929, having had a successful but not spectacular stage career. He made a series of well-received pictures, playing a variety of roles and established himself as one of the new talkies' major attractions. In 1932 he reinforced his position by winning the Oscar for *Dr Jekyll and Mr Hyde* (1931). Although March had previously avoided typecasting, in seven of the ten films immediately preceding *Star* he played dashing and romantic costume parts such as the title roles in *The Affairs of Cellini* (1934) and *Anthony Adverse* (1936) and Vronsky in *Anna Karenina* (1935). Since the earliest days of cinema, actors have employed a more mannered, one might even say more theatrical, performance style in historical films. March's recent film-making experiences, together with a Barrymore-esque conception of the role, might have caused him to employ the theatrically flamboyant style evident in the Academy Award and other scenes.

James Mason had achieved box office eminence and teen idol status in Britain in such films as *The Man in Gray* (1943) and *The Seventh Veil* (1945) portraying glowering, sadistic types who physically and mentally abused women, but whose anger, as in the latter film, often hid a secret sorrow. Moving to the United States in the late 1940s he determined to shed this image and played a variety of roles. In several of those immediately preceding his appearance as Norman Maine (*The Reckless Moment* [1949], *Rommel — The Desert Fox* [1951], *The Man Between* [1953] and *Julius Caesar* [1954] in which he played Brutus), his doomed, yet sympathetic characters were complex mixtures of good and evil, a complexity conveyed by Mason's always sensitive and intelligent performances. Was the Maine role Mason's 'cup of tea' because it resembled previous roles? And might these recent enactments of complicated characters have caused Mason to seek dimensions of the Norman Maine character to which Fredric March may have been less attuned?

Having examined the two scripts and the actors' possible motivations for their interpretations, let us explore the ways in which the performance and signifying practices of the 1954 film construct a more vulnerable Norman and permit the viewer greater access to his emotions. I shall compare two scenes in which the dialogue remains almost the same from 1937 to 1954. In the first of these, Norman has voluntarily committed himself to a sanatorium after disrupting the Academy Awards. Oliver Niles, the studio head, comes to visit and offers Norman a small role, which the actor's pride causes him to reject. The first film covers the action in thirteen shots, the important parts of the conversation filmed in medium two-shot and medium close-shot/reverse-shot. For the greater part of the scene, the two protagonists simply sit on a couch and talk to each other. The second film records the action in six shots (perhaps reflecting the difference between standard aspect ratio and CinemaScope editing patterns), while the camera tracks more frequently to follow the actors, whose movements create changes of shot scale within shots. The moving camera permits Mason to walk around and perform bits of business with props, expanding the available number of signifiers for externalizing Norman's mental processes.

In both films, Norman first appears in long-shot, walking down the sanatorium stairs to greet Oliver. The 1937 version shows Norman's shadow moving hesitantly and slowly on the staircase wall, but when the March/Maine comes into view he moves more confidently, as if readying himself for the encounter. The Mason/Maine seems to make no attempt to put on a false front, walking slowly downstairs, one hand on the banister and the other bracing himself against the wall. Instead of the slacks and shirt of his predecessor, he wears a terry cloth bathrobe of obvious institutional issue. Just as the bathrobe emphasizes the Mason/Maine's inmate status and hence degradation, so does a bit of business later on. When Oliver asks if he is comfortable, both Normans reply, 'Comfortable, it's positively luxurious. They even have iron bars [steel mesh in the 1954 version] to keep the draughts out.' The March/Maine delivers this line sitting on a couch, while the Mason/Maine walks to the window and lifts the curtain, allowing us to see the steel mesh and realize he isn't joking.

While both Normans deliver the same desperately upbeat dialogue, the costumes, staging, and other cinematic signifying practices combine to create different moods, reinforced by nuances of the performances. Throughout this scene, the March/Maine maintains a false, hearty bravado, while the Mason/Maine seems much more tired and defeated, less able to pretend a confidence he does not feel. March relies primarily on speech patterns and gestures to convey Norman's manful attempt to suppress his emotions. Mason augments speech patterns and gestures with subtle shifts in facial expression and body posture, changes in the direction of his glance, and the use of props – all these signifiers combining to create the impression of a Norman who lacks the fortitude to resist an inevitable decline.

March, of course, portrays Norman as a sick man, speaking more slowly and quietly and giving his movements an indeterminacy and lassitude that contrast with his earlier forcefulness. Only by comparison with the Mason/Maine does his Norman seem stronger. Throughout the scene, March talks more loudly and brightly than Mason, using conventional auditory signifiers to disclose his underlying nervousness: repetition of words; hesitant uhs and ums; nervous laughter; a sighed 'yeah'. March also uses conventional gestural signifiers both to reveal Maine's 'real' feelings and to indicate that he is trying to stifle them.[11] Consider, for example, March/Maine's reaction to Oliver's offer of a role. He first thinks that Oliver intends him to play the lead. Smiling, he straightens his shirt collar as if readying himself for the camera and asks, 'Who plays opposite me?' Oliver tells him that 'it's not exactly the lead'. The March/Maine's shoulders sag and he breathes out heavily. Trying to come up with an excuse for his refusal, he closes his eyes briefly and waves his hand vaguely side to side. As he says, 'Well the thing is, Oliver, I'm pretty well set at another studio', he pinches the bridge of his nose as if to contain his disappointment and hide his expression from the other man. Recovering slightly, he says of his supposed role, 'Every actor in Hollywood would give his eye-teeth to play it', kissing his bunched fingertips to indicate his relish for the part. Mason varies his vocal range more than March, alternating a real weariness with occasional bursts of animation, speaking more loudly and quickly as he lies to Oliver about his prospects, for example. Although he uses hand gestures, his movements seem idiosyncratic, less conventionally coded than March's. He relies more on facial expression than gesture to reveal Norman's vague confusion – slight smiles, hesitant blinks of the eyes, moistening and compressing his lips. His body posture reflects Norman's lack of strength. He walks with head lowered, in a halting shuffle, as if afraid of stumbling, and pushes himself up with his hands on the arms of the chair as he rises. As he follows Oliver to the door after refusing the role, his head bows, his shoulders slump, and he thrusts his hands in his pockets.

As Oliver offers Norman the role and Norman gives his excuses, the staging of the 1937 version forces March to rely upon dialogue and gesture and to look at the other actor or pointedly avoid eye contact. Mason walks around the room while delivering the same dialogue, conveying Norman's feelings through using props and by establishing and breaking eye contact, as well as by dialogue and gesture.[12] When Oliver first makes the offer, he hands the Mason/Maine a script. Mason/Maine looks down at it, smiling slightly, then looks up, arching his eyebrows, and flipping through the script as he asks, 'Who'll play opposite me?' As Oliver tells him he won't play the lead, his eyes shift away and he compresses his lips. Telling Oliver that he is 'pretty well set at another studio', he rises, puts down the script and feels in his pockets for money. Not finding any, he asks the attendant for a quarter. Then, as he says 'every actor in Hollywood would give his eye-teeth to play it [the role he will supposedly play]', he gets cigarettes from a machine. Oliver says that he will wait for Norman. The March/Maine turns to face him, but looks down at the cigarette pack as he opens it, avoiding eye contact as he lies about going to work in England. As he follows Oliver out of the room, he glances down at the script lying on top of the cigarette machine, Mason indicating with the glance that Norman is thinking of his lost opportunity or of his lost star status.

The final shot epitomizes the differences in the two actors' performances and the scene's overall effect towards the two Normans. Norman walks with Oliver to the door of the sanatorium and says, 'Good-bye. Thanks for dropping in.' The March/Maine simply shakes hands and delivers the line as if it were a conventional pleasantry, with no particular subtext. The Mason/Maine shakes hands and says, 'Good-bye'. Then as Oliver starts for the open door, Norman steps forward quickly and puts a hand on Oliver's arm, stopping him. 'Thanks for dropping in', he says quietly. The action of stopping Oliver and Mason's delivery of the line seems to suggest that both men know that Norman has no prospects of employment, that his pride prevents him from accepting Oliver's offer, but that he is none the less grateful. The connotations Mason's performance gives the phrase again emphasize the character's self-awareness and heighten the poignancy of his situation

The second parallel scene, in which Norman learns that Esther intends to sacrifice her career for him, is the character's emotional catharsis in which the Mason/Maine finally breaks down. Norman lies in bed, sleeping off a four-day binge, and awakens to hear his wife and his producer conversing in the next room. Gradually, the import of his wife's words sinks in: she plans to give up her stardom, the one thing that has justified his existence. Both films show Norman in close-up, his head on his pillow, surrounded by darkness. The lighting in the 1937 film shadows everything but the March/Maine's eyes, while the 1954 film shows the Mason/Maine's entire face. The 1937 version, which begins with Esther outside Norman's bedroom door, gives March three reaction shots. March signals his character's despair by moving his eyes very slightly and then closing them. The 1954 version, which begins with Esther looking down on the sleeping Norman, gives Mason five reaction shots, the first a full-length shot of him in bed. In the first close-up, Norman slowly awakens, moistening his lips and fluttering his eyelids. In the second and third close-ups, Norman gradually registers what Esther is saying, opening his mouth and his eyes in increasing shock and despair. In the fourth close-up, Mason registers the misery building in Norman over the past several scenes. He puts a hand to his forehead, tilts his head back, and opens his mouth. He then puts his hand on the pillow above his head and closes his eyes. Trying to suppress sobs, he arches his neck and closes his mouth. He then opens his mouth, sobs, squeezes his eyes shut, and swallows hard. Finally, he turns over and buries his head in the pillow, giving in entirely to the anguish that overwhelms him.

The earlier version externalizes Norman's emotions more through the lighting and the other characters' dialogue than through performance, preserving a certain reticence about exposing his feelings. The later version primarily uses performance, aided by more even illumination of the face. The March/Maine doesn't cry and the camera remains reticent about exposing his emotions. The Mason/Maine cries and the camera watches, the film cutting only when he buries his head in the pillow and his face is no longer visible. Despite their early disagreements about the proper interpretation of the role, Cukor by this point had decided to let the actor 'find out things for himself. In that last scene, where he breaks down and decides to commit suicide, I just let the camera stay on him for a very long time and all his feelings came out.'[13]

The above comparison of the two versions of *A Star Is Born* reveals that the construction of a character derives at least as much from performance and cinematic signifiers as it does from the words and actions of the script. But, as I argued above, other factors, such as the performer's conception of the character, also contribute to the realization of the script's instructions. Fuller comprehension of cinematic performance depends upon knowledge of extra-textual factors, particularly with regard to the conditions of production and reception for specific films. Star images function centrally in these conditions, informing the pre-production phase, actors' interpretations of their characters, and the audience's response to the performance. This essay concludes with a brief examination of Fredric March's and James Mason's star images in order to ground speculation about the performers' motivations and viewers' reactions in an historical framework.[14]

March's extra-textual image consistently stressed his Americanness and his 'ordinariness'. *Cue* magazine said of March in 1944 that he was 'as American as a streetlight shining through maple trees, a soda after the movies on a hot August night, the valedictorian's address at graduation exercises and that feeling you get the first day of your first job'. March's life was represented as fulfilling the American Dream. A blurb from the pressbook for *Strangers in Love* (1932) summarized the essential information endlessly repeated in other pressbooks and articles: 'distinguished himself at the University of Wisconsin . . . both athlete and manager of the varsity football team . . . participated in amateur dramatics and oratory, president of his senior class, leader in fraternity life and other activities . . . graduated with honors'.[15] March's married life conformed to those family values that have always formed such a central component of American national identity: 'The Marches are one of the notoriously happy couples of Hollywood', and 'He may be celebrated for the normality of his private life.'

In keeping with the all-American connotation that reverberates throughout the discourse about March, writers stressed his conventionality. 'He is normal . . . The perfectly conventional, upright, outstanding young man'. Indeed, so normal was March that he was said to have rejected the usual trappings of Hollywood stardom. 'He doesn't want to be a star. He doesn't want to be a matinee idol. He doesn't want to be a great lover. . . . He affects none of the folderol of movie heroism.' Obviously, a regular guy like this has no trace of pretence or stuffiness about him. Hence, 'it is only Fredric in the advertisements, to all who know him he is and always has been Freddy'. Even March's physical appearance conformed to the parameters of normalcy. A *Screenland* writer characterized him as 'good looking in a friendly way, as the president of a small town bank might be thought good looking'. A *Screen Book* writer concurred: 'He is the type, were you to pass him on the street, would cause you to remark mentally, "There goes an up and coming young member of some law firm – or else he's a young business executive".'

March's and the audience's knowledge of his star image may have resonated with the keying of his portrayal of Norman to the repression of emotion and the maintenance of false bravado. March was an all-American kind of guy who had played football and worked in a bank, while his Maine was an all-American kind of guy who attended the fights and chewed gum. March's conventionally coded good looks, within the range of 'normal' male attractiveness, may have reinforced the impression of Norman as an ordinary fellow. Contemporary cultural constructions of masculinity required that all-American types such as this not indulge in emotional expressiveness. Hence, the very conventionality of the speech and gestural patterns March used to convey both Norman's collapse and his attempts to disguise it was particularly appropriate. Contemporary audiences most probably would not have expected emotional displays from a character who seemed so 'normal' in other respects. Hence, the reticence the 1937 film displays towards Norman's emotions, the reluctance to dwell on his despair and humiliation, may have been in keeping with audience expectations of the character as embodied by this particular actor.

Mason too was perceived as diverging from the norm of Hollywood stardom, but certainly not because of his conventionality either as an on-screen personality or an off-screen 'real person'. His screen persona was described in phrases that linked Mason to the hero of a Gothic romance: 'the Briton who browbeats beauties . . . sadistic sensation', the 'romantic rebel', 'mean and lovely', the 'glowering, cinematic glamour boy', 'the man you love to hate', 'the magnificent man of mood and menace', 'that Mean Mason man', 'the screen's great romantic star', 'the menace', and 'British cinemenace'. Descriptions of Mason's appearance reinforced this image: 'somber, sensual handsomeness', 'glowering English actor', 'swarthy', 'slightly saturnine good looks', 'sullen good looks', 'saturnine and gripping', and 'dark, brooding masculinity'. In a review of *The Upturned Glass* (1947; a rather dreadful British film Mason produced and starred in) a female critic for the *Observer*, seeming slightly unbalanced by all this brooding, sullen sensuality, told how she read Mason's features:

> It is impossible not to feel that those somber eyes, brooding over us hauntingly from the screen, are not gazing into a portentous future; that those forbidding lips, magnified in close-up to an alarming size, are not closed on innumerable secrets of an enigmatic past. We look at Mr Mason and feel that we are being induced into a tragedy of the screen.

The uniform and extravagant descriptions of Mason's screen roles, complemented by the verbal portraits of his physical appearance, were balanced by supposed insights into the off-screen Mason. Hedda Hopper, laying claim to the inside scoop, emphasized the difference between the cinematic and the 'real' Mason:

> Those few whom he has permitted to become acquainted with him have discovered that he is mild-mannered, has a delightful tongue in cheek sense of humor, is highly intelligent and thoroughly charming.

Other writers stressed his differences from the typical Hollywood star (and perhaps the typical American male). Said a *Photoplay* writer:

He's as unlike the average Hollywood star as it is possible to imagine. Instead of the self-made boy . . . who heard about books and music and art after he made money, Mason attended Marlborough and Cambridge before he turned to acting.

An article in the American pressbook for the *Upturned Glass* stated:

Mason acquired his reputation as the most thorough going villain in the movies despite a personal background which includes just about every advantage likely to produce the perfect gentleman. Offspring of a wealthy British family, Mason received a first class education.

Writers emphasized Mason's intelligence, reserve, and independence while biographical details about his hobbies, which included reading, writing, and painting, as well as his well-known passion for cats, may have furthered the impression of Mason's divergence from the norms of both Hollywood stardom and American masculinity.

Mason's atypicality rendered him inappropriate for roles that required 'ordinariness'. John Ellis commented on the tensions between Mason's matinee idol status and his role in his second American film, *Caught* (1949). The director, Max Ophuls, wished to cast Mason as the eccentric and cruel millionaire (eventually played by Robert Ryan), but the actor, hoping to break with his sadistic beast typing, opted for the part of the kind and gentle doctor who rescues the heroine:

A desperately attractive James Mason is cast as the ordinary doctor in a poor district with whom Barbara Bel Geddes falls in love. Mason, the matinee idol, is meant to incarnate the ordinary and the honest. . . . The film multiplies the indications of ordinariness around him. . . . Yet it only succeeds in intensifying the paradox of the star image.[16]

Mason himself believed that his casting in *Bigger than Life* (1956) negatively affected the American reception of the film for much the same reason. Describing his role as that of a 'run-of-the-mill American school-teacher', he said that 'the US public could not accept me as such, since they knew that James Mason was an uncooperative import who should be seen only in glum foreign parts.'[17]

Mason's knowledge of his atypicality may have informed his interpretation of the Maine character. Viewers' awareness of his star image may have caused the original audience for the 1954 film to read the Mason/Maine in ways similar to my interpretation. I have argued that perceptions of March as normal and American gave credibility to the 1937 film's construction of Norman as an ordinary guy who became a movie star. In 1937 normal guys didn't expose their vulnerabilities and they most certainly didn't cry. By contrast, the emphasis in Mason's image upon his education, his habits of reading and writing, and his intellect may have strengthened the script's and the performer's construction of the 1954 Norman as having greater intelligence and self-awareness than the 1937 version. Mason's image may also have sanctioned Norman's greater emotional vulnerability. In terms of his off-screen persona, the audience, exposed to the anti-intellectualism and xenophobia of the 1950s, may have suspected that a well-educated, foreign actor who actually enjoyed such sissy pursuits as reading, writing, and painting might well be unable to suppress his emotions like a real man. In terms of his on-screen persona, we all know that underneath the brooding exterior of the Gothic hero lies a wealth of emotions just waiting to get out. As the *Observer* critic said, 'We look at Mr. Mason and feel that we are being induced into a tragedy of the screen'.

Mason's intertextual image, together with the script and his performance, created a Norman with greater depth than the previous version but also created a disjunction between the character and the narrative demands upon him. Both scripts fail to motivate Norman particularly well, never establishing the back-story for his alcoholism and self-destructiveness, but the March/Maine's relative lack of self-reflectiveness does not call attention to the script's failure. The Mason/Maine's intelligence, however, would surely cause him to have a certain contempt for Hollywood and the star system (as his real life counterpart did have) but the narrative requires that the loss of star status precipitates the character's total decline. Two quotes confirm my suspicion that the Mason/Maine's disintegration is not entirely credible. Said a 1954 reviewer, '[Mason] endows Norman Maine with so sardonic a sense of humour and self-criticism that one cannot understand why a man of such intelligence should mind whether or not he continues to be a success in so hysterical and flimsy a place as Hollywood.'[18] Twenty-five years later, Wade Jennings had much the same opinion of Mason's performance. Speaking about Maine's going on a four-day binge because a delivery boy called him 'Mr Lester' (his wife's stage name), Jennings said, 'Maine, as James Mason has played him, seems too intelligent a character with too much humor about himself to give in so completely to such an insignificant slight.'[19]

These estimations of Maine's intelligence may have derived as much from the commentators' intertextual knowledge of Mason's star image as from Mason's performance or other textual elements, all of these elements cohering in an interpretation of the Mason/Maine character as bright and self-aware. The same, of course, holds true for the March/Maine character, different elements cohering to produce a different interpretation of the character. In two films with roughly the same plot and several scenes with the same dialogue, two quite different Norman Maines emerge from the combination of editing, *mise-en-scène*, performance, and extratextual factors. And while performance cannot be analysed in isolation from these other factors, one might conclude that it is the actor's delivery of his dialogue, together with his facial expressions, gestures, and posture that most vividly endow a cinematic character with life.

Notes

1 The 1937 *A Star Is Born* was directed by William Wellman and produced by David O. Selznick. The 1954 CinemaScope remake was directed by George Cukor, produced by Transcona Enterprises (Garland and her then husband Sid Luft's company) and released by Warner Bros.

2 Of course, the astute reader may object that the difference in genres renders the comparison invalid. After all the 1937 version is a melodrama, while the 1954 version is a musical melodrama (if such a genre exists). However, while Mason's Maine lives in a world where other people sing and dance, he himself does neither (if one ignores the incorporation into Garland's act at the beginning). There is a second remake, from 1976, starring Barbra Streisand and Kris Kristofferson, but the film is quite dissimilar from the two earlier versions (and nowhere near as good!).

3 In fact one of the most famous of all film critics does agree with me about Mason versus Garland. Says Pauline Kael, 'The star's "fading" husband, James Mason, walked off with *A Star Is Born* . . . ' (Pauline Kael, *Kiss Kiss, Bang Bang*, Boston, Little Brown & Company, 1968, p. 283).

4 For more on this historical contextualization of formal analysis, see William Uricchio and Roberta E. Pearson, *Reframing Culture: The Case of the Vitagraph Quality Films*, Princeton, Princeton University Press, 1993.

5 Since judgments of this kind are so precariously subjective, I was pleased to find confirmation of my analysis of the two scripts in Ronald Haver's book *A Star Is Born: The Making of the 1954 Movie and Its 1983 Restoration*, New York, Alfred A. Knopf, 1988, pp. 57–60.

6 Haver, op. cit., p. 150.

7 James Mason, *Before I Forget*, London, Hamish Hamilton, 1981, p. 252.

8 Ibid., pp. 252–53.

9 William C. Young, *Famous Actors and Actresses on the American Stage: Documents of American Theatre History*, New York, R.R. Bowker, 1975, p. 62.

10 John Barrymore, *Confessions of an Actor*, quoted in Young, op. cit., p. 63.

11 This use of speech patterns and gestures to convey the character's 'real feelings' accords with what James Naremore calls 'expressive incoherence'. To quote Naremore:

> most film actors are acutely sensitive to the purely rhetorical need to make their 'thought' visible to the camera. Moreover, they must sometimes signal that they *act persons who are acting* [emphasis in original]. In these moments when deception or repression are indicated, the drama becomes a metaperformance, imposing contrary demands on the players: the need to maintain a unified narrative image, a coherent persona, is matched by an equally strong need to exhibit dissonance or expressive incoherence within the characterization. Thus, we could say that realist acting amounts to an effort at sustaining opposing attitudes

toward the self, on the one hand trying to create the illusion of unified, individualized personality, but on the other suggesting that character is subject to division or dissolution into a variety of social roles.

(James Naremore, *Acting in the Cinema*, Berkeley, University of California Press, 1988, p. 72).

12 Those of auteuristic inclination might be inclined to attribute this difference to the influence of the 'actor's director', George Cukor. The shooting of the 1954 film in CinemaScope, however, greatly complicates this point.

13 Quoted in Sheridan Morley, *James Mason: Odd Man Out*, London, Weidenfeld & Nicolson, 1989, p. 105.

14 Unless otherwise noted, all quotations are from material in the Fredric March and James Mason Clippings Files in the Billy Rose Theater Collection, in the New York Public Library for the Performing Arts at the Lincoln Center. Also, unless otherwise noted, all quotations precede the actor's appearances in *A Star Is Born*.

15 *Strangers in Love* Press book, Billy Rose Theater Collection.

16 John Ellis, *Visible Fictions: Cinema: Television: Video*, London, Routledge, 1982, pp. 96–97.

17 Clive Hirschhorn, *The Films of James Mason*, Secaucus, NJ, The Citadel Press, 1977, p. 133.

18 Quoted in Morley, op. cit., p. 106.

19 Wade Jennings, 'Nova: Garland in *A Star Is Born*', *Quarterly Review of Film Studies*, vol. 4, no. 3, Summer, 1979, p. 335.

6

LEE STRASBERG'S PARADOX OF THE ACTOR

Sharon Marie Carnicke

That Lee Strasberg's Method of actor training (for the Group Theatre and the Actors Studio) differs from Stanislavsky's System (at the Moscow Art Theatre) rarely raises professional eyebrows, despite popular belief to the contrary. Widely recognized and rightly criticized is Strasberg's transformation of the multivariant System into one that compulsively and therapeutically concerns itself with self-expression. James Naremore calls Strasberg's teaching 'rather parochial . . . fuelled by an excessive and very American obsession with the "self" ' (Naremore 1985: 44). Additionally, Naremore identifies the Actors Studio as 'an institution that was related to Stanislavsky in roughly the same way that psychoanalysis was related to Freud' (Naremore 1990: 198). Richard Hornby sees the Method as 'Strasbergian ideology' that 'shackles American acting' (Hornby 1992: 5).

Moreover, that Strasberg made his name as a guru of screen actors who excel in psychological realism (despite his avowed admiration for the stage and the classics) also represents common knowledge. Actors from Paul Newman to Robert De Niro, from Shelly Winters to Jane Fonda cite him as their mentor, often using panegyric phrases. Before taking Strasberg's classes, Fonda claimed, 'everything I'd done had seemed wrong' (Ross and Ross 1984: 99). Anne Jackson simply called him 'a saint for actors' (Ross and Ross 1984: 166).

An unexplored link exists between these two commonplaces. Generally, Strasberg's changes to the System are explained in terms of differing cultural conceptions of the self in Russia and America, or as aesthetic and stylistic developments from the late nineteenth century to the mid-twentieth. Yet, close examination of Strasberg's teaching shows how he also takes the System from stage to screen, thereby accounting for the Method's success in film. Ironically, Strasberg himself rarely addressed cinema, always speaking as if his actors aspired primarily to the stage. His one key discussion of film occurs in his 1957 entry on 'Acting' for the *Encyclopaedia Britannica*, in which he assumes that 'a properly trained actor moves easily from one medium to another without any diminution of his talent' (Strasberg 1957: 64). Yet Strasberg's attitudes towards the actor (so different from Stanislavsky's) led him to create adaptations in training that well suit cinema. At his worst, Strasberg invites actors to wallow in self-indulgence, but at his best, he gives them concrete tools with which to compensate for the practical conditions of film making.

Before examining how Strasberg reinterprets Stanislavsky in ways sympathetic to cinema, I invite you to recall the various ways in which the camera alters actors' work. Overall, film as a performance medium poses a major new question for acting theorists: who is the creator of filmed performance? The technology of montage suggests that the correct answer is no longer 'the actor'. Strasberg as director aptly observes that 'It is possible to put strips of film together and create a performance that never was actually given' (Strasberg 1957: 64). As Lev Kuleshov writes of his own experiments in editing, 'It became apparent that [I could] change the actor's work, his movements, his very behaviour, in either one direction or another, through montage' (Kuleshov 1974: 55). This cinematic technology significantly redefines the relationship between director and actor from one of collaboration to one of authority and control. Whereas Stanislavsky believes that the actor is an independent artist, freely collaborating with the director in the analysis of text, the creation of character, and the dynamics of performance, film repositions the director as the primary creator of performance. Method actor Kim Stanley comments that, 'No matter what you do in a film, it is, after all, bits and pieces for the director, and that's marvellous for the director, but it doesn't allow the actor to learn to mould a part. In films, it's the director who is the artist' (Ross and Ross 1984: 15). Non-Method actor, Robert Preston, agrees: 'Movies are the director's medium and his fun' (Ross and Ross 1984: 412). British-trained Cedric Hardwick more pointedly states, 'In a film, when all is said and done, good cutting can make a good actor out of a donkey' (Ross and Ross 1984: 24). At worst, the actor has little or no control. At best, the final performance, in Richard Widmark's words, 'is a combination of actor and director'. Recalling arguments by cinema scholars as to why acting in film cannot entail serious critical discourse, Widmark continues, 'There's no way of distinguishing between what the director does and what the actor does' (Ross and Ross 1984: 307).

Film also changes the conditions under which actors create. In the first place, when working in front of a camera, the actor's primary audience becomes the director (adding yet another complexity to the shifting cinematic relationship between them). True, in rehearsing a stage play, the director serves a similar function, what Tyrone Guthrie calls 'an audience of one' (Guthrie 1976: 245–46). While a live audience eventually replaces the director as spectator in the theatre, the eventual movie audience remains an abstraction for the film actor during the actual process of performing. Making a film, therefore, may be more akin to theatrical rehearsals, in so far as the director's eye remains the primary measure of the work. As Anthony Quinn comments, 'In movie making, the director is your audience and if he's pleased, you feel you've done your job' (Ross and Ross 1984: 378). Lee Remick similarly states, 'In making movies, you need to be able to rely on your director, because there is no other audience' (Ross and Ross 1984: 254).

In the second place, while stage actors rely on the progression of the play during performance to build towards climactic moments, film actors cannot. Filming scenes out of sequence disrupts and fragments the actor's experience of the role. The screen actor must often pull from the air on command emotional high points or reactions to other characters or to special effects that will be added in post-production. Some teachers of film acting make light of this difference by pointing out that stage plays are commonly rehearsed out of sequence (as does Tucker 1994: 15). In this argument, however, they ignore the reality of performance that ultimately puts the play back together and allows the actor to ride the dynamic waves of dramatic structure, something forever denied to the film actor. No wonder Strasberg observes that, 'Some actors find it difficult to perform scenes out of sequence, as is usually done in films' (Strasberg 1957: 64). At the Actors Studio, he spoke about nineteenth-century actors, such as Mrs Fiske (playing Ibsen's heroines) or Mrs Siddons (as Katherine in Shakespeare's *Henry V*), who staunchly stood backstage during whole performances, so as to better prepare themselves for their own scenes. He nostalgically acknowledges the loss of such a luxury (Strasberg 1956–69: Session A133, 8 March 1968). In preferring stage to screen, Dana Andrews points to this very difference. 'You get a much better opportunity on the stage to develop the character you're playing. Working in the continuity of a play – rather than in snatches, out of continuity, in a movie – gives you a better view of the work as a whole, and a deeper understanding of it' (Ross and Ross 1984: 295).

Finally, since the camera eye can change the apparent spatial distance from spectator to actor easily and quickly, film actors adjust their means of expression from theatrical full-body gestures in long-shots to subtle facial motions in the close-up. This 'freedom to place the actor at any arbitrary distance from the eventual viewer', to borrow Edward Dmytryk's words (Dmytryk and Porter 1984: v), defines an essential difference between stage and screen, as profound as the altered relationship between actor and performance. While stage training teaches some forms of expression (e.g. body work and meaningful blocking), it does not train the subtleties of motion and expression demanded by film. Dana Andrews states, 'The camera . . . picks up every little thing you do with your eyes and mouth. On the stage, you don't have to be conscious of every little gesture' (Ross and Ross 1984: 295). No wonder Strasberg writes that the extreme close-up 'can be intimidating' for the actor, and speculates that, 'Those who have been trained in the rhetorical and theatrical gesture approach, as many British and French actors have been, sometimes have difficulty in making the transition to films' (Strasberg 1957: 64).

The subtle, facial means of expression demanded by the cinematic close-up has led to pervasive, but deceiving, discourse around issues of sincerity, honesty, and truth in film. For example, Dmytryk concludes that the eye of the camera 'makes screen acting . . . a more honest art' (Dmytryk and Porter 1984: v). Similarly, Tony Barr teaches that, 'On the stage you can give a performance. In front of a camera, you'd better have an experience' (Barr 1997: 7). Acting truisms conspire to strengthen and extend this discourse, among them: Laurence Olivier's statement that 'truth [is] demanded by the cinema' (Barr 1997: 7); Alec Guinness's conclusion that it had taken him twenty-five years to learn 'to do nothing' for the camera (Barr 1997: 11); the oft repeated advice that on film 'do less' and 'make it real' (Tucker 1994: 4); and Michael Caine's warning that, 'If you catch somebody "acting" in a movie, that actor is doing it wrong' (Caine 1993: 4).[1]

While Strasberg never explicitly identifies the Method as an approach to film acting, the ways in which he redefines Stanislavsky's assumptions about the actor address not only the altered relationship between actor and director, but also the new conditions of work that film brings to the art of acting.

Strasberg's adaptations of Stanislavsky that adjust to the exigencies of film and help account for the Method's success in cinema, rest upon a major change in attitude towards the creativity of the actor. All the techniques that comprise Stanislavsky's System express the belief that the actor creates the performance, that the actor is 'auteur'. Strasberg, in contrast, shifts responsibility for the interpretive shaping of performance to the director, a shift clearly sympathetic to film. In the Method, the actor may be central, for the actor is the object of the audience's attention, but the director is 'auteur', sculpting the role's dynamics from the actor's credible, 'real', emotional life as if from living clay.

At the Actors Studio, Strasberg explicitly insisted on the authority of the director. In a series of sessions, in which an actor presented Andrey's third act monologue from Chekhov's *The Three Sisters*, Strasberg argues vehemently over the character's 'situation'. Had he given up all hope of a university career? Had he indeed become a hen-pecked husband? After much volleying, Strasberg expects the actor to concede to his interpretation, saying that such concession 'seems to me to be quite fundamental and primary in the understanding of my work, . . . or for that matter of any director's work . . . because [the situation] is what a director really creates.' He criticizes the actor for letting 'a drive towards originality' interfere with the director: 'You resent [giving in] because you feel your individuality is taken away.' Strasberg concludes that he, as director, would not care to work with such a difficult actor (Strasberg 1956–69: Session A138, 16 April 1968). Similarly, in another session, he explains that the director defines the thrust of any scene, and 'it isn't a question of who is right, but who is the director' (Strasberg 1956–69: Session 72, 6 March 1959). He gently coaxes another actor into letting her imagination flow more easily by telling her:

[We] absolve you of the responsibility for the scene. . . . That responsibility is the director's and your responsibility is only that of going on the stage, and regardless of whether you're doing the right or the wrong thing, of doing it easily, fully, following through logically, without too much thought.

(Strasberg 1956–69: Session 33, 31 December 1957)

In this often overlooked aspect of Method training, Strasberg teaches that, 'When the actor is capable of giving to the director anything that he wants, then I consider the acting problem solved' (Strasberg 1956–69: Session 165, 5 December 1961). Anne Jackson starkly testifies to this layer in the Method:

I started out as an instinctive actress who was absolutely terrified of taking direction and advice. I'd always say, 'No, I'll find it myself,' and then immediately get into a kind of contest with the director. I learned from Lee how to listen to a director. I learned how to take help from a director, and not care whether it was his idea or my idea to begin with.

(Ross and Ross 1984: 167)

How ironic, that only after studying with Strasberg does she reject the familiar stereotypical image of the Method actor as one who argues with directors and refuses their authority! Despite Strasberg's explicit teachings, the mistaken stereotype has a stronghold on popular discourse. One need only think of *Tootsie* as a case in point. Dustin Hoffman, a Method actor himself, plays Michael Dorsey, a Method actor who is hounded out of the business because he refuses to let directors direct. While playing a dying Tolstoy, Dorsey prefers to walk off the set rather than cross the stage as requested by the director. His character, he claims, is too ill and weak to walk. While filming a tomato commercial, he refuses to sit down as demanded. Tomatoes can't sit, Dorsey pleads; 'it's not logical'. His agent counters with, 'You are a wonderful actor. . . . But you are too much trouble' (Gelbard and Schisgal 1982). Strasberg too would have undoubtedly fired Dorsey.

Perhaps this particular disjunction between what Strasberg taught and what popular discourse believes he taught, stems from a double message to the actor inherent in the very institution of the Actors Studio, which was explicitly founded in 1947 to inculcate respect for the actor as artist. In his speech for the Studio's twenty-sixth anniversary celebration on 6 December 1973, Elia Kazan reminded its supporters that:

No one can appreciate what the Studio means unless he can recall what the actor was in Broadway Theater before the Studio existed, a part of a labor pool, his craft scoffed at. . . . The great body of the profession, like the longshoreman on the waterfront, shaped up every morning, hoped to be lucky, made the rounds, waited for a phone call, lived on the curb, had nowhere to come in out of the rain.

Kazan concluded that the Studio urged actors to get 'out of that goddamn Walgreen drugstore' waiting around to be discovered and to learn their craft (Garfield 1980: 46). Paradoxically, however, learning to respect their profession meant learning to give in to the director's authority. These two apparently contradictory premises easily create confusion in the minds of actors and the public alike. In regard to the acting techniques promoted by the Method, this paradox radically subverts Stanislavsky's view of the actor as 'auteur'.

One way in which Strasberg does so involves his redefinition of 'action'. Stanislavsky taught that playing a scene entailed making an event occur by carrying out a clearly delineated and purposeful action, which the actor discovers from the 'facts', like clues, set forth in the play. Stanislavsky saw action as the actor's most essential tool, harking back to the very etymology of the word 'drama' from the Greek *dran*, to do (Stanislavsky 1989: 88). Disagreeing with him, Strasberg explains that, 'Actions are valuable only when they define areas of behaviour which otherwise the actor would not create' (Strasberg 1957: 62). In sharp contrast to Stanislavsky, Strasberg taught that actions are given to the actor by the director, as addenda to the script, having 'nothing directly to do with the words of the scene'. Indeed, while 'it is very important in production, directionally,' he states, 'it's almost frankly better if the actor doesn't know what the action is' (Hethmon 1991: 136). While working on a scene from Noel Coward's *Private Lives*, Strasberg directs an actress to examine herself in a mirror in order to determine whether she has changed over the years since her divorce, explaining to members of the Studio that the actress 'would never play [this action] unless it were deliberately given to her because it is completely outside the words' (Strasberg 1956–69: Session 2, 10 April 1956). Did Strasberg really so underestimate the intelligence of his actors?

While Stanislavsky challenges the actor to create character through imaginative actions, Strasberg sees action as one way in which a director can manipulate an actor. He illustrates with an anecdote about an overly emotional member of the Group Theatre, whom he had calmed down in a particular scene by giving her an action – that of playing cards. When she resisted, telling him that no card game appears in the script, he had countered, 'I don't care, do it!' (Strasberg 1956–69: Session 2, 10 April 1956). This attitude is diametrically opposed to Stanislavsky's sense of the actor's creativity, but again sympathetic to the new relationship between actor and director as defined by cinematic editing.

By comparing Stanislavsky's treatment of the person of the actor to Strasberg's, their differing attitudes become crystal clear. Stanislavsky's concern for the actor's autonomy as artist is the source of his concern with the person on stage. As one of Stanislavsky's last students, Vasily Toporkov, puts it, 'Art begins when there is no role, when there is only the "I" in the given circumstances of the play' (Toporkov 1979: 156). Hidden within this statement is a basic assumption: that reactions to the play's specific circumstances generate character. Maria Knebel, another of Stanislavsky's last pupils, suggests how actor and character interact, when she writes:

> Actors must . . . work from their own individualities. That means –
> analyzing oneself as a human being/actor in the given circumstances
> of the play. But precisely because these circumstances are not at all
> those that formed the actor's personality in life . . . the actor learns
> what he must discard, what in himself he must overcome, which
> of his own personal traits can serve as 'building material' for the
> construction of the character.
>
> (Knebel 1971: 87)

In other words, actors transform themselves into their characters by paying strict attention to all the minutiae of the circumstances, what Stanislavsky calls the 'facts' of the play. In so doing, they think 'logically' and 'take action' as their characters do. Given this assumption, it is no surprise that much of what Stanislavsky teaches involves strategies for reading texts. The actor does not function without regard to text or scenario, else the transformative power of the artist disappears. Thus, Stanislavsky constructs a balanced relationship between 'the individuality of the actor' and 'the unified image' of the role, as Vsevolod Pudovkin put it (Pudovkin 1955: 211). Moreover, the System empowers the actor to interpret creatively, much as the director does in Strasberg's eyes.

It is easy to misunderstand Stanislavsky's statements about the 'human being/actor' as a directive to play oneself, and the Method wilfully promotes this distortion. Unlike Stanislavsky, Strasberg places great emphasis on the personality of the actor, thus 'feeding the star system', as Naremore notes (Naremore 1990: 198). Method actors do not transform themselves into characters, but find characters within themselves, through 'substitutions' of personal experiences for the 'facts' of the text. Moreover, Strasberg argues that Stanislavsky is theoretically mistaken in placing so much stress on the play. He rejects Stanislavsky's formulation of the technique known as 'the magic if', in which an actor asks, 'What would I do, if I were to find myself in the circumstances of the play?' Strasberg believes this question limits the actor to the play (precisely what the System means to do). He prefers a slightly altered query: 'The circumstances of the scene indicate that the character must behave in a particular way; what would motivate you, the actor, to behave in that particular way?'[2] This restatement easily allows the actor to substitute a director's request for the play, whenever necessary. In addition, Strasberg explains, this restatement 'not only requires the actor to create the desired artistic result, but demands that he make it real and personal to himself in order to achieve it.' In short, it forces the actor to use the self (Strasberg 1987: 84–87). Similarly, Strasberg rejects Stanislavsky's overarching concern with textual analysis, and warns actors against 'mental thinking'. In the System, he explains,

> the whole idea is in the analysis, that the actor analyzes, . . . [but] it's of no value. Every actor has done this from the beginning of acting, and it still does not lead to the particular results that Stanislavsky wanted or that we want.
> (Strasberg 1956–69: Session A142, 10 May 1968)[3]

During my work at the Actors Studio in 1978, I watched as Stanislavsky's and Strasberg's two opposing attitudes towards actors' responsibility to text came into direct conflict. Sam Tsikhotsky (a director at the Moscow Art Theatre who had worked closely with Mikhail Kedrov, Stanislavsky's last assistant) had been invited to direct a workshop production of Chekhov's *The Seagull*, cast exclusively with members of the Actors Studio. While they began work assuming that because they were all grounded in Stanislavsky they shared the same values, in fact, they soon learned that this assumption was faulty. Their differences were laid bare during rehearsals. The Method-trained cast often bristled when Tsikhotsky criticized them for not playing their characters. When one actress protested that he had asked her to play herself, he reminded her that she had not considered how the circumstances of her character would modify her normal behaviour. Her character wears a corset, whereas she does not. Her character was educated in a different system; grew up with values different to her own; lives in the Russian countryside, not in New York, etc. These circumstances, he said, would condition her behaviour as surely as they had that of her character. Placing oneself in the role does not mean transferring one's own circumstances to the play, but rather incorporating into oneself circumstances other than one's own. This relationship between text and self is the very one that Strasberg transforms through his personalization of the System.

The Method places new emphasis on the actor's use of self by redefining Stanislavsky's term, 'logic'. While Stanislavskian actors seek to uncover the character's unique logic, Strasberg asks actors to think in any way that will prompt required behaviour. 'It has often been assumed that the actor should be thinking exactly what the character is thinking. . . . But the important thing is that the [actor] be thinking about something real and concrete' (Strasberg 1956–69: Session 72, 6 March 1959), the content of the thought being less important than how it is read by the camera. From this point of view, it becomes easy to understand why the Method encourages actors to use analogous or emotionally appropriate incidents from their own lives ('personal substitutions'), instead of using the given circumstances of the play.

As Strasberg emphasizes, logic need not be a 'literal equivalent' to the play 'but a personal equivalent' (Strasberg 1956–69: Session 72, 6 March 1959). In short, a Method actor's 'logic' does not necessarily reflect the playwright's (Strasberg 1987: 86–87), but must result in whatever the director wants. If, at an Actors Studio session, Hoffman's stereotypical Method actor in *Tootsie* had refused to sit down as a tomato, Strasberg would surely have reprimanded him for not creating a personal logic that would allow him to do so.

Strasberg explicitly defines his attitude towards 'logic' at a Studio session in 1965 in response to Geraldine Page, who had performed Lady Macbeth's monologue, in which she learns that witches have promised her husband the crown. Page explains that she thought about how angry she becomes when her real life husband dismisses her praise of him, but accepts compliments from others (her 'substitution'). This personal logic aroused an unexpected anger during the scene (Page 1966: 249–50). In commending her work, Strasberg admitted that he could not detect the logic of her anger, but added that what takes place in her 'private imagination' concerns him only in so far as it 'serves the purpose of making the scene alive' (Strasberg 1956–69: Session 161, 17 November 1961).

In yet another session, Strasberg attempted to mediate between two actors who had performed a scene from Ibsen's *Hedda Gabler*. The scene partners were arguing about whether or not Hedda had actually had an extra-marital affair. Strasberg intervened with a firm 'That doesn't matter'. Since logic is personal and private, he sees no need for actors to work from the same premise. 'There are often times when the logic of each individual may not connect with the logic of what the other actor has chosen. . . . There is no right answer. The rightness is only what works for each individual, and what works for one does not work for the other' (Strasberg 1956–69: Session 32, 30 December 1958). In sum, Method training ultimately teaches that logic's value lies only in whether it 'helps the actor to play the scene with an aliveness, with a spontaneity, with a believability both for herself and for us'. After watching a successfully completed scene, in which personal logic 'helped the tears to come, helped the emotion', Strasberg praises the actor for 'the honestest work that you have done and the best' (Strasberg 1956–69: Session 72, 6 March 1959).

Strasberg's redefinition of logic – whatever makes the scene alive – leads quite naturally to key techniques in the Method, among them: the affective memory exercise (in which one recalls in full detail a highly charged moment from one's life in order to recreate a necessary emotional state) and the private moment (in which one performs in public an action as private as taking a shower).

Strasberg's redefinitions of 'action' and 'logic', as well as the techniques of affective memory and private moments, eloquently address the changed conditions of work from stage to screen, when scenes are not shot in consecutive order; when the actor may not have access to the full screenplay;

when an actor's partner is not present on the set to provoke appropriate reactions; when the actor must respond in a vacuum to sound and special effects that will be spliced in later. Strasberg's innovations provide actors with tools to cope with such work-a-day situations in cinema. His sense of action adapts the actor to the reality of the director's growing power over the final screen product. Personal, 'private' logic can be created without a script or partner, in the absence of a consecutive flow of story, in the absence of sound effects and atmosphere. The techniques of affective memory and private moments allow actors to maintain emotional continuity under the fragmented experience of film work. Using them, actors can pull emotions and reactions out of the air, as it were, and at will. Thus, while Stanislavsky proposed an ideal for artistic creation, Strasberg transformed it into practical tools for the contemporary business of film acting. Pudovkin wrote:

> Cinematography should not adopt the methodology of Stanislavsky directly, taking the results that he had obtained in the theatre without further developing them for the new technological conditions of film which are so complex and rich.
>
> (Pudovkin 1955: 211)

It is as if Strasberg were heeding Pudovkin's advice.

A final question remains. How does the Method's approach to actor training connect with cinematic discourse about truth and honesty? Obviously, Strasberg's notorious obsession with 'real' emotion, that had begun with his work at the Group Theatre in the 1930s and continued in sessions at the Actors Studio until his death in 1982, dovetails with naturalism as a filmic style. The Group's acting was seen as 'startling to the audience', who 'had not seen real emotion used to that extent on the stage', leaving them 'flabbergasted' (Phoebe Brand in Chinoy 1976: 515). An audience member once remarked that 'truthful emotions' on stage made seeing a Group Theatre production 'like witnessing a real accident' (Helen Westley in Chinoy 1976: 485). The Method's stress on the actor's use of self also sympathetically fits into the discourse. At the Actors Studio more than thirty years later, Strasberg reminded students that the purpose of the affective memory exercise is to produce 'a real emotion, which means something that is happening to the actor and which means that the actor actually created a true and real event, a true and real experience' (Strasberg 1956–69: Session A122, 2 January 1968). Such teaching surely prompts acting advice like Tony Barr's, cited above.

What may not be as obvious in considering naturalism and sincerity in the Method is yet another of Strasberg's paradoxical messages to the actor: While acting is indeed an instinctive natural art, it is also a craft to be honed through hard work. Under the influence of statements that encourage one to be real on screen and to do 'less' or 'nothing', actors can easily abjure all training. After all, one need not act, but behave for the camera. Or, to put it in terms of the

Method's jargon, screen actors 'play themselves'. Kuleshov had certainly urged the filming of 'types' rather than actors, 'that is, people who, in themselves, as they were born, present some kind of interest for cinematic treatment' (Kuleshov 1974: 63–64). Even more pointedly, he writes:

> If we simply choose a person, having no relationship to the theatre, and make him do what we need, we shall see that his work on the screen appears better than the work of a theatre actor and will give us more realistic material, from which it will be easier to construct a cinema film.
>
> (Kuleshov 1974: 57)

In the same spirit, Hollywood created its own myth of the 'natural', who is discovered by a sharp-eyed talent scout, while innocently sipping a soda at the corner drugstore.

Vsevolod Pudovkin, a member of Kuleshov's workshop, urged a very different response. 'As nowhere else is training of the actor [as] necessary [as] in the cinema', he writes. He assumes such training must take into account that, 'At base, an actor's work in film, just as in theatre, resides in the creation of a unified, living image', which depends upon a 'necessary organic link between the individuality of the actor and each moment in the life of the image depicted by him' (Pudovkin n.d.: 4–7). The working process of the medium, which disregards narrative chronology and fragments performance, demands more, not less training, especially in the actor's concentration and clarity of vision, in sustaining the 'unified image' of character. Only training, in his view, can compensate for the difficult and disruptive conditions under which the screen actor must work (Pudovkin 1955: 126, 130). Indeed, Pudovkin advocated not only Stanislavsky's System, which depends upon textual analysis, but also an 'actor's script' in addition to a 'shooting script' in order to allow the screen actor opportunity to create character in the same way as the stage actor does (Pudovkin 1955: 145). Needless to say, this suggestion has not been adopted by the film industry.

Strasberg's Method paradoxically embraces both these responses to training. Actors must use themselves fully and freely, creating credible inner lives for the camera to observe. For Strasberg the emotional life of the actor is therefore primary. The words of the text are the last element to consider; they do not initiate creation as they do for Stanislavsky. In this way, Strasberg too abjures training. 'There are feelings and experiences inside of you,' he teaches, 'that do not need to be worked for, in the same way that when you touch a piano, you get the sound of the piano. . . . Words [then] hit on the instrument and things come out' (Strasberg 1956–69: Session A1, 22 November 1963). However, he also teaches that actors are artists whose 'natural' behaviour must be carefully and rigorously trained. Social and psychological inhibitions interfere with self-expression. 'Instinct' is not enough; actors must 'tune' their 'instruments' daily in order to 'become completely responsive'. Only then, does the actor's 'instrument give forth a new depth of resonance. Emotion that has been habitually held back suddenly rushes forth' (Hethmon 1991: 92–93).

In conclusion, Lee Strasberg's paradox for the actor is twofold. While promoting respect for the actor, he places the director in charge of performance. While stressing that natural behaviour is the stuff of acting, he trains the actor in practical techniques. In both cases, he takes Stanislavsky from stage to screen. On the one hand, he teaches actors to cope with the authority invested in the director by the power of montage. On the other hand, he creates ways in which the actor can cope with everyday conditions of film work that fragment, disrupt, and essentially deconstruct the experience of performing. In short, the two predominant commonplaces about the Method – that Strasberg changes Stanislavsky and that his students succeed most in film – are indeed inextricably linked.

Notes

1 I find Tucker's frank rejection of these truisms and his willingness to show how film acting violates the real (especially in the close-up) quite refreshing. In addition, Walter Matthau turns these truisms on their head, when he implies that the stage is ultimately more real than film:

> On the stage, you're wide open. There are no tricks with the camera to make you look a certain way. Nobody is going to cut you out, either. The people are sitting out there, and they're going to see you full on. Nobody can fool around with your face. Nobody can fool around with your voice. You can taste and smell what the audience feels. You know if you're coming across. You know if you're being heard. You know if you're being understood.
>
> (Ross and Ross 1984: 421)

2 Strasberg correctly attributes the first question to Stanislavsky, and the second, mistakenly, to Vakhtangov.
3 Significantly, Strasberg belittled Stanislavsky's last experiments (called 'The Method of Physical Actions' in the West and more precisely 'Active Analysis of Text' in Russia). After telling the Actors Studio about the 'devices' that Stanislavsky worked out in his late years, Strasberg adds, 'I don't think they work' (Strasberg 1956–69: Session 7, 29 May 1956 and Session A161, 31 December 1968).

References

Barr, Tony (1997) *Acting for the Camera*, New York, Harper Perennial.
Caine, Michael (1993) *Acting in Film*, New York, Applause Theatre Books.
Chinoy, Helen Krich (ed.) (1976) 'Reunion: A Self-Portrait of the Group Theatre', a special issue of *Educational Theatre Journal*, vol. 27, no. 4.

Dmytryk, Edward and Jean Porter (1984) *On Screen Acting*, Boston, Focal Press.

Garfield, David (1980) *A Player's Place: The Story of The Actors Studio*, New York, Macmillan.

Gelbard, Larry, and Murray, Schisgal (1982) *Tootsie*, film directed by Sydney Pollack, Columbia Pictures.

Guthrie, Tyrone (1976) 'An Audience of One', in Toby Cole and Helen Krich Chinoy (eds) *Directors on Directing*, New York, Macmillan, pp. 245–56.

Hethmon, Robert, H. (ed.) (1991) *Strasberg at the Actors Studio*, New York, Theatre Communications Group.

Hornby, Richard (1992) *The End of Acting*, New York, Applause Theatre Books.

Knebel, M.O. (1971) *O tom, chto mne kazhetsia osobenno vazhnym*, Moscow: Iskusstvo. [Translations from this source are mine.]

Kuleshov, Lev (1974) 'The Art of Cinema', in Ronald Levaco (ed. and trans.) *Kuleshov on Film*, Berkeley, University of California Press.

Naremore, James (1985) review of *A Method to Their Madness* by Foster Hirsch, *Film Quarterly*, vol. 38, no. 4, p. 44.

—— (1990) *Acting in the Cinema*, Berkeley, University of California Press.

Page, Geraldine (1966) 'The Bottomless Cup', in Erica Munk (ed.) *Stanislavski and America*, New York: Hill & Wang, pp. 249–51.

Pudovkin, Vsevolod (1955) 'Rabota aktera v kino i "sistema" Stanislavskogo', in *Izbrannie stat'i*, Moscow: Iskusstvo. [Translations from this source are mine.]

—— (n.d.) 'The Stanislavsky System and Its Application in Cinema Art', typescript, Collection of Sharon M. Carnicke.

Ross, Lillian and Helen Ross (1984) *The Player*, New York, Limelight Editions.

Stanislavsky, C.S. (1989) *Sobranie sochinenii*, vol. 2, Moscow, Iskusstvo.

Strasberg, Lee (1956–69) 'The Actors Studio', Sound Recording no. 339A, Madison, Wisconsin Center for Film and Theatre Research (An Archive of the University of Wisconsin, Madison, and the State Historical Society of Wisconsin, Madison).

—— (1957) 'Acting', *Encyclopaedia Britannica*, 14th edn, vol. I.

—— (1987) *A Dream of Passion: The Development of the Method*, Boston, Little Brown & Company.

Toporkov, Vasily (1979) *Stanislavski in Rehearsal: The Final Years*, trans. C. Edwards, New York, Theatre Arts Books.

Tucker, Patrick (1994) *Secrets of Screen Acting*, New York and London, Routledge.

7

SUSAN SARANDON

In praise of older women

Alan Lovell

My initial relationship with Susan Sarandon was a pragmatic one. I asked a group of students who their favourite star was. They asked me to name mine. Their choices were inevitably current ones. Unprepared, and not wanting to introduce a historical dimension into the discussion, I was at something of a loss. Names of current stars I liked flashed through my mind, Joe Mantegna, Christine Lahti, Susan Sarandon . . . impulsively I chose Susan.

I haven't regretted my choice! On my part, at least, the relationship has become a more substantial and rewarding one. My initial enthusiasm for her work was immediate and direct but unreflective. In this essay, I have tried to become reflective without losing touch with that immediacy and directness. I have focused on two key themes: the way Sarandon's career developed and the quality of her performances. Sarandon's attitude and views on acting are also discussed, as is the role her physical appearance and voice have played in her on-screen personae.

The development of a career

The beginning was according to Hollywood myth. Although Susan Sarandon studied Drama at university, she had no experience of performance. In 1970, she went along to an audition with her then husband, Chris Sarandon. She didn't go in the hope of getting a part but to provide her husband someone to read with. An agent thought she had potential, signed her and, a few days later, got her a part in the film *Joe* (1970). On the basis of this accidental start, Sarandon established a strong career as a film and television actress. For nearly thirty years, she has worked consistently in the film and television industries. She has acted in something like forty-five feature and made-for-television films.

The early part of her career had no particular shape. She appeared in films that differed hugely in quality and character: big, expensive productions like the Jack Lemmon/Walter Matthau remake of *The Front Page* (1974), and

The Great Waldo Pepper (1975); limited, routine ones like *The Other Side of Midnight* (1977), *Checkered Flag* (1977) and *The King of the Gypsies* (1978); and a small-scale cult production like *The Rocky Horror Picture Show* (1975). She worked with a wide range of directors: from well-known ones like Billy Wilder, Sidney Lumet, and George Roy Hill to anonymous figures like Charles Jarrot, John Leone, and Alan Gibson. Her varied roles included among others, a cinema organist, a magazine writer, a gypsy fortune teller, a prostitute, a cinema attendant. The one constant in this patchwork was that she maintained the status of a featured actress, placed between the stars and the supporting actors.

If the early part of her career has any kind of shape, it is defined by two features: (a) she tended to be cast as an *ingénue*, the classic role for young actresses who are regarded as conventionally pretty; (b) she was frequently cast in comedies. Of the ten or so films she made in this period, eight are comedies.

Sarandon's own attitude to the development of her career at this stage was contradictory. She has said that she had no career ambitions, that she's 'never been smart in her career'. She also expressed cynicism about the possibility of doing so, 'You can't build a career. . . . You know how irrational this business is.' However, there's some evidence which goes against this. She changed managers twice because she didn't like the aims they had for her.

Two films directed by Louis Malle in the late 1970s, *Pretty Baby* (1978) and *Atlantic City* (1980) were crucial for the development of her career. *Pretty Baby* gave Sarandon more public visibility because of the notoriety it acquired. Sarandon's role was a prostitute whose 12 year old daughter was also a prostitute. The notoriety was heightened because the daughter was played by an actress, Brooke Shields, whose age was roughly the same as the character's.

Atlantic City was the more significant of the two films. It was both a critical and modest commercial success. More important for Sarandon, she was nominated for an Academy Award as best actress for her performance as the waitress, Sally – a tragi-comic role of a young woman who is trying to escape from the oppressive provincial world in which she has grown up.

The two films added another dimension which was important for the later development of Sarandon's career. Both films have strong erotic concerns. In *Pretty Baby* Sarandon appears nude; in *Atlantic City* she appears semi-nude. After these appearances, sexuality is always present as a factor in her career. If there is one image which provides a consistent reference point in responses to her, it is the opening image of *Atlantic City*, where Sally is seen squeezing lemon juice on to her breasts while she is voyeuristically observed by an old man (played by Burt Lancaster) from a window opposite.

The problems of building a career were demonstrated by what happened to Sarandon after *Atlantic City*. Despite her success in that film, her career in the first half of the 1980s continued to have a miscellaneous character. The feature films in which she appeared vary greatly in ambition and scope: a

Figure 7.1 If there is one image which provides a constant reference point in
responses to Susan Sarandon it's the opening image of her in *Atlantic City*
(1980)
Source: Courtesy of the Kobal Collection

misconceived reworking of Shakespeare's play, *The Tempest* (1982), with John
Cassavetes and Gena Rowlands in the cast; a lurid erotic horror film, *The
Hunger* (1983); and a plot-laden comedy, *Compromising Positions* (1985).

The one observable change in her situation was an improvement in her
status. In a number of the films, she played the central role. But the change
wasn't complete. In *The Hunger*, for example, she was a featured actress behind
the stars, Catherine Deneuve and David Bowie. Overall, her roles suggest she
was gaining recognition as an interesting actress without that interest being
strongly defined.

Sarandon was cast in the lead role in *The Witches of Eastwick* (1987),
opposite Jack Nicholson and alongside Cher and Michelle Pfeiffer. This casting
was a substantial step up for her. It was the kind of role, in the kind of film,
which would strongly confirm her as having star status. Then, just before
production began, she was told that she and Cher were to swap roles. She
described the whole experience of making the film as a humiliating one and
said that after it not only wasn't she an A list actress, but she wasn't on any list
at all. The film can't have had an entirely negative effect on Sarandon's career.
Although she lost the lead role, she had still played a prominent role next to
a major male star, in a big budget film which was successful at the box office.

A year later she was able to build on this when she appeared in *Bull Durham* (1988). It proved to be a key film in the development of her career. The main female character, Annie Savoy, is an original comic creation. When she read the script, Sarandon immediately recognized the opportunities the character offered. It was the one part she admits to having made a big effort to get:

> I knew they needed someone who could handle language and some of the woman's other attributes. I had to fly myself from Rome to L.A. which was quite a lot of money to meet with them to read . . . But it was such a wonderful script – surprising, sweet, did away with a lot of the myths and challenged the American definition of success. When I got there I spent some time with Kevin Costner, kissed some ass at the studio and got back on the plane.[1]

Her success in getting the part provides the one clear example where Sarandon was able to take control of her career and shape it decisively. The film gave her a much stronger definition as an actress. It powerfully associated her with roles that combined sexual attractiveness and intelligence. Annie Savoy goes along with Sally in *Atlantic City* as a key reference in discussions of Sarandon's work. Just as important, she had appeared in another commercial success (though of a more limited kind than *The Witches of Eastwick*) alongside another major male star (Kevin Costner).

Although their quality varies a good deal, the next four films Sarandon appeared in (*The January Man* (1989), *A Dry White Season* (1989), *Light Sleeper* (1991), and *White Palace* (1991)), have a more consistent character. They could be described as Hollywood art films – modestly budgeted, 'serious' films. All four films are thematically ambitious: *The January Man* deals with the relationship between big city politics and family and sexual relationships; *A Dry White Season* dramatizes the Apartheid situation in South Africa; *Light Sleeper* is an attempt to use a story about drug dealing as a way of expressing modern alienation; and *White Palace* explores the relationship between class and sex.

Given Sarandon's own liberal-left social and political convictions, and her expressed view that 'you can have entertainment in films which are about something', they are the kind of films with which you might expect her to be associated. However, if they are the result of more control over her career and more conscious choice, they also demonstrate the problems actresses/actors face when making such choices. Three of them are extremely limited in terms of the roles she plays. In *A Dry White Season* her part was cut so much that she hardly appears. In *The January Man* and *Light Sleeper* both the characters are underwritten, ill-defined, shadowy figures in dramas dominated by the male characters. Her part in *White Palace* is much the most interesting one. Nora Baker has echoes of Sally in *Atlantic City* and Annie Savoy in *Bull Durham*. A working-class waitress in early middle age, Nora is trying to make sense of her life. It's then complicated by a relationship with a young, rich, Jewish advertising executive. The role is a much more fully written and central figure than those in the other three films.

The third film to have a decisive impact on Susan Sarandon's career was *Thelma & Louise* (1991). On the face of it, her role in the film seems part of a grand career design. The character of Louise could be seen as a summing up of all the characters she previously had success with, especially Sally, Annie Savoy, and Nora Baker. Like Nora, Louise is a middle-aged waitress trying to make sense of her life. Like Sally and Annie Savoy, Louise combines sexual appeal with intelligence. However, far from being part of a grand design, Sarandon only got the part by accident. Meryl Streep was first choice for Louise, but because of other commitments, she had to turn the part down. Jodie Foster and others were approached. Sarandon was a late choice.

Her appearance in *Thelma & Louise* may not have been the result of a conscious career strategy but its success (mainly critical and mythological – it was only a modest commercial success) powerfully confirmed Sarandon's status as a star. As a consequence, at an age when she might have expected her career to be in recession, she got leading roles in substantial productions like *Lorenzo's Oil* (1992) and *The Client* (1994). Although she received Oscar nominations for both these films, in orthodox terms her career reached a climax in 1995, when she appeared in a more modest 'art' film, *Dead Man Walking* (1995). For her performance as the nun, Sister Helen Prejean, she won the Oscar for best actress.

The most obvious issue which emerges out of this sketch of Susan Sarandon's career is its slow development. Although she achieved some success by getting featured roles almost immediately, it took a long time – nearly twenty years – for her to become established as a star. In its trajectory, her career contrasts interestingly with comparable actresses of her generation like Meryl Streep, Jessica Lange, and Sigourney Weaver, all of whom achieved star status relatively quickly. The time it took Sarandon is an argument against the view that stars have a recognizable, innate quality which sets them apart from the general run of actresses and actors. She demonstrates that stardom can be worked for.

There's another issue of a more general theoretical kind which emerges out of a consideration of Sarandon's career. In discussions of their work, actresses (and actors) are often treated as quasi auteurs. Sarandon's work is often discussed in this way. She is associated with a modern type of woman, one who doesn't see intelligence and sexual attractiveness as contradictory forces. But to make such an association is to be highly selective. If all the roles Sarandon has played are taken into account, she could as easily be associated with more traditional mother figures (*Little Women*, *Safe Passage*, *Lorenzo's Oil*, *King of the Gypsies*, *Compromising Positions*). What is most remarkable about her career is the enormous variety of the roles she has played. There may be some pattern which can be discerned if they are all taken into account but I doubt it.

Attitudes to acting

Although Susan Sarandon never received any formal training as an actress, the views she expresses about acting are clearly within the naturalistic, Stanislavskian position which has dominated twentieth-century attitudes to acting. Acting is regarded as an important, creative form of artistic activity. It's a way of exploring human psychology:

> There are lots of aspects of yourself that you don't want to admit are there. And that's the challenge. If you're into experimentation with your psyche, and if human beings really interest you, it's the perfect job because you never get it right.[2]

She defines good acting in what are clearly Stanislavskian terms:

> If you're working with people who really listen and try different things and invest a lot and are very specific, it can be wonderful. It's just about listening and being specific.

From such a perspective there are two key acting challenges. The first is to give performances a sense of freshness and spontaneity. This is achieved by the actress 'listening' to her fellow actresses and actors, not coming to her performance with prepared responses. In line with this, Sarandon often emphasizes the importance of remaining 'open' in a scene. The second challenge is to give your character a strong sense of individuality. This is achieved by inventing responses that are 'specific' to your character.

Sarandon isn't a Method actress. In creating her characters, she is more dependent on the script than Method performers typically are. Again and again in discussing her performances she refers to the quality of the script. To support her reading of it, she generally uses naturalistic methods. In *White Palace* she put on weight because she thought it was appropriate for the character she was playing. In *Lorenzo's Oil* she got to know the couple the story was based on, the Odones, very well and modelled her performance on Christina Odone.

Because of her emphasis on the script, Sarandon often suggests changes when she feels a script isn't working. *Thelma & Louise* provides a very good example of how she works. Discussing the bedroom scene, when Jimmy tries to reconnect with Louise, Sarandon said:

> Originally in the script they were supposed to do a little marriage ceremony and sing songs and fuck, and I felt it just so unrealistic.

Not only would the film lose some of its tension, but also a woman who's just killed somebody because she's remembering having been raped – it's pretty hard to have sex under the circumstances and have it be great. Somehow that would cost us a lot of credibility.[3]

She persuaded Ridley Scott that the scene should be rewritten.

Sarandon's emphasis on the script also means that dialogue is of great importance and forms another reference point in her discussions of acting. She defined one of the main challenges in *Bull Durham* as 'handling language' and 'speaking all those words'. In *Lorenzo's Oil* the challenge for her was to make the exposition of scientific information 'immediate, passionate, funny and visual'. And she compares contemporary film acting unfavourably with 1930s acting in terms of a lost ability to handle dialogue.[4]

Physical appearance

A key part of the effect an actress or actor has in a performance is her or his own physical appearance. Susan Sarandon's build is a typical one for an actress. She is of medium height and slim. In many actresses, slimness goes with a figure which in outline looks like a boy's. Sarandon's shape, with its clearly observable curves, is evidently a woman's.

The most distinctive part of her appearance is her face. She has a relatively long neck which helps to draw attention to the face. Her face conforms to conventional notions about beauty in that it has a small, oval shape with a well-defined bone structure and high cheek bones. It is also well proportioned in terms of the size of her ears, nose, mouth, and chin. She has a distinctive palish red complexion which is set off by deep red-brown hair. Her face is prevented from being too perfect by two features. Her nose has a sharp outline with an upturned end which gives her a slightly 'cute' quality. But most striking are her large pop eyes. Because of their size and shape, they attract attention and give a powerful sense that she is interacting with other characters through the way she looks at them.

It is interesting to compare her with Meryl Streep. Both their faces have much the same basic character, except for the eyes and complexion. Meryl Streep has much smaller eyes and as a result her face often has an inscrutable quality. The combination of this with a delicate pale complexion and light blonde hair may in part be responsible for the coldness which critics often claim to see in her acting.

Sarandon's voice was quite high in her early films. It has become lower as she's grown older. The natural tone of her voice is pleasant but with a hard edge. Her voice doesn't appear to have a great range. She normally works in mid-range and any changes tend to be moves into a higher key.

Sarandon has presented herself physically in a variety of ways in her films. Her attractiveness is often heightened in conventional ways through the use of costume and make-up. But she has also been willing to present herself in less attractive ways, most obviously in *Dead Man Walking*, where she wears little make-up, has an unflattering hairstyle, and sober clothes. As a result the marks of age are evident, particularly in close-up. She has also presented herself in a directly erotic way by appearing nude in some sequences.[5]

Performances

Atlantic City (1980)

Atlantic City is a good place to start an analysis of Susan Sarandon's performances not only because of the quality of the performance but, more importantly, because there's enough information about the making of the film to allow reasonably confident judgements to be made about her work in it. I have access to a script which, while I'm not entirely sure of its status, seems very close to the final draft. It is therefore a fair indication of what the actors had to work with. And according to Sarandon's testimony, Louis Malle, the director, left the actors very much to their own devices. Because of this, I feel more confident about giving overall responsibility to Sarandon for her performance. According to Sarandon, *Atlantic City* originally had a very poor script. She suggested to Louis Malle that they get the playwright, John Guare, to rewrite it. Rewriting continued while the film was being shot. Certainly, the script which I have indicates quite a number of last-minute revisions.

Despite the problems in writing it, there is a basic dramatic strength in the way a vivid interaction between a range of characters and a distinctive setting is created. Atlantic City is portrayed as being on the cusp of change. A traditional, substantial seaside resort is being transformed to a glitzy gambling mecca. The characters are a detritus of the past and present. Lou and Grace are leftovers from a time when old-style gangsters dominated, while Chrissie and Dave are fringe hippies who have come to exploit the drug culture. The script's main weakness is structural: after a relatively slow narrative build-up, one dramatic event is piled upon another in the final part of the story.

Sally, the character Sarandon plays, is attracted by the possibilities the new city offers. They are an exciting contrast to what's on offer in the small Canadian town in which she grew up. In basic outline, the character of Sally is strongly drawn in the script. She isn't an unfamiliar character – the young woman who wants to expand her cultural horizons by exchanging small town crudity for urban sophistication. She is given a pathetic dimension by her romantic naïveté. She wants to be a croupier in Monaco because, for her, Europe represents class and sophistication.

Sally's situation makes her anxious and insecure. When her ex-husband and her sister reappear, these feelings are heightened and are joined by anger and resentment. She struggles to control these emotions as she is drawn into the destructive drama precipitated by her husband. The most striking feature of Sarandon's performance is the detailed and inventive way she plays Sally's struggle to express and contain her feelings. To get the right effect, she employs a variety of resources, voice and facial expression, gestures and movement.

Gestures and movement are the strongest indicators of the character's state of mind. An excellent example of how Sarandon uses these is provided by an early scene where Sally initially takes Dave and Chrissie back to her apartment. In the script they arrive by taxi. As eventually staged, they make the journey on foot. This is a very brief sequence without any great narrative significance but Sarandon gives it dramatic energy and meaning by using it to express the anger Sally feels. She strides rapidly in front of the other two swinging one arm vigorously while the movement of the other arm is constrained by the two bags she is carrying. She pauses for the other two to catch up, then strides on ahead. The pace slows as they go up the stairs. Then, as they come to the door, there's some particularly inventive business. On the landing, Sarandon walks quickly to the door while pulling a glove off with her teeth. Unceremoniously she drops the bags on the floor, takes the key from her pocket, opens the door, picks up the bags, and almost swings with them through the doorway. Despite the number of actions she has to perform, she keeps the pace up by treating them as if they were part of one continuous action.

Facial expression supports the use of movement and gesture. It's most marked by its absence. Sarandon is quite rigorous about this: the film is well over halfway through before Sally fully smiles. Much of the time her face remains expressionless. Occasionally, it shows signs of anger but in keeping with Sally's attempts to control her feelings, Sarandon makes the signs small ones; mainly it's a matter of a tightening of the facial muscles.

Sarandon keeps Sally's voice a 'small' one. She speaks quietly with no dramatic changes in volume. When Sally is angry, for example, Sarandon only increases the volume a little. She marks the anger by a change in pitch rather than volume. In the scene where Sally, having lost her job, tries to extract money from Lou and is thrown out of the casino, her voice goes higher and develops an ugly 'shrieky' quality. This quality, which recurs at various points in the film, recalls the harsh social world from which Sally is fleeing.

By giving Sally's emotional turmoil such a strong definition, Sarandon risks making her into an unsympathetic character. For much of the film, Sally is tense and constrained. Her emotions are mainly the negative ones of anger and unhappiness. However, because the turmoil is so strongly defined, the moments in the film when Sally relaxes have all the more force because of the contrast which is set up. The most powerful of these are the two sequences where Sally bathes her shoulders and breasts with lemon juice. Sarandon plays these in a relaxed way, with slow gentle movements as she cuts and squeezes

Figure 7.2 Using the body for comic effect – Susan Sarandon with Tim Robbins in
    Bull Durham (1988)
Source: Courtesy of the Kobal Collection

the lemons, then removes her blouse and bathes herself. The scene when Sally has lunch with Lou has a similar impact. Her big smile, when she kids Lou he has no fingerprints, has all the more powerful effect because Sarandon has been so disciplined in keeping Sally grim-faced previously.

Overall, the way Sarandon plays Sally is based on an intelligent reading of the script. The dramatic energy of the writing depends on a critical, anti-heroic perspective on the setting and the characters. The transition Atlantic City is undergoing is presented as a change from a legendary past to a tawdry present. The characters, who are the flotsam and jetsam of the past and present, are presented in a similarly anti-heroic way. Lou, in particular, is an exact portrait of the gangster as anti-hero. By making Sally's insecurities and anxieties so vivid, Sarandon keeps Sally firmly within the overall anti-heroic perspective.

Bull Durham (1988)

Susan Sarandon was right to see how good the script for *Bull Durham* was. It combines a romantic comedy with a sports comedy to very good effect. The two genres are given equal weight and their interaction is a great source for the narrative energy and comic invention of the drama. The interaction also provides another of the script's virtues, namely its strong characterization. The two central male characters, Crash and Nuke, are defined in baseball terms. One is an experienced professional, the other a promising rookie. Their sports status is then used to highlight their romantic status. The central female character, Annie Savoy, also helps to marry the genres by combining female romantic attractiveness with male baseball expertise. The script is also enterprising in the way it uses language: as well as conventional comic dialogue exchanges, Crash and Annie have a number of what are effectively monologues in which they discuss ideas, use abstract terms, and make, what are in the context of the film, obscure references.

The status of the script to which I had access is uncertain. Certainly it represented a relatively early draft with a number of significant differences from the finished film. But where scenes from the script are recognizable in the finished film, a comparison suggests they are a good indication of what the actors worked from. It also seems reasonable to assume the actors were mainly responsible for what is added to the script by their performances. *Bull Durham* was the first film Ron Shelton directed and by his own testimony he needed the support he got from Sarandon.

Annie Savoy is a genuinely complex figure, one of the most vivid female characters created in recent Hollywood cinema. She is in part a New Ager. She uses baseball as a substitute for religion: this is her way of making sense of the world. She has intellectual interests, reads poetry, and can discuss the distinction between metaphysics and theology. She is knowledgeable about baseball and can analyse the technical faults of batters or pitchers. She is a baseball groupie who has affairs with the players. But the affairs are governed by a feminist sense of the affairs as freely entered into, equal exchanges.

As one might expect from a film about baseball, *Bull Durham* is very physical. Although Annie isn't a player like Crash or Nuke, the physical demands on Sarandon are quite considerable. In the course of the film, Annie, among other things, has batting practice, climbs on a table, has sex in a variety of positions, jumps from the bonnet of car, and is lifted off her feet and carried away by Nuke. Sarandon makes a strong use of body language to define the character. Hers is a varied language encompassing the way Annie moves, stands, sits and gestures. The performance is designed to make an audience keenly aware of her physical presence and suggest a character who is confident about her sexual appeal. In this respect Annie is almost completely opposite to Sally in *Atlantic City*.

The tone is set in the opening images of the film as Annie leaves home en route for the baseball stadium. She walks with an easy, confident stride, her hips swinging freely. For the first half of the film all of her physical language has the same quality: she sits in a comfortable position with her legs apart and her body relaxed; she turns her head fluidly to talk to somebody.

Detail is added to the basic physical cues which the script gives which allows Sarandon to strengthen the character's physical presence. There's a very good example in the bar scene where Annie first meets Crash and Ebby. This is a brief scene but one full of physical detail. The two men have a fight over who should dance with Annie. They come back into the bar and sit exhausted next to each other. Annie, who has been dancing, moves behind the back of the their seat and says:

> You boys stopped fightin', pals now, that's good. I love a little macho male bonding. I think it's sweet, I do. Even if it probably is latent homosexuality being re-channelled but I'm all for re-channelling so who cares, right.

Annie's movements are choreographed in the following way. She moves behind the seat, tired from dancing, takes a long breath out, and leans forward between the two of them, her arms spread sideways with her hands being used to support herself on the back of the seat. It's a position in which she physically encompasses both men. As she makes this movement, she says 'You boys stopped fightin', pals now, that's good.' She then moves her arms in front of her and leans on her elbows to take up a more intimate position. As she does this she says, 'I love a little macho male bonding, I think it's sweet, I do.' She then reaches forward and picks up a glass of beer from the table and says 'Even if it probably is latent homosexuality being re-channelled but I'm all for re-channelling so who cares, right.' She then takes a swig of the beer, lets out a contented sigh, picks up a bag, puts her hand on her hip, and goes on to the next line, 'Shall we go to my place?' The movements not only give Annie a strong physical presence, they also underscore the lines. Overall, her moves 'intrude' her into the male situation in a way that mimics her verbal analysis of their relationship. And when she talks about macho male bonding, she gives the line an ironic inflection by picking up a glass of beer, a typical action in a bonding situation.

As well as making considerable physical demands, *Bull Durham* makes considerable vocal demands. Sarandon said that the biggest challenge of the film for her was delivering the dialogue. The script certainly provides a variety of challenges in this area. There are the predictable acting demands. A North Carolina accent is called for. A range of moods – happiness, anger, desire, frustration, bewilderment, amusement – have to be expressed through the use of naturalistic dialogue. But there are also demands of a different kind. At a number of points, Annie explains her 'New Age' ideas. These utterances tend to be longer than usual. They contain references to mysticism, poetry, science, and baseball. At other points she either reads poetry or quotes from it. She also provides voice-overs at the beginning and the end.

Unlike Meryl Streep, who aims at a detailed imitation of her characters' accents, Susan Sarandon tends to sketch and suggest them. To a British ear, the accent she uses for Annie sounds like a light Southern one (though this impression may be a function of the insensitivity of my ear to American regional accents!). Whatever accent she uses, it isn't strongly sustained throughout the film.

Her consistent vocal energy is the most impressive aspect of the way she handles dialogue in the film. Ron Shelton wrote some very good dialogue for Annie and Sarandon always tries to maximize its effect through the way she speaks the lines. She works mainly with rhythm and volume. Her natural pace of speaking is quite quick. She usually varies this rhythm not, as might be expected, by slowing down but speeding up, and then occasionally slowing right down on particular words or phrases where an emphasis is needed. In terms of volume, Sarandon makes Annie's usual voice relatively quiet. Her most effective variation is to speak even more quietly. She rarely speaks loudly so when she does, like when she berates Crash for messing up her sex life with Nuke, it's all the more effective. Overall, the changes Sarandon makes both in rhythm and volume aren't large ones. It's their consistency and subtlety which make the speech dynamic.

Sarandon always looks to give lines as much vocal energy as she can but not at the expense of the dramatic work they have to do. Indeed, one of the great virtues of her performance is her alertness to the place dialogue has in a particular dramatic situation and how its delivery can help the situation work. Whether it's the admiringly whispered line, 'Oh Crash, how you do talk' or when, in the tone and rhythm of a teacher reciting a lesson, she says to Millie 'You didn't get "lured". Women never get lured. They're too strong and powerful for that. Now say it – "I didn't get lured and I will take responsibility for my actions"', she gets full value from the lines.

The biggest dialogue challenge is the delivery of the 'New Age' speeches. The danger is that, because of their length and obscure references, audiences will find them boring and lose sympathy for the character. Sarandon's approach is to deliver these speeches in a light, playful tone. She speaks key sentences and phrases relatively slowly so the meaning of the speeches is clear. She speeds up the delivery of other sentences, risking throwing them away, but making sure the speech doesn't drag. For example, in the scene already referred to, the first part of the speech – 'You boys stopped fightin', pals now, that's good. I love a little macho male bonding, I think it's sweet, I do' – is delivered relatively slowly. The delivery of the second part – 'Even if it probably is latent homosexuality being re-channelled but I'm all for re-channelling so who cares, right' – is considerably speeded up with all the words after 'but' almost thrown away.

Susan Sarandon's performance makes a crucial contribution to the success of *Bull Durham*. Ron Shelton said that 'Annie could easily have been played as a flake'. Sarandon ensures that Annie is a vibrant character, funny, imaginative and intelligent, and more than able to hold her own with the two male characters. She surely deserved Shelton's tribute: 'Susan brought experience and commitment, substance and dignity to the part.'[6]

Thelma & Louise (1991)

Atlantic City and *Bull Durham* give an excellent idea of the range and quality of Susan Sarandon's acting. If this were a more extensive essay, her performances in a number of other films would warrant close analysis. Lack of space makes this impossible but *Thelma & Louise* and *Dead Man Walking* deserve some discussion.

Thelma & Louise is the film for which Sarandon is best known. She certainly deserved the acclaim she received. Callie Khourie's script is a very good one by any standards. It offers both Sarandon and Geena Davis excellent opportunities through the touching and subtle way it dramatizes a female friendship and the different problems two women face in trying to give their lives some meaning. Sarandon's performance enriches all the emotional subtleties of the script to produce a touching portrait of a middle-aged woman who is asking herself 'Is that all there is?'

The role is a demanding one because the acting opportunities are restricted. The film relies heavily on the exchange of words and looks in confined spaces like cars and hotel rooms. Sarandon, as might be expected, handles the dialogue very well. Interestingly, her performance highlights the importance of her eyes. Because of their prominence, they register strongly in close-up and intensify the sense of one character looking at another.

Overall, Sarandon's physical appearance is very important for the definition of the character. It establishes Louise as somebody whose appearance is being increasingly marked by the changes produced by age. While this is, in part, a matter of one kind of beauty being replaced by another, the changes underscore the importance of Louise's search for a different kind of life.

Apart from the restricted nature of the acting possibilities, there was another kind of problem that Sarandon and the other actors faced in *Thelma & Louise*. Ridley Scott is a director who isn't primarily interested in actresses and actors; he's much more concerned with visual effects, especially lighting. This concern often creates problems for the performers. Not long after the killing, there's a scene in a hotel room which is an emotional interaction between Thelma and Louise. This is an important scene because it's the first time they've recovered enough from the shock of the killing to take stock. Scott plays the scene against the background of a hotel window. This decision has a strong visual impact. By shooting the window head-on with a big light contrast – there's strong sunlight in the exterior – he emphasizes the window as an abstract shape. Added to this, in the background there's a swimming pool, a minor road, and a raised freeway with traffic moving at varying speeds in both directions. As well as being directly visible, reflections from the traffic can be seen on the open windows. The visual impact of all this inevitably distracts attention from the interplay between the two characters. In addition some of the subtleties in the performance are lost because the lighting forces Sarandon and Davis to play much of the scene in silhouette or half darkness.

This over-direction of scenes at the expense of the actors is very strong in the first half of the film. Another key scene, where the importance of Texas for Louise first becomes apparent, is played at a level crossing with a freight train rumbling past so that the actresses have to shout their lines! It's a tribute to Sarandon and Davis that they managed to produce such good performances despite this kind of direction.

Dead Man Walking (1995)

If an Oscar were a true measure of acting, *Dead Man Walking* would be the climax of Susan Sarandon's career since she won the Best Actress award for her performance in the film. Undoubtedly hers is a fine performance, but I think Sister Helen as she emerges in the film is, dramatically, a less interesting character than Louise, Annie, or Sally.

The problem is created by the way the script shapes the character of its heroine. Helen Prejean's autobiography,[7] on which the script is based, reveals a remarkable woman. As a Catholic nun, her day-to-day work was in a project to improve the social conditions of poor blacks. Out of this work she became the spiritual adviser for prisoners awaiting execution and this led her to become a leading anti-capital punishment campaigner. It also led her to work with support groups for both the relatives of the victims and the relatives of the executed men. The book provides a very lively account of all this. Particularly impressive is its analysis of the way capital punishment is deeply woven into patterns of class and race – the most likely people to be executed are poor blacks.

A two-hour screenplay has to exclude much of this material. Tim Robbins' adaptation of the book condenses Helen Prejean's relationships with prisoners into one, Matthew Poncelet, and concentrates heavily on it. There's one other substantial theme, the relationship between Helen and the parents of the young people who were murdered. The consequence is that the script puts Helen in what is almost always a reactive role. Effectively, the focus of the dramatization is her emotional reactions to other people's intense pain.

In the book, Helen Prejean describes her reactions and discusses them at some length. She also tries to understand the situations by placing them in a broader context and explaining what she did to deal with them. The screenplay only has room for the direct expression of the emotional reactions. The resources available to Sarandon for this expression are very limited. Robbins provides her with serviceable, naturalistic dialogue which she makes good use of, but the dialogue isn't rich enough to give the character's emotional reactions much depth. The setting also limits what the actors can do: much of the action is played in restricted spaces. In the case of the central relationship between Helen and Matthew, they face each other through a glass screen and most of their scenes are played in close-up. As a consequence, everything has to be played on the face – there are few opportunities for the invention of movements, gestures, or the use of props to strengthen the emotion. Sarandon uses her face very well but this is inevitably a limited form of expression. And Tim Robbins isn't a director with the ability of a Robert Bresson or a Carl Dreyer to handle such situations.

The concentration on Sarandon's face also poses other kinds of questions. With a man and a woman in close physical proximity for long periods in a situation of intense emotion, questions about the sexual nature of the relationship are bound to surface. In tune with the film's seriousness of purpose, Sarandon plays the part with very little make-up, with the marks of her age (49 when she made the film) evident, and with an unflattering hairstyle. However, the fact that she has a beautiful face can't be hidden. The basic character of the face – its overall delicacy, its well-defined bone structure, the high cheek-bones, the large eyes which catch the light – are still evident. If anything, the absence of make-up gives it a refined, austere, erotic quality.[8] As such, it encourages questions about the nature of the relationship beween Helen and Matthew and whether there's a sexual dimension to it.

The relationship between sexuality and spirituality is a large theme which has been dramatized in a variety of ways. *Dead Man Walking* has many virtues but its dramatization of this issue isn't one of them. It doesn't do much more than acknowledge the issue. The consequence of all this is that the character of Helen enjoys limited dramatic possibilities. In the key situations, she is passive, reacting to other people. Most of her reactions have to be communicated through facial expressions alone. For an actress like Sarandon, that's an important limitation, because her strength isn't in a particular form of expression but in her ability to use a variety of forms – voice, movement, gesture and the use of props.

Helen is also a character who, in modern acting terms, has no subtext. As she's written, there are no nuances for an actress to draw out. Within the limits laid down, Sarandon's performance is a fine one: sober and controlled, it gives Helen presence and dignity. But the fact that she won an Oscar for it is more an indication of the Academy's tendency to give awards for the performance of noble, suffering heroines in serious films about important issues than it is of acting quality.

Conclusion

Why in the end do I respond so strongly to Sarandon's performances? Why do I value them so highly? In the first place Sarandon's work is marked by an expressive energy. She consistently finds strong and varied physical movements, gestures, and facial expressions to define the characters she plays. She demonstrates the same kind of vocal energy: lines are shaped and pointed so that they have maximum effect.[9]

Crucially this expressiveness is combined with intelligence and this is what marks Susan Sarandon out for me. Energy on its own isn't enough; it can produce undisciplined, over-the-top performances. Nor is her technique outstanding – there are other actresses who have equal or stronger techniques. But again and again in watching her performances, I have been struck by the sense that the choices she has made are the right ones. But I want to say something more than that. To describe her choices simply as correct is too weak. They are correct because they are based both on a deep understanding of the dramatic context she is working within (she is a very good reader of scripts) and on the human context to which the dramas refer. So I want to characterize her intelligence as both mature and sophisticated.

I also value Susan Sarandon for the consistency of her performances. Whatever my final estimate of them might be, I can't think of one where she doesn't show a commitment to making the part work as well as she is able to. Her long career testifies that these qualities have been recognized by producers and directors. She more than deserves that recognition.

Notes

1 I originally read the article from which this quotation is taken on one of the Internet sites devoted to Susan Sarandon: 'The Susan Sarandon Shrine'. This site has now disappeared and I have been unable to identify where the article was originally published.

2 Ben Yagoda, 'The Prime of Susan Sarandon'. This was also taken from an Internet site which has disappeared.

3 Gavin Smith, 'Uncompromising Positions', *Film Comment*, XXIX/2, March–April, 1993.

4 Sarandon discusses *Bull Durham* in Smith, op. cit. The references to *Lorenzo's Oil* and contemporary film acting are in Roy Grundmann and Cynthia Lucia, 'Acting, Activism and Politics', *Cineaste* vol. 20, no. 1.

5 Sarandon has probably appeared nude more often than any other actresses of her age and status. This might appear odd for an actress who is keenly aware of the position of women in the movies and in society. She has expressed an uneasy attitude to such appearances: 'Who wants to do nudity any way? I've never wanted to do it. It's tough . . . You can completely upstage yourself with nudity; people don't hear a thing you're saying for at least ten seconds when they see breasts' (Grundmann and Lucia, op. cit.).

6 Yagoda, op. cit.

7 Helen Prejean, *Dead Man Walking*, London, HarperCollins, 1996.

8 It is instructive to compare Sarandon's face with Helen Prejean's. Prejean's face is rounder and fuller, the bone structure is less obvious, the cheek-bones lower and less evident. Hers is not the kind of face that is conventionally described as beautiful, but one more likely to attract adjectives like 'friendly' and 'open'.

9 That this approach inevitably has its limitations is suggested by *Twilight* (1997), Sarandon's latest film which I saw just as this essay was being finished. Sarandon's approach makes the characters she plays dynamic. Catherine Ames in *Twilight* is a passive 'iconic' figure, an ageing actress whose major successes are in the past. Sarandon can bring little to such a figure and as a result this is one of her least interesting performances.

8

HELEN SHAVER

Resistance through artistry

Susan Knobloch

In a 1996 episode of the TV horror series *Poltergeist: The Legacy* entitled 'Do Not Go Gently', Helen Shaver's character kicks a male villain to the floor. Derek DeLint dashes in to dispatch him as we cut away from the 'rescued' Shaver. But before the camera leaves her, Shaver helps DeLint shove the villain back. The actress's small shove intensifies our sense of her character's self-sufficiency. When I showed Shaver an earlier draft of this essay, which read feminist meanings from such textual details of her work as an actor – an imaged body and voice in a camera and microphone-defined frame – she said the shove symptomized broader choices on her part:

> You cited when I kicked the guy. . . . That was not in the script. . . . I said to the writer and the director, 'So I'm supposed to stand around and go, "Oh, oh"? That's crazy, I can do a great kick, I'll put a short skirt on, and it'll be very cool. Let everybody get a whack at the guy.' Because what is that saying if I'm just standing there? I don't want to say that.[1]

Shaver is one of the thus-far untheorized class of 'industry famous'[2] working actors, with many credits but little popular press.[3] Her proficiency is visible not only in textual analyses informed by a reading of acting handbooks and reviews but also in her prolific but relatively anonymous presence since the mid-1970s in both supporting and leading roles on American, Canadian, and British stage, screen, and TV.[4] Moreover, Shaver's physical choices consistently provide a feminist critic with material to mine for 'resistance through artistry'[5] to sexist stereotype. Her acting amplifies filmic themes influenced by popular 1970s American feminism: equal opportunity and responsibility at work; pleasure and choice in relationships between women and men; and mutual reliance, esteem, and love of all kinds between women. (Shaver's first leading movie role came in Hollywood's first happy lesbian romance, Donna Deitch's 1985 *Desert Hearts*.[6]) When such feminist idea(l)s are not engaged or endorsed around Shaver, her imaged body and voice introduce them, in ways that allow us to explore how screen acting can be read for its political significance precisely because it in and of itself does signify, adding and even changing meaning.

Mildly typecast by the qualities she projects, Shaver has neither pursued nor been offered characters who function purely as sex objects: 'I'm most often asked to play very intelligent, strong women.'[7] She does not 'consciously' work or live 'with any concern for feminism . . . But I live as a whole person, which to me is the definition of feminism'. Such 'wholeness' she elaborated to me in terms of a universal human capacity to understand, and in a spiritual sense to be, both male and female classic stage characters. Her gender philosophy thus evokes the same ideas which resonate with her technical approach to acting: Constantin Stanislavsky writes to his actor-readers, 'We have in us the elements of all human characteristics . . . [D]iscover . . . methods of creating an infinite number of combinations of human souls'.[8]

Embodying principles of 'good' modern acting – which cross between her discussion, Stanislavsky's writings, and the modern acting textbooks influenced by his various Anglophone heirs – Shaver creates readable feminist effects in two ways. A fact-based 1992 NBC TV film, *Fatal Memories*, falls into the fairly roomy category of post-1970s Hollywood projects featuring fictional women of institutional authority. In it, Shaver works 'with' a feminist-influenced text by playing convincingly (in accordance with historically grounded ideas about good acting) her well-integrated supporting part as a happily unmarried prosecutor helping a grown daughter convict the father who, she believes, sexually abused her and killed her childhood friend. On the other hand, *The Craft*, a 1996 feature, illustrates feminist-friendly acting 'in excess' of an ideologically retrograde text. Shaver plays, in a small and narratively unintegrated role, mother to a teenage witch whose power, derived from solidarity with three other girls, the film condemns as causing only violence, insanity, and death. But Shaver enacts a character subtly sharing and delighting in her daughter's rage against poverty and abusive men. In moments from these two very different projects, and from her current, erratic TV series *Poltergeist*, Shaver works in response to the pressures of TV and film sets to make her (and her co-stars') characters 'live', more liberated from clichés, sexist and otherwise, than they might otherwise be.

The body in the frame

Michael Chekhov, inspired by his associate Stanislavsky, sums up one of the most central ideas about actors' work found in modern acting textbooks:

> every role offers an actor the opportunity to . . . collaborate and truly co-create with the [script's] author and director . . . not [by] improvising new lines or substituting business. . . . *How* he [*sic*]

speaks the lines and *how* he fulfills the business are the open gates to a vast field of improvisations . . . in which he can express himself freely.[9]

Shaver says in the same vein,

> Most scripts ain't Shakespeare. And even Shakespeare, he'll have a bunch of actors standing around onstage while [of them, only] three people talk. So you're supporting. You don't want to take all the focus. . . . But your story has to stay alive. . . . All characters have to be alive all the time. Particularly in television, where you shoot an hour in seven days, and the concerns of the director are oftentimes getting his day done . . .

Working actors in particular are positioned by recent textbooks' credos about industrial as well as artistic practices not as manipulated objects but responsible subjects:

> The director would also like to feel that if he [*sic*] doesn't give you any direction at all, you will still deliver a good performance. . . . [T]he very nature of the beast [i.e., of tight production schedules] frequently makes it mandatory that he give all of his time to the stars.[10]

Shaver confirms:

> A really good director might come and remind you [about your character's last scene, since scenes are usually shot out of story sequence]. But most often that's the work an actor's expected to do on film. . . . Whereas on stage you rehearse for four weeks and explore. . . . I know actors who are great actors with directors, but if they've got a bad director, they can't do a thing – so I try not to do that.

When I asked Shaver to talk about her sense of creative freedom and responsibility in the frame, she began by talking about her development of her character well before she arrives on a set. Her discussion finds many parallels in Stanislavsky, not least his idea that actors should exercise their own imaginations so as to be no director's pawn.[11] With wry resolve, she said:

> You have ultimate freedom to do what you do when the camera rolls. Obviously if you don't do it where the marks are set, it won't be in focus, and you have the opportunity to do it again. If you don't do it in the context of the script, it won't end up in the movie. [But] no one can make you do anything unless you choose to be made . . .

Within the context of a project's complete narrative, Shaver concentrates upon

> the story I'm telling with my character. . . . Much of which comes from my imagination because most times a lot of the character isn't in the script. . . . [12] Whilst I'm working on a character – which happens generally from the first time I read the script till after I finish shooting the character – I, at all times, am consciously or unconsciously seeing the world through two sets of eyes, one of which is mine and one of which is the character's, or it becomes the character's. [13]

As Stanislavsky would advise, Shaver 'collects' connections between behaviours and emotions, in 'small things that happen' in her life. These connections fit themselves to her role before, and as, she performs.

Stanislavsky-influenced textbooks reiterate that an actor signifies by his chosen physical responses to patterns set around him. Acting is the 'physicalization' of thoughts and feelings provoked by (in Lee Strasberg's phrase) imaginary stimuli,[14] and 'physicalization refers to *anything, however subtle, that the film audience can detect*'[15] through sight and hearing. Shaver thinks an actor should not wear the smallest item unless its specifics suit the character: 'You don't put on a ring except that it means something to you in real life. Onscreen, everything that you do has to be that specific, and at all times in a scene.'

Screen acting also involves all the physical effort, hidden to the audience, demanded by film production. While criticism has tended to see the technical features of film as limits to an actor's expressive capacity, acting textbooks suggest that they in fact partially constitute it. Director-teacher Patrick Tucker writes, 'When you act, part of your brain deals with the acting side and another part . . . must function as your own private technical director'.[16] Shaver compares acting for the camera to her 8 year old's description of playing drums: making the steady accomplishment of many tasks at once look effortless.

With regard to on-screen physicalizations, teacher Tony Barr advises student-readers not to be afraid to move in the frame, after determining what the length of a shot and hence the limits upon their movements will be.[17] Shaver asks the cameraman, 'Where are you cutting[18] this frame? . . . You should be able to see me doing this because this is important – but if you can't [frame me so the gesture is visible] then I can do this [as she moves her hand from chest-level to face-level] to tell the same story.'

Convincing screen actors physicalize a script's meanings by moving along whichever bodily axes (the eyes, chin, neck, shoulders, waist, and so forth) a particular framing by the camera makes visible, shaping each movement or series of movements in the Aristotelian narrative pattern (start, middle, end),[19] and pacing their movements to be legible for the camera. Arguing, like Barr, that good screen actors are not static, Tucker feels that the shoulders especially should move on camera: 'If a character is facing us with her shoulders [perpendicular to the camera], and she turns away from us, we might feel rejected. . . . But if a character is *not* facing us with her shoulders, and she turns towards us, it . . . makes us feel good.'[20]

In one *Fatal Memories* scene, Shaver uses her shoulders to underline her character's public authority. 'We're going to have to include the rape testimony in the trial', Shaver's prosecutor tells her hesitating star witness (Shelley Long). Shaver stands facing the camera, framed at her chest, with her left shoulder nearer to the camera than her right (see Figure 8.1a). We cut to Long, then back to Shaver, in a subtle reframing, as we can see with reference to an easel behind her (Figure 8.1b). Shaver is now closer to the centre of the frame, but with her shoulders still angled the same way. The new framing allows her – or her thought-out dynamic calls forth the new framing in order – to spin her right shoulder forward, to be more even with her left, and 'appealingly' more available to the camera, as she continues to make her case to the camera/Long (Figure 8.1c).

In a later scene Shaver demonstrates the same principle in a tighter framing. Long's character says, about accusing her own father of the sexual abuse and murder she believes she has just remembered, 'Some days I wake up scared. And other days I wake up and feel . . . ?' Shaver's character suggests, 'Free?' Framed by the camera just below her shoulders, Shaver sits holding in her left hand a water glass which obscures her mouth and directs attention to her steady look at Long (see Figure 8.2a). In three steps, Shaver organizes her movements around the axis most available to the camera, her chin. She moves it slightly up and to her left to mark Long's switch to a questioning tone (see Figure 8.2b); she drops her hand to reveal her mouth but not her chin before speaking herself (Figure 8.2c); at last saying her line, she tilts her right ear towards her right shoulder, her lateralized movement keeping her face in focus as she lets the shifting weight of her head lift her chin just above the upper rim of the glass (Figure 8.2d). With each of Shaver's delicate movements (the shot is four seconds long), her face progressively becomes more 'free' to the static camera, a visual correlative for the characters' shared emotion. The imaged body of a woman taking the determination of meaning on to itself echoes and enhances both characters' self-determining, patriarch(y)-overcoming actions.

Always, after having developed her character from a script, Shaver uses the framelines consciously, working on the one hand with the technical limits of the production plant, and on the other with deep-seated ideas of visual pleasure:

> Some actors depend very much on the director to control the frame, and they're the accident that happens within that frame, and that also

Figures 8.1a–c Helen Shaver moves on a bodily axis made prominent in the frame. Shaver angles her shoulders (a) . . . holds the position in a new camera set-up (b) . . . and heightens her 'appeal' by moving on a bodily axis made prominent in the frame (c)
Source: Twilight Motion Picture XXII Limited Partnership/Green's Point Productions Inc.

Figures 8.2a–d Shaver physicalizes dialogue within a frame's tight limits. Shaver listens to Shelley Long off-screen (a) . . . marks Long's switch to a questioning tone (b) . . . prepares to answer (c) . . . and physicalizes the 'free' feeling her character wishes Long's character (d)
Source: Twilight Motion Picture XXII Limited Partnership/Green's Point Productions Inc.

works. . . . For me, in order to free myself to the inspired side, I have to give the conscious part of my brain something to do. The best thing is for it to be aware of the parameters of the frame that it's working within, and to amuse itself with the moving pictures it's creating. So I'm aware of the space, of what it means if I move my hand into that space beside my face, if I turn away. . . . I'm aware of that from how it affects me if I'm seeing it, but I think again that's a whole collective thing of classic images that we're all aware of. . . .

So freedom – I think it's really easy for an actor on a film set to feel restrained. The obligation is to deal with your own feelings about that, to find your center, and to be able to return to it quickly because time is money. . . . I've developed little Pavlovian tricks with myself, so that I can use the touch-up of the make-up artist to annoy me . . . to make me giggle . . . as a sensual thing . . . I can let the environment be whatever I need.

For me it doesn't work to pretend the camera isn't there . . . to pretend the lights and the technicians aren't there. . . . For me it is to accept . . . the mark, to accept the limitation that if I want the camera to rise with me, I need to do it like this [she demonstrates a 'TV rise',[21] head up, shoulders straight, movement slow and controlled]. But I can do it like this and know that on the camera it looks like I'm doing this [she leaps from her chair as anyone would]. I can do it at the speed that is necessary to capture it on the film. . . . It's not for me to have the jive of jumping out of the chair, it means nothing unless between me and the camera we can get it on this piece of silvered plastic. So I love all of that.

The voice in the frame

Tucker suggests the most important thing competent screen actors do is play to the frameline vocally as well as bodily. Convention positions the listener just outside the frame, Tucker explains, so 'the *effective* distance [actors] should project [their voices] to varies according to the *size of the shot*'.[22] That is, actors in close-up should speak as if to a close listener; in long-shot, as if to one further away. Because the boom microphone is positioned just above the top frameline as defined by the camera, the ideal listener is present(ed) to the actor by the mic just as the viewer is by the camera.[23]

For Tucker, actors seem 'too theatrical' and unnatural on-screen – i.e. they violate convention – most of all when they set a consistent volume which is too loud for the shot.[24] Tucker argues that a large part of the modern screen actor's craft involves speaking quietly and physicalizing vehemence or other extreme passion through a patterned variety of vocal as well as bodily movements. Stanislavsky and the screen again intersect: 'Stanislavsky advised that the actor . . . think about the strength of . . . his speech rather than volume, which [strength] was to be found in the intonations and range of the voice, not in loudness.'[25] Stanislavsky writes that actors should have enough control of fully formed words, spoken at an intelligible speed, that they are able to vary the 'tempo – rhythm' of their speech 'on purpose for the characterization of a part'.[26]

In *Fatal Memories*, Shaver does all that these acting theorists advise to add the same kind of punch vocally as she does visually. Framed at sternum-level, trying to convince Long's character to testify, Shaver begins ('Eileen, I am here to support you . . . ') by talking quickly rather than shouting to convey her character's passion. She raises her volume just a little; and then slows down and speaks with a comparatively much softer and higher voice. She reaches her highest, softest notes at her speech's end, when she pleads about her witness's reluctant testimony, 'Look, just, just sit down and try it with me – once. Okay?'[27] Shaver here invokes 'motherspeak', the high, soft, sing-song intonation adults use with infants. As with her body above, her varied, ordered use of her voice deploys screen conventions in order to play persuasively her character's professional persuasiveness. Yet when Shaver's character ends up reaching Long's by speaking in a high, soft voice – a conventionally feminine voice – femininity appears where, until recent decades, it was not conventional: in a commanding position, connecting with another woman in order to defeat anti-female violence.

In *Poltergeist*/'Transference' (1997), the way Shaver speaks two words changes their meaning, refusing to play up (to) a man's protection. The series positions Derek DeLint's character Derek as a godlike, ghosthunting father-figure who assumes command over Shaver's psychiatrist character Rachel. While Rachel seems structurally primed to serve as flattered helpmeet, Shaver's acting often (and the very uneven writing sometimes) shows no joy at his self-satisfied paternalism. Investigating a lunatic out to get Rachel, Derek stops to reminisce with a male cop whom Derek's preternatural powers saved from an 'Aztec shapeshifter' long ago. Shaver in close-up frowns and interjects, 'all right, okay' in a flat, hurried voice. Shaver told me:

> [The line] that was in the script, I don't know if it was intended the way I played it. I mean, it was for me to affirm what Derek was saying. I threw the spin on it of, 'It's enough now, let's go. We've got a serial killer after me. Let's get real.'

The actor between frames: acting and editing

Stanislavsky recommends that actors ground both their (inner) evocations and (outer) representations of emotions in 'physical action' – 'some ordinary, small, natural movement'[28] – and that actors work in 'communion' with each other. Touching upon the latter concept, Shaver says: 'If you're just aware of yourself in acting, it's not working. Because, like in dancing or like in making love, your intention is the effect you're having on the other person.' Stanislavsky finds that actors may commune with – that is, physically express attention towards – themselves, present persons or objects, or imaginary ones.[29] This last power of (the physical representation of) focus serves screen actors well, since they speak, gesture, and look 'to' the framelines as if the framelines were fellow Stanislavskian actors in need of careful attention and negotiated contact. More than film theory has realized, acting helps to direct the audience's attention, and to interconnect shots smoothly.

In the courtroom in *Fatal Memories*, Shaver uses her eyes to highlight people and spaces either not clearly visible, or not present, in the frame. One shot features Shaver in the left foreground framed at her chest, with the defendant father in blurry focus in the right background. Before questioning her witness (Shelley Long) about what she 'saw', Shaver turns her head and shoulders to her left and towards the rear of the frame, where he murkily is (see Figures 8.3a and 8.3b). Shaver's acting thus parallels Long's character with her own, Shaver looking at the man Long will say she saw at the crime scene. Later, walking framed at her waist as the camera pans with her, Shaver casts her eyes in what we remember to be the father's direction, well before the father becomes visible in her fuzzy background when she and the camera stop moving.

Having won a subsequent point at the bench against a male defence attorney, Shaver walks towards the camera in long-shot, tossing her eyes and a confidence-inspiring grin to her left. The spatial configuration of the scene suggests that the jury is her object, but we never cut to the jury. In this feminist-influenced film,[30] Shaver's character emerges victorious, her social firepower represented not by her alignment with the camera's eye (as feminist film theory finds that classical Hollywood represents male authority) but by her own telling movements before it.

A more usual on-screen 'communion' occurs between separately framed actors each playing a character whom both the other and the camera see, in a shot/reverse-shot pattern. It might seem obvious that everything actors can do to connect with other actors within the same frame, they can do to connect characters between shots. But coordination and effort, and a set of generative conventions, underlie the obvious impression. In *Fatal Memories*, Dean Stockwell, as a detective assigned to her character's prosecutorial office, collaborates with Shaver to feed the editing and convey mutual respect. When Long's character asks to visit the father whom she's just put in prison, Stockwell, in a two-shot with Long, bites his lip before we cut to a medium-shot of Shaver. Shaver begins a quick series of expressions by biting her own lip, Shaver's character picking up on the expression Stockwell's has 'just' shown her, and Shaver herself using her imagination and probably her memory because her shot may have been filmed hours or days apart from his. Here the direct exchange of signs of attention between stage actors becomes an implication in the frame(s).

Figures 8.3a–b Shaver's movements stress a background character otherwise unemphasized in a shot. Shaver turns to mark the blurry presence of the defendant father (Duncan Fraser) (a) . . . and then looks forward again while he remains obscure behind her (b)

Source: Twilight Motion Picture XXII Limited Partnership/Green's Point Productions Inc.

Shaver experienced positive reverberations from her carefully conceived physicalizations in communion with another actress (Sarah Strange), and with herself across frames, both in the TV text and behind the scenes of *Poltergeist/* 'Fear'(1997):

> One of the producers said, 'This cut really works.' I said I designed it that way. He said, 'What do you mean?' The end of this one scene, I'm talking to this girl [in a mental ward, who is having aural hallucinations, and holding them off by pinning her ear shut with a safety pin, all bloody]. We cut to my reaction. I feel my ear, and I take this [right] hand [of mine] down and leave this [left] hand up [see Figure 8.4a].
>
> Next scene is a walk and talk outside [two characters walking in long-shot] . . . So I made sure as my head comes up the hill and into view, I've put my hair back and I'm playing with my [left] ear [see Figure 8.4b]. So the cut cuts right from my hand on my ear, to my hand on my ear, like it's a continued gesture. But you have to think about that stuff.

Shaver's design to help the editing creates an identification between her character, a doctor undercover as a mental patient, and the young woman patient who has killed her abusive male lover and is now bedevilled by voices (personified by a male demon, whom Shaver's Rachel eventually obliterates) telling her to kill herself. Shaver goes on to finger her ear throughout the episode when a male authority figure (Derek, the demon) 'bugs' Rachel (who herself hallucinates insects when talking to these men). Shaver thus typically extends her character's physicalized affinity with another woman across frames, both immediately and across lapses of fictional time.

Reading acting ideologically: 'communion' in the frame

When Shaver similarly attends to other actors inside the same framelines, her embodiment of this acting norm maintains her character but also, often, resists otherwise unopposed sexist remarks or behaviour, or adds female–female bonding where it need not be. Across a wide variety of projects, Shaver denies physical contact or verbal encouragement to men who approach her character in domineering terms, and she acknowledges other females through touches, glances and words. A Stanislavskian emphasis upon physicalized interconnections between the actor and the world also seems to inform Shaver's characters' routine readiness for physical combat with men, women, or natural forces. Shaver's work in *The Craft* is organized around her vocal and bodily 'communion' in the frame with other actors and with objects, as her character Grace finds happiness in literally focusing upon the feminine.

117

Figures 8.4a–b Shaver reprises a gesture in consecutive shots of different lengths, feeding the editing. Shaver helps the editing from ear (a) . . . to ear (walking with Rosemary Dunsmore) (b)

Source: MGM Worldwide Television Productions Inc..

Grace's witch-daughter Nancy (Fairuza Balk) wills their kitchen to catch fire and spur a fatal heart attack – and a hefty life insurance settlement – for Grace's live-in lover Trey (Nathaniel Marston), after he ogles Nancy and belittles and shoves Grace. Nancy and her friend Sarah (Robin Tunney) explicitly debate whether the members of their coven, female (and, in one case, black) victims of male (and racist) violence, have the right to rebut their tormentors violently. Thinking so, Nancy winds up ranting alone in a padded cell. Ultimately deciding not, Sarah, who excuses a would-be rapist but attacks her former coven mates, winds up sane and still witchily potent. The film's punishing of Nancy and her loyal friends for punishing their tormentors equates them with their tormentors, thereby effectively collapsing the sexist and his abused target, the racist and hers. Such a collapse reactionarily denies the existence of differences in power among social groups, particularly females and males.

Shaver's contributions to this film, in contrast, suggest that male violence impedes happiness, which females together may find. Her acting grants Grace a full humanness: though she mostly rages at Trey's oafish indifference (groaning derisively when he implies his sexual expertise redeems his indolence), Grace briefly laughs with him. And her grief at his death is made convincing in the role's one break from black comedy, when Shaver escalates her volume on a single repeated line ('What's happening to him?'), from silent mouthing to a wail. However, Shaver, with Fairuza Balk, celebrates Grace's otherwise unstated kinship with her daughter over and against her loss of Trey: Balk holds a burning cigarette in her right hand while Shaver holds one in her left, as they sit side by side, first learning of their insurance windfall (see Figure 8.5). The cigarettes synecdochically recall the fire that removed the man, even as they make mirror images of the two women, suggesting that Grace at some level shares in Nancy's fiery, anti-patriarchal rebellion.[31] In the same scene, Shaver works with the framing to imply one action and then reveal another, using this longstanding film actor's joke-form to emphasize Grace's pleasure at the substitution of money for man. When she drops her hand from her mouth after the insurance agent mentions a dollar figure, we see that Grace is laughing, not crying.

Shaver's longest *Craft* scene is shot in one long take, which she organizes (the acting effectively editing within the frame) around female or heavily feminized foci: the four girl-witches, and a jukebox. Set free from male mistreatment and poverty, Grace welcomes Nancy's friends to her new, big, bright apartment. Exemplifying Shaver's typical affirmations of other women, Grace touches Sarah and Bonnie (Neve Campbell), murmuring, 'You look so pretty', and pulls Nancy into a full-bodied hug, patting her on the rear as she releases her.[32] Grace then sprawls on the only piece of furniture in the room, a couch whose 'cash' purchase (with her dead man's blood money) she proudly recounts.

Figure 8.5 Shaver and Fairuza Balk's props play up their characters' incendiary
mother–daughter bond
Source: Columbia Pictures

Shaver's ardent attention to Grace's jukebox – expressed through voice, eyes, hands, another object, and another actor's body – definitively frames Grace's new place as her version of an all-girls' paradise (see Figure 8.6). Grace runs from her couch to the jukebox, gasping, 'Oh, oh, oh!' and keening merrily. She tells Bonnie and Rochelle (Rachel True) that the jukebox fulfils a girlhood dream by playing only 'Con-nie Fran-cis rec-ords' (like the one on the soundtrack). Shaver matches the rhythm of her gleefully separated and held syllables with one hand's three-step caress of the jukebox, a gesture she ends by grabbing her second cigarette of the scene from a pack on the machine. The cigarette prop again subtly associates the mother's delight, and now her liberation through and into a feminized object and its music, with the daughter's witchery. Shaver hugs Rachel True, literally leaning on her to encourage her character Rochelle to appreciate Connie Francis as much as Grace does. Unfortunately, Rochelle has never heard of Francis, and the girls leave Grace, across the intergenerational divide.

None the less, her overflowing joy in the girls and the girl singer's jukebox unsettles the canards about the evil power of female groups that the story otherwise upholds, especially because Grace is never punished for profiting from the death of an abusive male 'beloved'. She just disappears from the film after the jukebox scene, something which I find unsatisfying in light of Shaver and Balk's indication of complicated but fierce ties between Grace and Nancy. It seems strange that Nancy winds up in a mental institution alone, with no sign of her mother. However, marginalized by the main storyline as her

Figure 8.6 Shaver celebrates an all girls paradise with Neve Campbell, Rachel True, and a Connie Francis-only jukebox
Source: Columbia Pictures

character's story is, Shaver's use of proper acting tools creates a space for a literal woman-centredness which feels giddy and electric, due perhaps to the director empowering the actors. The first *Craft* script Shaver read gave the character she was being offered some three lines, in three scenes, but meeting with director Andrew Fleming, she said:

> 'You have to let me do her, really do her . . . I want a wig that looks like I went to the Cut and Curl three months ago and told them to do me a platinum Meg Ryan.' So he let me go with that, and I worked with a designer and found tacky enough clothes . . . and all of that stuff [beyond the very sparse original dialogue], that's all improvisation.

Grace could easily have been a mere caricature of a shrew. But in Shaver's hands she appears, amidst everything, unexpectedly brave: dazed after Trey attacks her and Nancy ignites their home, Grace still runs, alone, to beat down the flames with a dish towel.

Conclusion

I have used the work of Helen Shaver, an actress whose oeuvre meshes liberal themes with well-received if not universally famous performances, to model a critical method for

121

1   outlining significant physical and philosophical elements comprising screen actors' specific discourse;

2   reading actors' physical choices in light of the present era's standards of competence as marked out in actor training textbooks and reviews; and

3   interpreting the details of actors' physical choices in terms of their feminist potential.

Modern, post-Stanislavskian training manuals ask screen actors to organize a wide variety of bodily postures and vocal textures into the classical narrative pattern with a clear beginning, middle, and end, always cognizant of how much of the body (and voice) the framing makes available for the audience to perceive. In thus constantly if microcosmically telling stories, contemporary screen actors have quite broad opportunities to add, subtract, or alter meanings suggested by a film's other constitutive forms. Actors' uses of their eyes, voices, and bodies may inscribe agency and desire, without, or in excess of, the editing formations that theory has generally held to be the primary way of physically inscribing them.

Shaver's work on TV and film, in support and in the lead, provides strong evidence that female characters' solidarity and self-determination can be not only illustrated but also embellished through the technical details which comprise an actorly prowess, even without a superstar persona. Such elaboration may occur, in fact, especially without one, given that Hollywood practices today leave working actors to shape their characters by themselves at least as much as and probably more than stars. Within the Hollywood industry, it may be that Shaver is free to play (up) feminist and other liberal themes because she is not a star, outside of relatively small subcultures, like fans of lesbian films or sci-fi TV. It may also be the case that she is not a star in part because her qualities and abilities seem so fit(ted) for such themes. Some publicity which she received at the time of *United States* – Larry Gelbart's formally daring 1980 sitcom which ran for about a month and was Shaver's first lead role in the USA – explicitly suggests a threat to mass success in the conjunction between gender representation and Shaver's ability to act 'well':

> [A] television series must depend . . . on its stars. Here is where *United States* may run into some problems. . . . [T]hese two disparate types produc[e] a marriage of unequals . . . [Shaver] can use the simplest dialogue or business to show that she is in the grip of conflicting but deeply felt emotions, and even of conflicting ideas. [Playing her husband, Beau] Bridges . . . never seems to have more than a single feeling. . . . It seems significant – *some would even say ominous* – that when [the wife] finally welcomes her husband into bed . . . it is after he has yielded to her in an argument . . . and is seen to be wearing one of her slips.[33] [my italics]

Read as ominous or invigorating, a liberal humanism thrives in Shaver's playing. She believes that actors and storytellers are 'a very important thread in the social fabric', and that her job is

> to disarm the audience with laughter or mystery . . . or romance . . . so that part of their minds is occupied and the judgment is taken away, and at that moment they can then see themselves and their humanness – our humanness. And it's in that identification that there comes the possibility of growth, and I think that's why there are actors.

Although film scholarship has to this point focused almost completely upon star images, Shaver's case shows that to recapitulate the film industry's and the culture's relative marginalization of certain performers, and of the particulars of screen performance itself, is to miss many likely pockets of resistance in the mainstream to sexism and other 'sets of ideas and representations'[34] that attempt to crush rather than foster human beings.

Notes

1   Helen Shaver spoke with me on 20 May 1997 in Los Angeles. All her subsequent comments date from that interview except where noted.
2   Hollywood calls actors whom professionals but not the general public know 'industry famous'. Shaver's industry fame surfaces on-screen when other characters praise her characters' skills but express regret that they/she never receive due recognition.
3   Shaver has more than sixty screen credits, and she has won several awards, including a 1978 Genie (Canadian Oscar). But I have found less than ten North American magazine articles about her, excluding reviews, which tend to applaud her briefly, mourning her under-utilization. On 9 March 1982, John J. O'Connor wrote in the *New York Times*, 'The actors drag themselves through . . . this dramatic mud with more dignity than one has any reason to expect. One of these years, Miss [*sic*] Shaver . . . will get the television vehicle she deserves' ('TV: "Between Two Brothers", thief in candidate's family'). On 6 April 1992, John Simon expressed similar sentiments in *New York*: 'Knowing this Canadian actress only from her solid work in some flimsy movies, I was delighted by the shadings, the innuendoes, the complexity she could manage in person [in the Neil Simon play *Jake's Women*].' ('Confessions or Confections?', pp. 106–7).
4   Her first high school play won Shaver a summer scholarship to study at the Banff Academy of Fine Arts. Returning to her native Ontario, she got roles in nearby amateur and then professional theatre, but her only further formal training consisted of a few classes at the University of Victoria, and, later, one professional acting class with an alumnus of the Neighborhood Playhouse. In Canada in the early 1970s she gained experience in children's theatre, an improv company, and 'films, plays, radio plays, commercials, voiceovers'. She has read some

Stanislavsky and other acting texts, but 'my education has really been learning on the job . . . asking questions and watching movies'.

5 I build from R. Dyer, 'Resistance through Charisma: Rita Hayworth and *Gilda*,' in E.A. Kaplan (ed.), *Women in Film Noir*, London, British Film Institute, 1978, revised edition, 1980, pp. 91–99.

6 The late casting director Tim Flack considered Shaver his 'first choice' for Deitch's film (K. Garfield, *'Desert Hearts:* a Lesbian Love Story Lights up the Silver Screen,' *The Advocate*, 18 February 1986, pp. 43–47, p. 44). Performed for scale wages six years into her Hollywood career, it was 'the first time I ever carried a film', Shaver told Lawrence Van Gelder ('At the Movies', *New York Times*, 4 April 1986). She remains proud of a project so 'significant to such a significant group of people', lesbians and all supporters of implicit universal human worth.

7 Shaver quoted in Van Gelder, 'Movies'.

8 C. Stanislavsky, *An Actor Prepares*, trans. E.R. Hapgood, New York, Theatre Arts Inc., 1939, p. 168.

9 M. Chekhov, *To The Actor*, New York, Harper & Row, 1953, p. 36.

10 T. Barr, *Acting for the Camera*, New York, HarperPerennial, revised edition, 1997, pp. 157–58 (originally published, Boston, Allyn & Bacon, Inc., 1982).

11 Stanislavsky, *An Actor Prepares*, p. 54.

12 Stanislavsky (*An Actor Prepares*, p. 60) tells actors, '[W]hen the author, [and] the director . . . leave out things we need to know . . . [we discover] an inner chain of circumstances which we ourselves have imagined'.

13 'To reproduce feelings . . . identify them out of your own experience' (Stanislavsky, *An Actor Prepares*, p. 23).

14 S.L. Hull, *Strasberg Method: A Practical Guide For Actors, Teachers and Directors*, Woodbridge, Connecticut, Ox Bow Publishing, Inc., 1985, p. 19. Stanislavsky (*An Actor Prepares*, p. 142) teaches, 'Come to the tragic [emotional] part of your role . . . by carrying out correctly your external sequence of physical actions.'

15 Barr, *Acting for the Camera*, p. 18.

16 P. Tucker, *Secrets of Screen Acting*, New York, Routledge, 1994, p. 158.

17 Barr, *Acting for the Camera*, p. 177.

18 Shaver uses the slang 'cut' to refer not to the editing between shots but the definition of the framelines, which also 'cut' the actor's body at certain points.

19 Chekhov (*To The Actor*, p. 9) advises actors, 'Create strong and definite *forms* . . . [T]hink of the beginning and the end of each movement you make.'

20 Tucker, *Secrets of Screen Acting*, p. 37.

21 The term appears in Tucker (*Secrets of Screen Acting*, p. 46), who reminds his readers that even moving up and down is a technical feat on-screen.

22 Ibid., p. 67.

23 Ibid., p. 68.

24 Ibid., p. 67–73.

25 J. Martin, *Voice in Modern Theatre*, New York, Routledge, 1991, p. 50.

26 C. Stanislavsky, *An Actor's Handbook*, trans. and ed. E.R. Hapgood, London, Methuen Drama, 1990, p. 129.

27 Twice in this speech Shaver repeats a word as if her character's tongue outpaces her mind, a 'realistic' effect which Stanislavsky-influenced textbooks encourage.

28 Stanislavsky, *An Actor Prepares*, p. 8.

29 Ibid., p. 196.

30 In reality, the 1990 conviction upon which the film was based was overturned in 1996. Mary Curtius, 'Man won't be retried in repressed memory case,' *Los Angeles Times*, 3 July 1996.

31 Flawed and darkly comic, Grace never completely harmonizes psychologically with others, because Shaver makes Grace's attention slightly disregarding, lagging, and impeded, connoting drunken self-absorption in her own unregulated emotions. Cigarettes, for example, are not a healthy, wholly effective bond between mother and daughter. Shaver physicalizes this idea when Grace, hugging her, cannot fully touch Nancy because of the cigarette in Grace's hand.

32 Balk grabs her butt, stalks away, and wordlessly fires an imaginary gun at Shaver. Thus Shaver helps Balk develop her leading character, as, again, they accentuate Grace and Nancy's attachment, however conflicted.

33 A. Lurie, 'Are we ready for marriage-1980s style . . . with no sugar added?', *TV Guide*, 26 April 1980, pp. 4–8, 6–8. An audition tape for *United States* (UCLA Archive) pairs Bridges with Shelley Long, opposite whose sunshine he seems the rougher, more complicated one. Gelbart and company probably cast Shaver partly because she and Bridges together make the wife seem more difficult than her husband.

34 Richard Dyer describes ideology as the 'set of ideas and representations' through which a social group understands its material circumstances in *Stars*, London, British Film Institute, 1979, p. 2.

9

ACTORS AND THE SOUND GANG

Gianluca Sergi

This essay will focus on one of those key acting tools that have constantly been overlooked: the voice. My aim is not to assess the ideological implications of the male and female voice, nor to form a canon of good actors' voices for future reference. I am more interested in whether we can identify the many ways in which the voice is employed as an acting tool, recorded by film crews, and integrated into the soundtrack in contemporary film acting.

This means looking not only at acting *as* a performance, but mainly at acting *in* a performance. This involves considering the actor's use of his/her voice, the understanding and interpretation of it that other actors and crew need to have, the many ways in which that voice is mediated and put into the larger framework that is the film's soundtrack, and the technical boundaries that may expand or limit its effectiveness (and their time/financial implications).

In movies actors do not just speak, they are recorded. This suggests that we should devote some interest and attention to two consequences: there are people who record them and there is the technology to do so. Similarly, we don't just hear movie actors speak, we hear a reproduction of their voices in a complex sound construct called a soundtrack. This suggests that there are further consequences to look into: there are people (not actors) who construct that soundtrack, and there is a place where we are offered that reproduction of the actor's voice.

These considerations, simple as they may sound, suggest the kind of parameters we should seek and the areas where we may find them. For argument's sake, we can divide these into two main segments, whilst always keeping their relationship well in sight. The first segment is concerned with those factors that are solely under the actors' control. The second segment deals with those factors that are outside the actors' direct control but still within the film-makers'.

Factors that are solely under the actors' control: awareness of own voice and awareness of medium

Commenting upon his film *Se7en*, director David Fincher describes Morgan Freeman's approach to his character, detective William Somerset, as follows: 'Here is Morgan who was like "I will take these lines and make them work for me . . . Tell me where to go, what to do and I will do my thing within those confines".'[1] This quote emphasizes two key aspects. First, there is the actor's desire to 'interpret' those lines according to his/her own characteristics. The aim of this would seem to be an attempt to understand how he/she is going to deal with those words on the scripted page whilst working within the framework of his/her own skills and limitations. Those words need to be spoken, how am I going to do this? Second, Fincher points at Freeman's understanding that, as an actor, he is working within a context. His performance is not a stand-alone, but is subjected to the specific conditions of the medium in which he is working.

In other words, the first two parameters that we can isolate answer the following questions: Are actors aware of their own skills and limitations? Do they take these into account when approaching a new character? Do they understand the context in which their performance operates?

As Fincher suggests, an actor works within specific confines, and good actors are always aware of that. Awareness of this understanding can be found in various aspects of an actor's vocal performance. A script, be it good or bad, presents the actor with some clear constraints. The most obvious one concerns the quality that the character's voice is going to have. Let us work on three of Freeman's most famous roles: detective Somerset in the aforementioned *Se7en*, 'Hawke' in *Driving Miss Daisy*, and 'Red' in *The Shawshank Redemption*. These three characters are very different and the script presents Freeman/the actor with a series of clear limitations as to how to interpret them.

The character of Hawke in *Driving Miss Daisy* is a fairly poor and ignorant man, though honest and hard-working. His ignorance does not come from being stupid, but from having been repressed by a racist system into a constant position of subordination. Once again, his financial situation forces him to seek employment as a subordinate, this time as the driver of an elderly and wealthy Jewish woman, the Miss Daisy of the title (played by Jessica Tandy). The script defines this master–driver relationship straight from the start: he will always be addressed just as Hawke (i.e. by first name); Tandy's character will always be addressed as 'Miss' Daisy.

Here Freeman/the actor is given a rather difficult brief. The script suggests a lot and leaves little room for manoeuvre. The man will speak with a strong Southern accent (indeed, the script reminds us that Hawke has never been out of Georgia before). Moreover, his accent will also reflect his limited social and cultural background. The interesting aspect of the performance would thus appear to be, if we were to follow conventional wisdom, how faithfully

Freeman/the actor can reproduce those characteristics in his voice. In short, if he 'sounds' like his character, it is a good performance. I would like to suggest that we need to go further and deeper than that if we are seriously to assess Freeman's performance. The important questions here do not merely pertain to whether the actor's accent is good. For Southern-born and bred Freeman, putting on a Georgian accent is probably not strenuously hard (I am not discounting the skills that go into understanding what that accent sounds like and then reproducing it faithfully).[2] The key to his performance is how he is going to use that accent.

In the case of Hawke, Freeman chooses to make it sound not just like a poor, ignorant black man from Georgia: Hawke sounds like a child. His voice often breaks into a kind of nervous laughter which highlights his willingness not to upset the master. Most importantly, it lacks the kind of lower tone and pitch typical of the grown man he is: indeed, his voice often shrieks. Metre and pitch are therefore the instruments that Freeman uses to underline the fact that his character's subordination is not merely one of financial means, but one of a cultural and racist nature. He is forced to behave in a childlike manner: he must be the good slave.

That this is Freeman's skilful choice and not accidental can be clearly seen/heard when we are finally given the 'positive' version of that 'negative' accent in the film. Whilst driving Miss Daisy to one of her relatives' birthday party, Hawke feels the urge of nature and asks permission to stop the car and relieve himself. When Miss Daisy denies that permission, his voice suddenly assumes those 'grown-up' qualities I have highlighted above as he affirms for the first time in his relationship with Miss Daisy his right to be treated as a grown man.

The script informs the choices – Freeman actually says 'I ain't a child, Miss Daisy' – but it is the actor who needs the skills to be able to make those words work for him, find ways to interpret the character behind the lines, and translate that into something more than just an accent or a 'talk'. Although Freeman already shows his skills in the way he masters the accent as required by the script, it is that change of gear, that ability to use accent as an acting tool, which ultimately provides us with some clues about the quality of Freeman's performance.

Compare now the choices of that performance with the ones involved in Freeman's portrayal of detective William Somerset in Se7en. Freeman understands his character, in his own words, as follows: 'A police detective whose gift is cerebral, who is not necessarily action-oriented'.[3] The situation here is as far as it could be from Hawke and the *Driving Miss Daisy* script. Freeman has very little constraints. Race is not an issue in the film, nor is location (indeed, the film-makers went to great lengths to camouflage the location and make it look and sound like any other American city to avoid identification). Somerset is an intelligent and educated man, who is close to retirement, tired of what he has seen over the years on the job. Most importantly, he hates the urban environment in which he lives (the film originally opened with a scene where Somerset buys a house in the countryside). In other words, Freeman is given a huge palette with which to work: accent, metre, pitch, tone, and speed of delivery are all open for interpretation. However, showing once again great understanding of the brief to which he is working, his chosen approach is one privileging reduction rather than amplification.

One of the key elements in the film is Somerset's desire to leave the job and the city behind him. This incompatibility is as much aural as it is visual. In one of the early scenes, we are shown Somerset in his home at night. The noise of people screaming and ambulance sirens fill the air with jarring sounds. More importantly, this sound has no specific metre or rhythm to it; it is a cacophony of sounds. In his desperate attempt to impose some order on that chaos, Somerset starts off the metronome he keeps on the bedside table: it is a slow tempo, on which he tries to concentrate hard to find the necessary peace to fall asleep. This very well-executed scene – there is no dialogue here – is a blueprint for Somerset, and it is what Freeman latches on to for his interpretation of the character.

He interprets Somerset as a guy for whom method and economy of action and words are a philosophy of life. Unlike Hawke in *Driving Miss Daisy*, he chooses to keep his voice and tempo down to a constant beat. This matches perfectly Somerset's attempt to achieve a rhythm more congenial to him and his life than the one that the city threatens to impose. Speaking in a constant tone, limiting the amount of words spoken, and pausing before answering a question, become Freeman's way to interpret Somerset. As for the first characteristic, the scene where Somerset tells his boss that they are facing a serial killer is exemplary: Freeman never loses his beat or raises his pitch or level. He makes a point of keeping his voice constant, playing off Brad Pitt's interpretation of his own character, detective Mills.

Indeed, this scene illustrates well another key skill in a good actor's repertoire: the ability to play off other actors. Pitt's character offers the perfect foil to Freeman's character: his meter is impatient, often changing in rhythm, unable to impose his authority without considerably raising his voice level. Freeman plays off this: where Mills raises his voice, he lowers his; where Mills answers questions without thinking, he pauses before answering; and so on. This shows an understanding on Freeman's part of the way(s) in which his acting partner employs his voice and of its main characteristics, so as to be able to interact with it creatively and efficiently.

This is one of the most important vocal acting skills that a good actor must possess. For instance, the script may call for a situation where a character must impose his/her voice (i.e. authority) over that of another character. How can this be achieved? Is sound level enough (i.e. is it enough to speak louder)? One may suggest that raising the voice level, whilst signalling the character's desire to impose his/her authority, might in fact suggest the exact opposite: screaming is a rather extreme reaction and could be seen as a rather desperate attempt to achieve control, rather than expressing actual authority. On the other hand, a resourceful actor might choose his/her strategy in relation to his/her counterpart's voice. He/she might choose to suggest: (a) difference, by adopting a different pitch, (b) independence, through adopting a different metre, syncopating[4] the lines where he extends his and vice-versa (i.e. rejecting his attempt to impose a certain rhythm to the exchange), (c) authority, by setting the tempo of the exchange.

In an earlier scene of *Se7en*, Freeman gives a great and subtle example of this skill. When Mills and Somerset first meet, the former seems to reject outright Somerset's attempt to get to know each other. The script calls for Mills to exhibit a few of his characteristics from the beginning of the movie: he is eager to prove himself and is very arrogant and selfish. Freeman plays his lines accordingly.

At first, he keeps his questions and answers at a distance from Pitt's. He seems to cut some slack for Mills, to give him the benefit of the doubt. But when he realizes that this attempt to establish a channel of communication has failed, he is ready to establish his authority as the older and more experienced detective who is also in charge of the investigation. Which brings us to the question above: how to establish such an authority? In line with his character, Freeman chooses to shorten dramatically the time of response to Pitt's delivery. He increases the tempo of the exchange by eliminating all pauses: it becomes a short, quick-firing exchange of words, rather than a slower, more 'friendly' discussion. Actors themselves refer to this kind of interaction via a musical analogy, as in this comment from Dustin Hoffman: 'There is a synergy that takes place, and for a moment, you feel like you're in a jazz group.'[5]

The skill above is also useful for actors to create time for their performance by choosing the appropriate metre for their characters. When confronted by a few lines of a script, the choice is not just what accent to employ, what pitch and level, how to play off other characters, or how fast the delivery should be. Several questions need to be asked of those lines: Are you going to deliver them as one long sentence? Are you going to pause? If so, where? Do you consider this as incidental dialogue or as core dialogue? If the latter is true, where are you going to put the emphasis? Which words are you going to put the stress on? The ability to answer these questions shows an awareness of some key issues: how to identify key lines; how to identify the key words within those lines; how to impose a certain metre and tempo to them.

The Shawshank Redemption is an interesting film in this respect. For all the lines the actors have to play with, this is still not a terribly actor-friendly script. Most noticeable is the scarcity of props with which the actors can interact (which is perhaps to be expected, given that the film is set in a maximum security prison). Interaction with props happens at an aural level as much as at a visual one. Indeed, the ability to interact creatively with props and surrounding soundscape can be identified as a further important skill which a good actor needs to master. The skill we are exploring now could be defined as the actor's awareness of soundscape, or how to interact with surrounding sound elements. It concerns mainly two aspects.

First, it concerns the issue of how an actor interacts with the sounds surrounding him/her. For instance, in *Bull Durham*, there is a scene in which Susan Sarandon and Kevin Costner discuss the possibility of having a relationship during the current baseball season. The discussion takes place in a batting cage (an area where a metallic net is employed to protect bystanders during batting practice). In turn, both Costner and Sarandon swing a baseball bat. What is of interest to us here is the way in which the two actors actually interact with their surrounding sound (in a manner similar to the way in which they may use the baseball bat as a prop). Where Costner seems unwilling to take any risks (he makes sure that his lines are never disturbed by other sounds, especially that of his bat hitting the baseball), Sarandon uses the latter sound creatively to give an edge to her lines (listen to the way in which she stresses certain words as she swings the bat). This way, she achieves a way of punctuating her lines by employing the sound of a bat hitting a baseball (a useful sound as it 'peaks' quickly and it is thus apt to function as punctuation, more than, to remain within the baseball aural palette, the much more constant sound of a runner sliding on to base).

Second, there is, of course, also an objective factor: the screenplay itself. Randy Thom has already noted how screenplays rarely give actors the possibility to 'listen' to their surrounding sound environment.[6] This can limit both the actor's performance (e.g. there is a difference between uttering the words 'I love you' in a crowded street of LA and professing the same feelings in a quiet spot somewhere in the Mojave desert or in Yellowstone Park), and the work of sound editors/designers (i.e. there is little you can do with sound if there is constant wall-to-wall dialogue, over-the-top music, or incessant explosions all around it).

An actor who does not understand these dynamics involving the combination of his/her own voice, that of other actors, and the sound surrounding him/her will not be able to perform well. Indeed, his/her performance might hinder the overall construction of the soundtrack just as much as a speech-redundant script that does not allow time for the characters to listen to their environment.

Issues outside direct actors' control: the kindness of strangers

The film voice, unlike that of the theatre, is not a given, fixed value, but a variable. The film actor does not simply speak: he/she is recorded. In other words, like any other aspect of filmic performance, the voice is mediated. Furthermore, this mediation is itself negotiated through a series of technical choices: how many microphones to use, which type, and so on. Some of these choices have little to do with 'artistic' integrity and more to do with practical necessities.

From a recording point of view, to quote but one important example, matching sound perspective is more important than allowing actors absolute freedom of movement. This is a matter of time and money: to go for total acting freedom might later mean huge headaches in post-production. Mismatching perspectives might be audible in the soundtrack when cutting between shots, leaving the film-makers little choice as to what to do: either to leave it as it is (but this would mean attracting audience attention to the soundtrack for all the wrong reasons), or to reconstruct the whole scene through extensive ADR and adding background sound (assuming that a recording of location background sound for that particular scene was indeed carried out and is usable).[7] This would mean a considerable waste of time and money as the actors would have to be called in for an ADR session and the whole scene would have to be mixed again. With some dubbing stages costing upward of $1,000 per hour, usability inevitably takes precedence over complete artistic freedom.

Most good actors understand this need for continuity and will aid it by avoiding huge changes in the way they deliver the same lines over a number of takes within the same scene. However, others show less awareness of this complex jigsaw puzzle, which, of course, involves both sound and visual elements of a performance, as John Lithgow reminds us: 'He [the editor] said, "You have no idea how I've had to save actors' performances who don't pay any attention to continuity".'[8]

There is also a huge pressure on both actors and production sound mixers to 'get the dialogue right'; that is, to record intelligible production dialogue that can be used in the final mix. This is mainly because directors will nearly always try to employ production dialogue – and also because most big stars do not like long ADR sessions. Unfortunately for both actors and sound crew, dialogue/voice is the sound element which is in the least controlled environment, and thus very often ends up being the worst sounding element in a scene.

Choices will eventually need to be made that will affect our perception of the acting performance. Which microphone to choose? The answer is by no means a foregone conclusion. Different mikes will have different character-istics that translate into certain advantages and disadvantages. In a perfect world, sound recordists would have time to visit the scene, study the best placement for the mikes, and choose the type according to the amount of background sound, reverberation, and other factors (for instance, there may be some unexpectedly strong winds in the area). They would have time to discuss camera placement, actors' movements, where shadows are going to fall, etc. They would also have time to test their choices and correct possible problems. They would have time to record some wild tracks and ambient sound should that be needed later. Most importantly, all recording of a given scene would happen in equivalent sonic conditions.

Again, all this would require the kind of time and money that is rarely available. This is not to suggest that a bad performance should be attributed to the production sound crew.[9] On the contrary, the latter will do their best to accommodate the actor's needs, given the objective limitations mentioned above, but there has to be an understanding between actor and sound personnel as to the specificity of the medium, the technical requirements, etc. This understanding is not always present, as Larry Blake reminds us: 'Getting good production dialogue recordings during the shooting of a film is a notably under-appreciated, misunderstood part of the film making process.'[10]

To underestimate the importance of these production issues can seriously damage our ability to appreciate the distinction between what sounds good and what is good. A voice-over performance recorded in a studio, in a sonically dead room with very little reverberation, with a directional mike (e.g. a shotgun mike) may sound under control, devoid of blurred areas – in a word, professional. On the other hand, the scene mentioned above with Sarandon and Costner, recorded on location, in a very large space with a very high reverberation time (a baseball stadium) and with many other sounds going on at the same time may sound less 'clean', more edgy, less controlled.

However, in terms of skills and complexity, the latter scene is far more demanding than the voice-over: it requires the actor to understand the conditions of his/her vocal performance, that he/she is being recorded in the space we have just described, not in a studio. The degree to which Sarandon understands that in our example is a measure of her acting skills and experience. It would be unwise, however, to give all the credit to the actor. It is up to the production and post-production sound crew to understand and aid the actor's performance in the final mix (by, for example, not overly 'filling up' the background, and highlighting certain sonic interaction, like that between Sarandon's voice and the bat). In other words, actors are not in a position to 'impose' their chosen style of performance: they can only 'suggest' it to the sound crew and hope that they will pick up on it, and expand it.

After an actor has spoken the words, after they have been recorded and all the post-production clean-up and replacement have taken place, one might be excused for thinking that the actor's performance has now taken its final shape. This is not the case. Indeed, perhaps the most important of all manipulations of an actor's voice is yet to take place. This last step is not about massaging the voice recording into a higher or a lower pitch;[11] it is about the place that the voice will have in the final mix, the actual finished soundtrack. This is perhaps the most underestimated factor influencing our assessment of an actor's performance, at least in vocal terms. It is safe to say that, in Hollywood cinema, dialogue intelligibility is still 'the' rule overseeing the construction of a soundtrack. There are, of course, moments of incidental dialogue where it is more important to convey the rhythm and tempo of the dialogue rather than focus on its literal meaning.

The opening sequence of *Saving Private Ryan* is a good example. When I recently asked Gary Rydstrom, who was responsible for the sound design for the film, about the opening sequence of the film, he confirmed that the sound of the bullets – whizzing past, hitting bodies, conveying the notion of a 'nowhere to run' situation – is the structuring element for the scene from an aural point of view, not the dialogue. The latter serves the important purpose of emphasizing the dramatic mood of the scene, but it is not always important to understand exactly what is being said amongst the dozens of men fighting and amidst all manner of explosions, screaming, bullets, machine-guns and mines going off. However, the example above is the exception confirming the rule. In other words, although dialogue can be employed for its 'musical' qualities, it is its literal meaning which remains central to the construction of the final mix. However, to know that soundtracks are built around actors' voices is only the first step. Two further issues inform our judgement of the actor's skills.

First, there is the issue of masking. It is important that the actor's voice, no matter how well recorded and 'cleaned up' it may be, occupies its own frequency range without too much interference. In other words, to have two actors with a very similar voice talking to each other in an environment where most surrounding sound has similar characteristics is a recipe for problems and lack of clarity. This of course applies to all elements of a soundtrack, including music. The importance of the harmonization of sounds is most evident in the casting of star voices for animated pictures. All the key voices in *Toy Story*, to quote but one recent example, were cast for their aural characteristics so that they could occupy different frequency areas in the soundtrack and complement each other (especially Tom Hanks as 'Woody' and Tim Allen as 'Buzz Lightyear').[12]

Second, there is what we could define as 'supporting sound'. This refers to the many ways in which editors and directors can in fact give an edge to line delivery, without necessarily interferring with the voice itself, but rather by arranging the surrounding sound environment. One of the best examples of this can be found in Andrew Davis's film *The Fugitive*. Tommy Lee Jones plays Samuel Gerard, the US marshall who is in pursuit of escaped murderer Dr Richard Kimble, the fugitive of the title (played by Harrison Ford). Jones won an Academy Award for his role and his performance was widely praised. Jones's considerable skills notwithstanding, part of that Award is probably owed to the sound crew and picture editor who worked on it.[13]

The scene I am discussing happens immediately after Kimble escapes his guardians after a car versus train crash, in which the latter derails. Amidst scenes of death and destruction, Samuel Gerard makes his entrance. We do not yet know him, so it is crucial that his authority is established promptly. He listens to the account of one of the guards who were involved in the crash and ascertains that Kimble might have got out of the crash alive. At this point Gerard/Jones stands up and delivers his instructions.

Stambler and Levaque emphasize Jones's delivery by fading out most of the background noises. Indeed, you can still see in the background of the shot all the dozens of people working on the train wreckage, but you can't hear any of the loud sounds made by them. Moreover, the sound of the leg chains that were on Kimble's legs can be heard clearly, adding poignancy to Gerard/Jones's words. In a sense, it is as if Jones's performance were being 'protected', guarded from extraneous sounds which might mask his voice or detract attention from it. What can be heard supports his performance, gives it weight and body – the leg chains have a very high pitch, occupying a different portion of the frequency range than Jones's own voice. In other words, Jones has no competitors.

Apart from protecting him, the soundtrack also supports him. This is mainly achieved through editing. As Gerard/Jones stands up and starts delivering his orders, the music kicks in to give more body to his voice, almost as if to vouch for his authority (he is the one who can summon up the music). Moreover, there is a very effective editing between Gerard/Jones's voice and that of Kimble/Ford. The latter voice has been massaged and turned into something that closely resembles the grumble of an animal out of breath, rather than a human being. The juxtaposition between the hunting marshall and the haunted fugitive is thus established beyond the literal meaning of Jones's words. This example of supporting sound shows how a performance can be greatly enhanced in the final mix. The careful arrangement of effects, music, and silence (and their editing) in relation to the actor's voice can have a major impact on our perception of the performance.

Thus, it should not be surprising when actors acknowledge the impact that post-production has on their performance, as this quote emphasizes: 'It is interesting that so many actors acknowledge that this final stage of the film [i.e. post-production] will determine how their performance will be received.'[14]

Conclusion

The adjective 'film' does more than just indicate the type of acting. It works as a structuring element indicating the relationships at the core of the acting effort. These relationships – between actors and script, between actors themselves, between actors and technology, between actors and crew, and between actors and their knowledge of their own skills and limitations – become the areas to explore. This exploration can help unhinge old misconceptions about film acting and replace them with a new awareness of and admiration for actors' skills. It is clear from what we have seen when dealing with the voice that our perception takes place after a complex series of mediations between actors and the medium in which they work.

Actors have limited control over their voice. They have no control over the way in which it will be recorded, manipulated, and placed in the overall soundtrack. Moreover, they have no say in deciding whether their voice will be challenged by other sound elements or supported by them. Their skills however, reside in understanding this complex dynamic involving a mike and fifty other members of the crew. Indeed, recognizing medium specificity is the first step towards a more comprehensive grasping of the dynamics of film acting. Actors work in a context, not in splendid isolation. They have to deal with dozens of other crew members whose work will impinge not only on their performance but also on the way the audience will perceive it.

Luckily, as we have seen, that context can be investigated. Moreover, our investigation can inform our assessment of an actor's skills and limitations without the need to revert to too many vague notions and terms. Discrete areas of assessment, and even criteria for assessment, can be identified. Actors' ability (or lack of it) to show an awareness of script confines, of other actors, of their surrounding soundscape, of technical issues, of being recorded, and of the need for continuity, is at least as revealing about their skills as the ability to 'sound like Gandhi', get the right accent, and project their voice. To put it simply, a good actor will always know that, ultimately, his or her performance will depend on that of others, as Linda Seger reminds us: 'Actors all must ultimately rely on the kindness of strangers.'[15]

Notes

1 David Fincher, audio commentary of the film *Se7en*, Laserdisc Criterion Edition, 1997, commentary soundtrack.
2 Morgan Freeman was born 1 June 1937 in Memphis, Tennessee.
3 Morgan Freeman, audio commentary of the film *Se7en*, Laserdisc Criterion Edition, 1997, commentary soundtrack.
4 This is here intended in its linguistic meaning. In the 1997 edition of the Cassell *Concise Dictionary*, to syncopate is described as: 'to contract (a word) by omitting one or more syllables from the middle'.
5 Dustin Hoffman as quoted in L. Seger and E.J. Whetmore, *From Script to Screen*, New York, Owl Books, 1994, p. 181.
6 Randy Thom is one of Hollywood's most prominent and experienced sound designers.
7 ADR or Automatic Dialog Replacement, also known as 'looping'. It is the process by which production dialogue can be replaced during post-production in a studio-controlled environment. Main actors are always contracted for a certain amount of hours of ADR per picture.
8 John Lithgow in L.Seger and E.J. Whetmore, op. cit., p. 189.
9 Although it is useful to remember that audiences are less forgiving, as Tom Holman suggests when he says: 'Today, if an actor can't be understood it is routinely thought to be a technical fault, no matter how much of a mumbler the actor is.' In Tomlinson Holman, *Sound for Film and Television*, Boston and Oxford, Focal Press, 1997, p. 25.

10 L. Blake, 'Slumming with the First Unit', *MIX*, April 1998, vol. 22, no. 4, pp. 34–42. Larry Balke is a sound editor/re-recording mixer.

11 The practice of massaging or manipulating an actor's voice is surprisingly unusual. There are obvious exceptions, but it does not constitute common practice. Moreover, actors also seem to be wary of any changes to their voices.

12 Conversation with Gary Rydstrom, sound designer on *Saving Private Ryan* and *Toy Story*, Marin County (CA), July 1998.

13 Bruce Stambler and John Levaque were nominated for an Academy Award for their sound design on the film. However, when I asked him about the film, Bruce Stambler suggested that the success of its soundtrack was mainly due to their good relationship and understanding with the film's picture editor, Dennis Virkler.

14 L. Seger and E.J. Whetmore, op. cit., p. 189.

15 Ibid.

10

SECRETS AND LIES
Acting for Mike Leigh

Paul McDonald

Mike Leigh is well known as a film director who works intensively with actors. At a most basic level, Leigh's working process can be understood as requiring actors to work without a script, developing their own characters in ways that involve a deep exploration of every possible aspect of the character's life. This chapter investigates this process through a descriptive account of how Leigh worked with his actors on one particular project. Using interviews with Leigh and the actors Claire Rushbrook and Ron Cook, the chapter explores in detail the rehearsals for *Secrets and Lies* (1996).

Leigh's first theatrically released feature was *Bleak Moments* (1971), developed from a stage production performed in London during March 1970 at the Open Space Theatre. The film is a portrait of Sylvia (Anne Raitt), a young but lonely woman confined by her caring responsibilities for her retarded sister Hilda (Sarah Stephenson) and unsuccessful attempts to build intimacy with others. It would not be until 1988 that Leigh would make another feature. Coming at the end of a decade of Thatcherism, *High Hopes* (1988) mapped a tripartite set of relationships to illustrate some of the key social and political trends shaping the period. In *Life is Sweet* (1990), the relationship of different characters to food becomes the means for exploring the ambitions and anxieties of a suburban family. Leigh would eventually receive international critical recognition with *Naked* (1993), which took the awards for best director and best actor (David Thewlis) at the Cannes Film Festival. Set against the dark urban landscape of London, the film follows Johnny (Thewlis) as he wanders the city expounding his cynical guttersnipe philosophy. As Michael Coveney suggests, the film's title 'carries connotations of sexual activity and spiritual emptiness'.[1]

In *Secrets and Lies*, the narrative centres on the relationship of Hortense (Marianne Jean-Baptiste), a young black woman who, following the death of her adopted mother, discovers and befriends her white birth mother Cynthia (Brenda Blethyn). While the racial difference of daughter and mother is one of the film's secrets, it does not become an issue debated by the film. For

Maurice (Timothy Spall), Cynthia's beloved younger brother, his marriage to Monica (Phyllis Logan) is severely strained by their problems with having children. Maurice runs his own photography business and, periodically, the film steps to the side of the main narrative for a succession of short vignettes in which various individuals, couples, and groups are photographed by Maurice in his studio. Each is literally a portrait, capturing succinctly the personality and private dramas of Maurice's subjects. As these vignettes feature dozens of actors who have appeared in Leigh's previous films, they become reflective of the director's own dramatic preoccupations. At the conclusion of the film, when the whole family, including Cynthia's other daughter Roxanne (Claire Rushbrook), learn the secrets of Hortense and Cynthia's relationship and Maurice and Monica's private problems, the shock and surprise first divides but ultimately unites the family.

Secrets and Lies began from Leigh's usual starting point: no script and no characters. Unlike conventional methods of casting, in which script readings are frequently used in order to find the performer who will adequately fit the role, in the absence of a script and an established list of roles, auditions for Leigh's films involve a more open process. Leigh is quite guarded about exactly what the process involves. Usually actors will be invited for a 20 minute interview and then, if recalled, will spend a further hour working with the director. In many cases, it has been Leigh's experience that he may see an actor for one film but will not use him or her until a subsequent project. While all actors are cast because of their performance abilities, Leigh's auditioning process places less emphasis on the actor's ability to perform a specific role and far more on a general sense of acting skill.

Leigh's use of improvisation has led commentators to see associations with the films of John Cassavetes and Robert Altman.[2] However, while Leigh admires the work of Cassavetes and Altman, he would not directly credit those directors as influences on his work. Instead, Yasujiro Ozu, Satayjit Ray, and Jean Renoir are the actual influences he prefers to acknowledge, identifying as he does with the spirit of their films. Although Leigh uses improvisation throughout rehearsals, Leigh is always keen to emphasize that what appears on film is not a record of actors improvising in front of camera. Leigh works in such a way that improvisation is only the means to arrive at a tightly rehearsed end product. In *Secrets and Lies* it is only in the briefest of moments during a few of the photographic vignettes that there is anything which could remotely be described as spontaneous improvisation on film. Leigh points out, 'the little kid, sitting on a miniature *chaise longue* putting his finger up his nose, that is not the result of six months rehearsal . . . that is a 2 year old putting his finger up his nose. And the dog with Alison Steadman was not doing Stanislavsky.'

It is Leigh's opinion that the fascination with improvisation amongst commentators on his work has led to a total emphasis on the start of the process by which he creates his films. For Leigh, it is only ever the quality and effectiveness of the end product that can justify the use of such means. Leigh believes it is misguided to see his use of improvisation during rehearsals as in any way a special method, for he regards improvisation as inherent to any creative process: 'All art is a synthesis of improvisation and order. . . . You arrive at it by improvising and distilling that down. Putting order on it and working and working until you have something which is refined and precise.' While Leigh's working process starts without a script, through rehearsals the actors arrive at highly structured dialogue.

However, the purpose of improvisations is not simply to arrive at the words. Leigh is interested in actors developing a whole event for the circumstances in which they find themselves. Improvisation is used to explore and analyse the motivation of characters. From this work, actors develop the subtext for scenes so that, in Leigh's words, 'what is going on is not simply what is being said'. For Leigh, the rehearsal process is always directed towards creating a precisely organized drama. The director and the actors work at 'distil[ling] out of all of the [inputs] . . . to pin it down and pin it down so that we do start to work from improvisation through to something which is very structured, very very thorough, and finally word perfect and moment perfect.' What is found on screen in Leigh's films is therefore not improvisation but the results of improvisation.

While Leigh will start with an initial idea, through rehearsals that idea is continually developed and revised. In the case of *Secrets and Lies*, Leigh began work with many ideas, including the theme of adoption, which was influenced by knowing people who were close to the experience of adoption. What emerges from the work with actors is what Leigh describes as the premise of the film. The premise is a product of the rehearsal process, and as the core idea is arrived at, so the premise comes to inform the final ordering of material. Before shooting, the director will have developed a structure based on the premise and, in their various ways, the actors will understand the premise relative to their character's point of view. However, this does not mean that shooting simply becomes the recording of a set structured drama. Leigh frequently finds that the structure he devises remains open ended. In the case of *Secrets and Lies*, three-quarters of the film had been shot without a clear idea of how the film would end. Only then was the final act of the film, the scenes around Roxanne's birthday, actually created. New improvisations were therefore conducted on location alongside shooting. Further work on structuring the drama was then continued into post-production. Leigh therefore retains an open approach to the creation and ordering of material.

Leigh's work with actors usually takes several months. Before rehearsals begin, he will gather the actors for a social meeting to introduce the principles by which he will be working. However, after this initial collective gathering, the whole cast are unlikely to meet as one again. Leigh starts rehearsals by meeting actors individually, gradually creating and developing a character through discussions followed by improvisations. Ron Cook had previously worked with Leigh on *Ecstasy*, performed at the Hampstead Theatre in 1979. In *Secrets and Lies*, Cook appears for one scene only as Stuart Christian, a drunk and emotionally destroyed individual who, prior to emigrating to Australia, sold his photography business to Maurice. Cook's description of how Leigh and himself created Stuart provides a detailed account of the procedures used by the director with his actors:

> You come in with a list of names of people that you know or who you have met. . . . With *Secrets and Lies* . . . Mike said it can be any class, the age range, white, Caucasian obviously. . . . you go in and you sit there with Mike one-to-one and you just go through the list of names. You start at the top and he says right, describe them. So you do little sketches and he notes those down. . . . I think I had about seventy-five names. . . . Everybody else is doing the same thing, one-to-one. . . . There's an absolute secrecy. Mike is the only one who knows . . . what it's about as it develops. . . . So eventually he pins it down to one character . . . Then at some point you create a parallel character. . . . You then jettison the original person you knew. . . . [and] make a name for them.

Once actors arrive at a name, Leigh stipulates that actors always speak of the character in the third person so as to give life to the role and encourage actors to believe in the person they create. From this basic idea, Leigh has his actors develop their characters through extensive research. To support actors, researchers are employed to investigate and make contacts relating to the histories constructed for characters. Cook explains:

> You start working on the whole history. You work all the way back to grandparents, or great-grandparents. . . . Between you, you start inventing. Stuart . . . was based on someone I was at college with . . . but in the end was nothing like him. . . . We decided he came from Grays, Essex. . . . So then I go off down there . . . go to the library, read up about Tilbury. . . . I picked out the actual house and the school he went to. Walked the route to school . . . going into cafés. . . . The researchers . . . find someone who went to that school about the time Stuart would have gone. You ring them up. Meet them. . . . We decided that Stuart's father was such an influence on him. I was discussing it with Mike and saying he has to have been an amazing guy that Stuart could never live up to. . . . The father would have been at the age when he would have been in the war. So I had this idea of Bomber Command. . . . I talked to this guy who was in Bomber Command, rear-gunner. . . . Amazing stories. In the end I

said to Mike, I want to play the dad, I don't want to play Stuart at all! . . . And I went up to the airforce museum in Hendon, climbed inside Lancasters, because that is what Stuart would have been taken to.

Even though the history of a character may become highly detailed and complex, actors do not write things down, but instead must carry the history of the character as a set of memories, feelings, and emotions.

In the finished film, Stuart appears in Maurice's photography shop for one scene only. To build the relationship between the two characters, improvisations for another situation, in which Stuart sells his business to Maurice before departing for Australia, were conducted. This situation was only used to develop the relationship between the two characters and was not intended to be rehearsed as a scene for the final film. It may not be immediately apparent why the shop scene is in the film. Stuart's scene does at first seem to stand apart from the main narrative. The director did face pressures to cut the scene in order to reduce the running time. However, Leigh retained the scene for several reasons:

> First of all, the structural reason why it is important is because . . . by that time you're gagging to know what's going to happen to Cynthia, and you need a breather from that. You need to go back to Maurice and Monica. And I felt there was nothing else to go back to. If you went back to them at home you'd learn nothing new at all. It was important to see them in another context, just to throw a different light on their relationship, and on the nature of, basically, what sorts of people they are. By putting them in a situation where they are confronted by having to care for somebody, and in the case particularly of Maurice, of dealing with somebody, firmly.

Out of the solo work of actors, Leigh begins to bring actors together to explore possible productive meetings and relationships between characters. Appearing in only the one scene, Cook created Stuart mainly in isolation from the rest of the cast. However, Cook entered into some initial work with Timothy Spall to explore links between Stuart and Maurice:

> We tried to work out what Stuart did for a living. . . . I said photography. . . . There was an original idea to make Stuart and Maurice competitors. . . . Tim and I went out and met photographers at the same time, passed on information to each other . . . [Originally] Stuart was actually very successful. . . . Suddenly Mike came in and he said 'He meets this Australian girl. What happens then?' . . . Mike sent Stuart's character on this tailspin of disasters.

In rehearsal, Stuart's visit to the shop was set up as a surprise for the other characters. The first improvisation started with Stuart sitting across the road from the shop on a bench, drunk. Emma Amos, who plays a woman scarred in a car accident, failed to recognize Cook when she left the shop at the start of the scene. Cook recalls that when Stuart said to her 'Hello darling', Amos responded quite genuinely with 'Just fuck off'. From an initial lengthy improvisation between the characters of Stuart, Maurice, Monica, and Jane, rehearsals worked towards achieving a tight, highly structured scene. The detail of this work required the actors continually to refine the minutiae of their performances. For example, Cook had Stuart imposing himself on Maurice and Monica with the request 'I'd love a cup of tea.' Leigh modified this line to 'I'd *kill* for a cup of tea', a single word adding resonance to Stuart's bitterness and desperation. During editing, Leigh cut a moment from the scene where Stuart questions why Maurice has not removed a pillar that stands in the studio. Spall had Maurice responding by pointing out that if the pillar were removed, then everything would fall in. At this point, Stuart broke down. Leigh chose not to include this moment because he believed it introduced a highly emotional scene too early. However, this omission does indicate further the importance of the scene, for Stuart represents the state of despair with which other characters are struggling, and which will only become completely evident in the final act. Stuart's demise is therefore integrated into the film through its thematic significance. Although only a single scene, Cook's performance succeeds in immediately bringing to the screen an entire history and set of personal circumstances that reflect on the film as a whole.

For Claire Rushbrook, *Secrets and Lies* was her first film work and first experience of working with Leigh. To create Roxanne, Rushbrook underwent the same general procedures as Cook. However, as the work of creating a character is always tuned to the specific individual case, actors will inevitably experience those procedures in different ways:

> We very slowly started going through this list. First on my list was [a girl] I went to school with. She was my best friend when I was a child. . . . And Mike would say 'Was there money in the family?' 'Any brothers and sisters?', drawing out what you may not necessarily think to say about that person. . . . At the very beginning, Mike wanted to use a bit of two people from the list. There was a girl from home, who was the girlfriend of one of my mates. . . . I didn't feel I had much to say about her when I first wrote her down. Then I remembered hearing that she had an uncle who was a bricky and her mum ran a pub. And the characteristics of that person are what Mike is coaxing out of you. She was rather sullen and prickly. . . . With the other girl, it was her mannerisms which were of interest. She was all twitchy and chewy and nervy. . . . Still working one-on-one . . . you

do this exercise to inhabit the character and not do much. . . . It's quite scary the first time you get on your feet because you want to get it first go. It's all about retraining your attitude. You want to show off or be perfect . . . and of course you can't because you haven't really got a clue what you are doing. . . . To help the acting, Mike does this exercise where you start as your character at your age. You just walk around the room, play and just get into their head. Then he takes you down year by year so you get to being that character when she was 10 . . . right down until you are a baby.

These one-to-one sessions may suggest that actors are encouraged to be isolated from one another. However, this early individual work becomes the basic elements from which Leigh builds a complex and more highly integrated form of ensemble playing. After creating their individual character, an actor will be introduced to the characters created by other actors. Roxanne belongs centrally within a complex of familial relations. After working one-to-one with Leigh, Rushbrook met with Brenda Blethyn and Timothy Spall to develop the relations of daughter, mother, and uncle. Together, the actors constructed a family history that went back to when Roxanne was 2 years old. From these foundations, further discussions and improvisations between Rushbrook and Blethyn developed the daughter/mother relationship.

Although these meetings are in some respects experiments in character interaction, it has to be plausible that such characters could meet. A key principle in Leigh's work with actors concerns the distribution of knowledge between characters. In conventional rehearsals, at the first meeting actors frequently read the script and generally talk together as a group in order that the cast can assemble a global overview of the whole narrative and all the roles in the drama. With Leigh, actors are required to keep private the individual decisions they arrive at between themselves and the director in the construction of their role and the character's circumstances. Information shared between actors is monitored by Leigh on a need to know basis. The reason for this is that Leigh hopes that the all-important first improvised meetings between characters will only be informed and motivated by what individuals would plausibly know of one another in that situation. None of the actors will know everything about everybody, resulting in individuals having a greater or lesser understanding of immediate circumstances and the narrative as a whole.

The first improvisation of any scene, what Leigh calls the 'master improvisation', is an unrepeatable stage in the devising process. For the first time, actors approach a situation totally from the limited knowledge they have of other characters. After the master improvisation, actors inevitably approach any subsequent improvisations of the scene with different insights. *Secrets and Lies* is served well by Leigh's working method because the whole drama is predicated on the gradual revelation of major secrets hidden between

Figure 10.1a & b 'Leigh's way of working situates actors as a series of links in a
chain. Characters will join with some and not with others.' In
10.1a, Claire Rushbrook (centre) with Phyllis Logan and Lee Ross
and in 10.1b with Marianne Jean Baptiste in *Secrets and Lies* (1996)
Source: Courtesy of Thin Man Films

members of a family, with scenes dealing with the immediate responses of individuals to those revelations. For example, Cynthia's big secret is that she gave away her first child for adoption. Since the adoption, Cynthia has no other knowledge of her child. Hortense knows she is adopted but does not know the identity of her birth mother. The first meeting of Hortense and Cynthia is arranged by phone. Blethyn and Jean-Baptiste had not met in rehearsals and the meeting between Cynthia and Hortense was arranged through the actors using mobile phones in different parts of the rehearsal rooms in Stoke Newington, North London. In the film, the meeting occurs outside Holborn underground station. However, for the master improvisation of this crucial scene, the actors agreed to meet outside a cemetery across the road from the rehearsal rooms. Leigh explains the outcomes of the meeting:

> They agreed to meet outside this cemetery . . . in the rehearsal mode. Obviously at the very beginning of the rehearsals of the film . . . I get all the actors together . . . and I just sort of talk about, not the film, but simply the technical parameters of what we are going to do. . . . Certainly anybody that doesn't know anybody else will see that person, say hello to them, and then really never see them again basically. So Brenda, she knew there were two black actresses in it, and she sort of knew who they were to a degree because she had seen them in a play they were in at Stratford East. It so happened, that at the back of her mind . . . she thought that the person she was going to meet was whoever the character was that was going to be played by Emma Amos [who appears briefly as a scarred car crash victim photographed by Maurice at his studio]. She was waiting for this girl, and she was aware of a black woman standing there . . . and she, in reality, didn't think it was her. She'd forgotten what she looked like. She didn't think it was her anyway. So when she said 'I'm Hortense', it was a genuine organic thing. . . . They went and did it and sat in a pretend café in the rehearsal room. And then they had a version of what was the scene in the film.

Although only a two-hand scene, such examples are fundamental to understanding the ensemble principle in Leigh's work. Rather than forming the collective from having everyone know everything, Leigh's way of working situates actors as a series of links in a chain. Actors will link up with some characters and not with others. However, an ensemble is nevertheless formed as the sum of those individual links.

The film builds to the final scenes of the barbecue for Roxanne's birthday party at Maurice and Monica's house. Here the controlled flow of information between actors was essential to the dramatic dynamics of the scene and the film as a whole. At this point, Cynthia and Hortense know that they are mother and daughter. Maurice and Monica know that Cynthia had a child who was adopted but do not know that Hortense is that child. Roxanne does not know about the adoption and so has no idea who Hortense may be. Maurice and Monica have kept secret their unsuccessful attempts to have children and the strain this has had on their relationship. Outside this family circle, the only other characters attending the barbecue are Roxanne's boyfriend Paul (Lee Ross) and Jane (Elizabeth Berrington), Maurice's assistant from the photography shop, neither of whom can have any clue as to the family secrets they are about to hear revealed.

As previously mentioned, most of the film had been shot before the conclusion was even devised. Leigh regards working with actors in actual locations as very important, 'so that the defining of the thing in visual and cinematic terms and the blocking of the action is integral with the actual dynamics of . . . the dramatic situation'. For Roxanne's party, a nine-hour master improvisation was conducted at the house in Southgate used as the location for Maurice and Monica's home. Roxanne is placed in a situation where she is the centre of attention because the afternoon is intended to celebrate her birthday. However, she is also the member of the family who knows the least about the secrets to be revealed during the course of events. For this reason, Roxanne is probably the character with the most to respond to in the sequence. Rushbrook describes her experience of the scene:

Brenda and I and Lee Ross were in Stoke Newington at the rehearsal rooms. Tim and Phyllis were up at Southgate . . . Cynthia and Roxanne had a cup of tea. Paul came round. . . . We got in a real mini-cab. Stopped off to get some booze. Drove up to Southgate. Got lost. Brenda had to ask the cab driver as Cynthia 'Where're you going?', 'Where are you?', 'You know, I think you don't know where your're going, do you?' [We] drive down this incredible street full of huge houses. Get out. It is the first time that any of us had seen that house. . . . When we improvised the revelations, it freaked me out. I didn't have a clue. How it is in the film is pretty much how it happened except we were sitting outside when we improvised it. . . . When Marianne's character arrived, that was weird. We asked the questions you see in the film . . . But when Cynthia said 'This is my daughter' I could not believe my ears. . . . I remember Mike asking me 'Did you really have no idea?' because of course he had been so diligently keeping this secret for months. . . . I don't think that I could have played it as honestly as I had if we'd worked on it any other way. I remember feeling as Claire, as an actress, and no doubt it helped my performance, . . . really appalled that these other actors kept it from me, and that Mike had been working out this whole other secret, and I felt like an idiot. . . . This is a side which came very easily for Roxanne.

Numerous improvisations then developed the scene before filming. The actors investigated and reinvestigated the motivations of their character. When Roxanne learns of Cynthia's secret, Rushbrook was adamant that the character should leave the party never to return. While Roxanne still leaves the party, making her way to the bus stop, Paul eventually persuades her to return. This change serves the pragmatic purpose of giving a resolution to the scene and the film but it was only achievable through Rushbrook exploring Roxanne's change of motivation.

As Leigh has suggested, the same process of improvisation and order permeates the work of everyone on his films. Dick Pope, the cinematographer who has collaborated with Leigh on all his films since *Life Is Sweet*, has to work without a script. Therefore Pope must be openly responsive to whatever the actors have prepared:

> I arrive on the set the first day of the shoot, I've got *not-a-clue* as to what any scene will really involve . . . We have a location, but what happens in it is a complete mystery to everybody, apart from the actors maybe.[3]

Pope aims to 'prepare an area for the actors to work in that is free of any encumbrances'.[4] In the case of the barbecue sequence, the use of a long-take to film the seven actors around the table outdoors suited the ensemble feeling of the conclusion:

> You just hold the one shot and all the characters are all well featured, they're in, they're out, they're foreground, they're background, they're moving around here and disappearing out there, and coming back around there . . . you feel like you are actually sitting there at the table observing them.[5]

In keeping with Leigh's general emphasis on the orderliness of his work, Pope is clear that the actual shooting of any sequence is highly disciplined and refined:

> Once [Mike's] blocked a scene with the actors and we've worked how we're going to shoot it, that scene is buried in concrete. It is written down and that scene is shot conventionally . . . There is no improvisation whatsoever.'[6]

However, Leigh regards Pope as having a major input into how scenes are finally filmed. On the one hand, the camera must respond to the action that the actors have rehearsed. Equally, on the other hand, the introduction of the camera introduces new opportunities for adding to scenes. For example, during Roxanne's party, when Hortense leaves the dinner table, it was Pope's suggestion that the camera should be placed inside the bathroom, so as to capture the character's response to what is going on downstairs.

Leigh regards the process of improvisation as fundamental to all forms of artistic creation. Yet his way of working does allow actors opportunities that are distinctively different from working on other filmed features. Rushbrook found that the extended rehearsal period she experienced on *Secrets and Lies* contrasted with all the television work she had done before and her subsequent film work. After *Secrets and Lies*, she went on to take the role of Deborah in *Spice World: The Movie* (1997). Rushbrook recalls how when she met with the producer, director and fellow actor Richard E. Grant, 'I said "How long's our rehearsal period?" and they laughed and said, "We don't rehearse. You've been working with Mike Leigh too long".' Rushbrook found that her character was not very different from herself and so did not need lengthy preparation. She met the PA for the Spice Girls, on whom the character of Deborah is based in the script, picking up gossip and insight into what the job involved. With the film focusing on the high jinks and capers of the Spice Girls, together with Grant providing an expert performance of parodic hyperbole as the group's manager, Rushbrook decided she would not seek to compete for comic effect but instead offered a relatively quiet and reserved performance.

Ron Cook's career includes the role of Mews, the accountant in Peter Greenaway's *The Cook, the Thief, His Wife and Her Lover* (1989). Leigh's insistence on the discipline and orderliness of his film making is masked by the improvisatory appearance of some scenes. However, in the case of Greenaway, the highly stylised *mise-en-scène* of his films makes very obvious the control of elements on screen. In *The Cook, the Thief, His Wife and Her Lover*, actors seem just one set of components integrated with cinematography and art direction. For this reason, it could be presumed that the work of actors is highly constrained compared to the relative freedom enjoyed by actors in Leigh's films. However, for his part in the Greenaway film, Cook found that actors were still granted a fair degree of independence:

> I thought it would be 'Ron raise your eyebrow a little more to the left'. But no, he allows you to do your own thing. Then he begins to control it. There was a bit where he showed us a picture . . . a painting. He said, 'Now look at it. Don't copy the picture but look at one of the poses. Do something similar to it or do the same thing.' Then you do it and he'll go, 'Right, yeah that's good, stand over there.' So he will arrange it.

In Cook's opinion, the absence of a script is the simple difference which distinguishes Leigh's ways of working from the majority of film-makers. Without a script or characters, Leigh's rehearsal methods grant considerable creative independence to actors. However, Leigh is not interested in such liberty *per se*. For Leigh, improvisation is just a means to an end:

> The actual substance of the film, the actual quality and the discipline and the order and the form of the film, must go beyond being merely people improvising. . . . Obviously you try and make it as natural as possible . . . You could say it aspires to the condition of improvisation but even that is to miss the point, which is that it aspires to the condition of reality. And obviously people in life are improvising.

Leigh is regarding improvisation as fundamental to actors achieving a sense of realism. His work for stage, television, and film has become well known for its observations on contemporary British culture. So well known is this work, that Leigh's name is commonly referred to outside references to dramatic fiction as a shorthand definition of everyday British life. For example, one journalistic profile of the Labour member of parliament Ken Livingstone opened with a description of the MP's office as 'cosy, with Mike Leigh mud-brown sofa and Mike Leigh flowery curtains and Mike Leigh nets shadowing the flowery curtains'.[7] On the occasion of a rare victory for England in a cricket test series, one sports reporter commented that 'The soap opera that is English cricket appeared so bleakly ordinary, so depressingly repetitive a short time ago that it might have been scripted by Mike Leigh.'[8] Leigh's success comes from the recognizable and familiar sense of British ordinariness found in his dramas. It is this vision of British life which has led some to choose to invoke Leigh in their observations on Valentine's Day kitsch,[9] the pleasures and frustrations of camping,[10] the practicalities of the camper van,[11] the pretensions of posh restaurants,[12] the social manners of serving wine,[13] and the sex lives of swingers,[14] amongst other things.

Critics of Leigh's work argue that many of the characters found in the films are only ever stereotypes.[15] Additionally, critics have charged Leigh with creating caricatures, which poke fun at the ordinary lives that the films represent.[16] A degree of social typage is an inevitable and necessary part of all realist representation. Certainly some but not all the performances in Leigh's films do work through a heightened sense of realist observation. Accents are more distinct than in everyday life and all characters have their twitches that are forever foregrounded. However, this heightened quality gives the performances in Leigh's films a distinctive quality. Characters appear as both clearly representative of ordinary lives but also extraordinarily idiosyncratic. Part of the comic quality of certain characters comes precisely from the acute accuracy of performances. If these performances evoke laughter, then it is a humour based on recognition. However, Leigh's films consistently switch between dramatic and comedic moments, a change achieved also at the level of individual performances. Across these changes of tone, what emerges from the heightened quality of performances is the means for discovering both the comedy and the tragedy of ordinary lives.

Notes

My thanks to Ron Cook, Mike Leigh, and Claire Rushbrook for their contributions to this chapter.

1 M. Coveney *The World According to Mike Leigh*, London, HarperCollins, 1977.
2 J. Hoberman, 'Cassavetes and Leigh: Poets of the Ordinary', *Premiere*, vol. 5, no. 3, 1991, pp. 25–26.
3 M. Most, 'Dick Pope Talks About *Secrets and Lies*', *Eyepiece*, vol. 17, no. 3, 1996, pp. 14–15.
4 Ibid., p. 14.
5 Ibid., p. 15.
6 Ibid., p. 14.
7 S. Hattonstone, 'Lazarus of the Left', *Guardian*: G2, 3 Dec. 1997, p. 6.
8 P. Weaver, 'England's Cast Hits Right Notes at Last', *Guardian*: Sport, 20 Feb. 1997, p. 23.
9 L. Gamman, 'The Fluff That Dreams Are Made Of', *Guardian*: G2, 14 Feb. 1994, p. 10.
10 M. Sawyer, 'Meaningful and in Tents', *Observer*: Life, 6 Aug. 1995, p. 10.
11 M. Seaton, 'We Also Surf . . . ', *Observer*: Life, 30 Nov. 1997, p. 53.
12 J. Lanchester, 'Eating Out', *Observer*: Life, 22 May 1994, p. 39.
13 T. Atkin, 'Chill Factor', *Observer*: Life, 20 Oct. 1996, p. 45; 'Fair Weather Friends', *Observer*: Life, 29 June 1997, p. 37.
14 A. Karpf, 'Wave Riding: Sex With Auntie', *Guardian*, 2 Nov. 1996, p. 7.
15 A. Pulver, 'Enfield of Dreams', *Guardian*: G2, 14 Sept. 1995.
16 G. Adair, 'Provocations: See Me after School, Leigh', *Guardian*, 11 Oct. 1997, p. 6.

11

AN INTERVIEW WITH IAN RICHARDSON

Making friends with the camera

Carole Zucker

Introduction

The difference between British and American acting was a recurrent issue in my 1995 book, *Figures of Light: Actors and Directors Illuminate the Art of Film Acting*. Some of the comments made by American actors were:

> What we're great at is this kind of organic, shoot-from-the-hip, react-off-the-other-person, casual arena of acting. What we're not so good at is the control – voice work, interpretation, clarity, being able to use the text . . . It's what the English are so good at, and why we love their theatre.
>
> (Lindsay Crouse)

> It's a very complicated relationship between the British actor and the American actor. There's a kind of mutual envy and a mutual inferiority complex. American actors tend to think the Brits are the great stage actors, and the Brits tend to think the Americans are the ones who act truly from the guts.
>
> (John Lithgow)

The implications of these statements are that British actors are technically proficient, but somehow – compared to the Americans – lack raw emotional power. Such statements do not begin to account for the vigour, authority, complexity, and emotional depth of performances by British actors.

I have attempted, through empirical study, to develop a fuller and more complex notion of the core stylistic traits and impulses that are emblematic of British performance. After interviewing twenty-six British and Irish actors – an excerpt from one interview follows – I have located a number of consensual ideas and feelings actors have about their profession.

The foundational element of British acting is most certainly its basis in language. Actors repeatedly stress their subservience to the text, and indeed British theatre, film, and television are often noteworthy for the high quality of the writing. This would be quite in opposition to the behaviourism that marks American acting, which is especially suited to film rather than the theatre. (My wish is not to position British and American performance styles in an ill-begotten competition in which history, politics, education, and culture would need thorough discussion.) British actors were asked about 'the Method' and, as a rule, they objected to the lack of technique and emphasis on pure emotion that dominates (for them) 'Method acting'. For most of them, Method actors seem self-indulgent, playing out their feelings of the moment rather than basing those feelings on the emotional trajectory of the text. Further, more than a few actors did devastating imitations of the pausing, hemming, and hawing, and basic inarticulateness they felt were valorized by the Method. They claimed that in their encounter with Americans, 'real' people never spoke in the broken language that they found characteristic of the Method.

In spite of the classical training of the large majority of the interviewees, most actors believe that acting cannot be taught. One can learn to use one's voice, and to move with greater panache, but genuine acting talent is – for them – an unlearnable gift. The ability to observe human nature, and to maintain an attitude of active curiosity about people and the world around them, was also considered an essential ingredient of good acting.

The actors were more divided in their opinions of film acting. More than a few expressed Helen Mirren's candid reply when asked about the difference between stage and film, which was 'money'. Some actors liked the pared-down nature of acting for the screen. Natasha Richardson quoted Peter Brook who said, 'It's much harder to act truthfully loud'. Many of the interviewees noted the delicacy of intense moments of quiet concentration that mark screen acting, while others lamented the lack of the dynamic between audience and actor that one experiences in the theatre. Other actors appreciated the ability of the camera to act as a microscope, revealing hidden, unspoken feelings with a subtlety unavailable to theatre performers. Natasha Richardson also noted that in film one has the opportunity to repeat a take, whereas in a play there are many times when she felt she had started on a wrong foot, but could not rectify her path, as she might in a film. Quite a few actors found themselves gravitating towards film because of their increasing boredom with long runs in the theatre. Others remarked on the more permanent nature of film performance. Fiona Shaw expressed this best when she talked about acting for the stage:

> To choose a way of life where you give your life's blood to concentrating and perfecting events that pass in a second and only live in the memories of people who are watching it, is an incredible throw-away relationship to eternity.

Perhaps one of the most interesting differences between American and British actors is the fluidity with which actors move amongst film, theatre, and television, and their lack of hierarchical feelings about the media. One of the most pervasive feelings amongst the interviewees is that good acting is good acting, and achieves the same goals regardless of the medium. The endeavour of the actor is perhaps best expressed by Helen Mirren when she says that acting is 'placing yourself within the kaleidoscope of human character, and seeing yourself as clearly as you can. It's not looking at yourself egotistically, but looking at yourself as a human being, and what being human means.'

Interview

CAROLE ZUCKER: When you were attending drama school in Glasgow, do you remember what the orientation of the school was?

IAN RICHARDSON: The principal of the college was a great exponent of Stanislavsky. So consequently everything we did, no matter what, was geared towards the Stanislavsky System. Now, let me make one thing quite clear: there is no connection whatsoever between the Method theatre as we understand it, and the Stanislavsky theatre. They are poles apart, because unlike the Method, Stanislavsky is never overindulgent, which the Method is. Stanislavsky is controlled and technically polished, which the Method could never be. So consequently I was trained in the very best ways of approaching a role – playing it from a deep emotional centre, with motivations from everything one does, and subtexts to build the character so that it isn't a facile piece of presentation which won't stand on its own feet on a public platform for more than three weeks without falling apart. There's a bedrock of preparation and reality behind it, and that goes for farcical comedy as well as the great tragedies; it's the same for all presentations – they must be based on truth.

We had, as well, a rigorous voice training. I remember, having come out of the army, that I'd picked up – as well as losing any trace of a Scottish accent – one or two curiosities of army language, and so I was coming out and saying with clipped flattened vowels 'Now look heah' and things like that. I remember the voice man saying 'What are we going to do about your accent?' and I said 'Good heavens, what accent?' So I had to do an exercise which went 'Rolling home to Rio' which I had been saying as 'Rayling hame to Riaou.' [*laughs*] It was a wonderful three years.

CZ: What do you find is the big difference between the sort of training and background you received, and that of younger people coming up now?

IR: The one thing I notice is that they talk a very different kind of language. There was a young man in this production [*The Magistrate* by Arthur Wing Pinero] who said to me 'I won't be comfortable until I've found my space', and I said 'What do you mean, "found your space"? We're going

154

to do it on stage, that is your space.' He said 'No, no, my personal space.' 'I've never heard such rubbish,' I said. But fortunately, we all get on very well together, and they're very sweet and very talented.

CZ: There still seems to be a dichotomy between places like the Drama Centre and East Fifteen versus the Royal Academy of Dramatic Art and the London Academy of Music and Dramatic Art. The Central School is some place in the middle. That goes back to what you were saying about the Method, because people always say, 'I can spot a Drama Centre actor the minute they get on stage.'

IR: Well, of course, I suppose my training must show on stage, although people never mention that, because I have developed a technique, which I use fully in this farcical comedy that I'm doing at the moment. If that is the stuff of a particular brand of training, then I can only say that particular brand of training is best. It's all very well for people to say that people from a certain school are noticeable the moment they walk on stage; what they mean is that they are arrested by a certain presence, as opposed to a shambling, insecure, indeterminate piece of doubtful presence. You see the trouble with doing it for 'the moment' is that you cannot maintain it. There's a complete disregard for the people on stage with you, which is something that, in my training, was constantly dinned into us: that you must be aware that you are on stage with other people. They are saying dialogue as well, to which you must listen. The whole art of working as an ensemble is the art of listening as well as speaking your own dialogue. Now, I maintain that if you come out of a school that teaches you about this business of 'your space' and all the rest of it, they are instilling in their students an utter selfishness, which means that they're out there 'doing their thing' and to hell with anybody else. That's not what it's about! Also if they do prepare their performance in that way, there is no guarantee that it's going to be the same the next night, or the night after that; it'll be different every night, because they've got no bedrock of preparation at all!

CZ: I wonder if there aren't performances by actors who would be called Method actors which have impressed you. I'm thinking of actors like Marlon Brando, Robert De Niro, Harvey Keitel, Christopher Walken, or Al Pacino.

IR: I think some actors are born just being able to do it, and in that case their training, whether Classical or Method, is probably irrelevant. They may be great actors in spite of their training. It's not that the Method is all bad, indeed, in its essence it is simply what actors of any sense or sensitivity would do anyway. What is wrong with it is that it ignores the technical tools such as projection and clarity of diction, and however truthfully you may be feeling something, if nobody can hear or understand what you're saying, it's a total waste of time. Brando at his best is splendid, and he is quite capable of giving up the grunt and mumble when he chooses, as witness his Fletcher Christian in *Mutiny on the Bounty*, with an English accent, no less!

CZ: In watching a lot of Royal Shakespeare Company performances at the British Film Institute, it seems to me that in the 1960s there was almost a sense of radicalness about what you were doing. I saw your performance in *The Comedy of Errors*, and I saw *Marat/Sade* as an adolescent. What was it like to work with Peter Brook?

IR: Frightening to begin with, and then absolutely marvellous thereafter. He and I got on famously. Perhaps the most important thing was that he established an ensemble style. He brought back the observations of the iambic pentameter in Shakespeare. We were all given training and voice exercises.

CZ: What was it like working on *Marat/Sade* [1965], since it created such a great scandal?

IR: If you remember, we were all, first and foremost, lunatics in an asylum. We had a rehearsal period unheard of outside Russia, I think, of sixteen weeks. For the first eight weeks, we never looked at the text. We were invited to bring, to each day's rehearsal, actual case histories of lunatics that people had observed, or had managed to get to see. I myself got an introduction to the director of the Tooting Bec Mental Institute who agreed, very reluctantly, to escort me around his Institute, which he did, which was enormously interesting but frightening too. But more important was that he talked to me for about two hours about mental illness and, in general, the things which can go wrong inside people's heads. We were all doing this kind of thing, the whole cast, and we all contributed. So we had, if you like, a dossier of case histories. And at the end of the first eight weeks, Brook said, 'Right. Now, you have all been given roles to play, and it's perfectly obvious that you cannot be someone who has speaking problems if you have one of the larger speaking roles. So you have got to choose a case history, or an amalgam of case histories, which will enable you to perform, although at the same time remain faithful to your established illness in its reality.' So that's how we did it. Before I played Marat, I played The Herald, who was the kind of master of ceremonies. I found the best thing to do with him was that as long as everything was ordered and going smoothly, he was fine. But the moment anything unexpected or untoward happened, he became exceptionally violent. When I played Marat in the bath, I could only find the case history of extreme schizophrenia to be my case history. I regretted that shift in the casting, terribly. I was not entirely right, nor was I entirely happy, playing Marat. I build my characters sometimes, not just from the heart out, but from the feet up as well. I enjoy physical characterization, as well as mental and emotional characterization, and to put me in a boot-shaped bath meant that I was reduced to the animation of a glove puppet, whereas when I was playing The Herald, I had the full scope and the languidity of Jean-Louis Barrault's clown in *Les Enfants du Paradis*. I played it very much along those lines. *Marat* was not a happy experience.

CZ: How do you generally go about choosing your roles? Obviously that's changed over time, and as you've achieved a different status, but are you generally looking for change?

IR: Yes. Especially since the quite astonishing success of *House of Cards* [1990], because that character I played – which was wonderful and brought me a recognition that I had not hitherto enjoyed – stamped me in such a strong way on people's imaginings of what I am like that I have been purposely looking for something totally different since then.

CZ: Do you think that doing Francis Urquhart opened up a lot of doors for you in terms of doing American films?

IR: Unquestionably so, but they wanted more of the same. Unless, of course, greed got in the way, and they offered so much money that I would have been out of my mind to say no.

CZ: I want to talk about how you develop characterizations for different roles, and to be quite specific in our discussion. I'd like to concentrate on Francis Urquhart, since it's a programme which has been seen by so many people. How do you work breaking down a script? How do you deal with a character's basic desires and obstacles? How do you make a role personal for yourself? Do you use imagery, personal memories, things like that? Would you create a story about Francis, about why he was so cynical and manipulative and murderous? In other words, do you need to have a reason for why he behaved the way he did, why he craved power so intensely and had so few ethical values?

IR: There are some texts, some scripts that you get, where the characterization or the basis of the character is so incredibly sketchy that you have to invent an enormous amount of background before you can even begin to understand, and thereby interpret, the way the character behaves. With *House of Cards*, I was told by Andrew Davies, the scriptwriter, not to read the novel till afterwards. He presented me with a script that leapt – to use the old cliché – off the page at me. However, to have just played what leaps off the page is not enough. I have to tell you that there is a typical kind of Establishment Englishman who still exists today in the same way that he existed in Victorian times. They have a code of behaviour and I knew such a diplomat very well indeed. When I started off my search, not just for the character but for the character idiosyncrasies: the way he holds, how he drinks, how he sits, whatever he does – I brought back to mind the body language of this charming diplomat that I knew, who was also as hard as iron in his dealings. But he did it in the established, diplomatic way.

I then decided that I needed to invent a kind of sexual orientation for the character, simply because it was going to be necessary to do so, because of what the demands were of the character's sexual behaviour in the piece. I studied a book about people in power, and how they needn't necessarily be like the film stars girls swoon over, but they have this incredible aura about them, of power. So I thought 'How do I establish this aura so that when I'm on camera, it is a measurable chemistry?' You know Stanislavsky talks about the circle of concentration; you imagine a band around your head, which you expand outward and outward until it touches the audience. Well, I wanted to create the same band but create it with an aura of power. I realized that the most essential ingredient in achieving that was self-confidence, enormous self-confidence, and this was an aspect that was amply filled by my director, and indeed by Andrew Davies who actually said on one occasion that when I walked on to the film set to do a scene, I brought this particular aura with me. So I was winning, I was getting there. Don't ask me *how* I achieved it. It's like asking me, almost, how I make love. I can't tell you because I don't want to tell you and if I did tell you I might spoil it for myself, you know. I don't quite know how I got there, but I did, and it was just through digging deep, deep, deep.

Now, the other thing is, how do you play a man who is so incredibly ruthless and cruel to the point of pathologically murdering? Fear is the next thing. The man has, inside him, a terrible fear or a guilt which goes back to his youth and a burning, burning ambition fed in the same way as Macbeth's ambition is fed, by his wife. As I said to the director at the time 'If Collingwood had kept his promise and promoted Francis Urquhart from being the Chief Whip to being the Home Secretary, Urquhart would never have gone on a path of blood.' He comes back, if you remember, from having been told he's to stay exactly where he is, and his wife says 'Well, why don't you do something about it? Why don't you bring him down?' and that begins it. There's a wonderful line that Macbeth has: 'I am in blood, steeped in so far that, should I wade no more, returning was as tedious as go o'er' – to go back would be as tedious as to go on. That's what happens with Urquhart. First of all, that drug-sodden press agent has to go, then poor Matty has to go, then before you know it there's another girl in the next series and somebody else; the newspaper editor has to go, and then even his aide has to go, and it becomes almost Jacobean.

The other thing that I decided was that the only way to make this monster acceptable to a viewing audience was to give him what my diplomat friend had, which was enormous urbanity, wit, charm, exquisite manners, beautiful dress – always Saville Row – and a cultured kind of knowledge which left you breathless. So I prepared all those things because I'm not like that at all [*laughs*]. And so I built the character up steadily until it all began to fall into place. I did most of this on my own because most things now have pitiful budgets. There isn't the luxury of rehearsal time although we did have two weeks. I did most of the research and the preparation in my own study with the result, too, that I came to it knowing every single word of every single episode. It was a lesson I learned from no less a person than Alec Guinness when we were doing *Tinker, Tailor, Soldier, Spy* [1980] together. He said that he learns the whole thing because it's the only way to place each scene – shot out of sequence as they always are in movies and in television – in its position on the graph of your entire performance. So I came knowing every word of it, which in a way, too, helped the self-confidence required to establish this aura. I remember, too, leaving my dressing room at Ealing Studios. There was a great mirror, and the dresser used to put me into my Saville Row suit, and just as I went to reach for the door handle, I would suddenly see Francis Urquhart in the reflection and not me any more.

CZ: Did it help that you had played Richard III?

IR: Yes, I think it did. There are very, very strong similarities between the two. Curiously enough, when Richard achieves his ambition, which is the crown, the part and the play itself are on a downward course from there on. And the same is true of Francis Urquhart. That's why the first episode was such a strong one compared with the second. In the second one, he is Richard III facing his Bosworth.

CZ: The next question I want to ask you is a technical one. Since there are so many close-ups in the series, does that affect the scale of the performance?

IR: I always asked to be told what lens they were using so that I knew the size. I've always found that, particularly in television, cameramen are very forthcoming. When they realize that you need to know how close they're going to be – because the camera doesn't always move physically towards you but the lens does, you know. In close-up the blink of an eye is as big as a wide, policeman-like street gesture, halting traffic, or waving them on. So the first thing you have to train yourself to do is to hold your eyes open during the take. Not permanently, otherwise it seems a bit of a worry, but not to blink too much. The other thing is to keep your eyebrows steady, because, again, the eyebrows are like extravagant gestures, especially if they're dark. And stillness, utter stillness. No gestures whatsoever, so that the performance is all coming from behind the eyeballs. The only thing I used to find a little bit scary was if they put a filter into the matte box, and I'm talking to the camera, I used to be able to see my own reflection, which I found very off-putting so I used to get them to put just a little mark on the underside of the matte box, because I didn't want to look at my own face speaking. I played it all to that little spot. It makes me very cross, incidentally, because people think I probably had an auto-cue for those speeches – not a bit of it!

CZ: What I found interesting was that the use of close-up would seem to provide a lot more intimacy with the audience, but even while you have this whole series of direct addresses to the audience, at the same time we have very little access to the interiority of the character.

Figure 11.1 'How do you play a man who is so incredibly ruthless and cruel?' Ian Richardson as Francis Urquhart in *House of Cards* (1990)

Source: Courtesy of BBC Films

IR: That's right, because he's not going to give anything away to you either. The device was to make you, the audience, as guilty as he is, partners in crime with him. I remember there was one scene, particularly, where I say 'Oh, come along now, you know very well . . . ' and I was thinking of all those poor unfortunate people in their drawing rooms and sitting rooms at home, with their televisions, and this guy is actually turning around and saying 'You're just as guilty as I am,' in a big close-up. It must have been quite a shock! But that was one of the reasons for the device. Appearing to take the audience into your confidence, and not giving anything away. I remember during *Tinker, Tailor, Soldier, Spy* a very clever director, John Irvin, took me to one side and he said, 'I haven't got a great deal to say to you, except to say when we see your eyes as you're speaking to us, if we look carefully at your eyes, we should realize that you're thinking about something else. Although you're saying one thing, your eyes are actually doing something different; in other words you're hiding something.' Which sounds like a vague and rather difficult instruction to give an actor, but actually it's pure gold, and I used that very much for Urquhart. The eyes would be there, and I would say something, and I used to shoot my eyebrow up, because I expected them not to believe me, and I quite enjoyed the fact they didn't, you know. It was a wonderful challenge . . .

The very start of your question was about the preparation. I was told at the outset they thought I might be rather worried and frightened by the business of speaking directly to the audience through the camera. I said 'You mustn't think that for a moment,' because one of the things Peter Hall established in Shakespeare playing all those years ago, was instead of the soliloquy being addressed vaguely towards an exit light in the back of the first circle, or to a place just by the proscenium arch, he established the pattern of saying a Shakespearean soliloquy *to* the audience, taking the audience into your confidence. So I said 'I'm not at all frightened of doing it to the camera.' In fact, I rather enjoy it; it's rather nice because it's a tremendous feeling of power. There's no other actor around me, there's just me, the camera, and the audience, and I loved it. I had the prospect of holding the audience, metaphorically, in the palm of my hand, and that's wonderful, especially if you're playing someone who has this enormous sense of power.

Also, there was something else. I said to Andrew Davies that the only way that the television audience are going to believe that a beautiful young girl is actually going to invite me to take her to bed is if they have seen for themselves, through their contact with me in close-up, talking to them, the kind of bolts, charges of chemistry that are hitting the girl. The audience must feel that too. He agreed and he wrote some soliloquies for me as a result of that, so that the audience could see for themselves that it would be perfectly easy for an impressionable young girl to fall into the trap.

CZ: I think it is. But I also get the sense that you don't have any kind of relationship with your wife.

IR: No, Diane [Fletcher] and I talked at great length about that. She said that they slept in the same room, but in single beds, but they had something quite different in their relationship. If you like, it was sort of sexual, but it wasn't actually physically sexual. And that was fine. Andrew, again, agreed with that, and it was decided to intimate that possibly Mrs Uquhart had lovers.

CZ: What do you think you have learned about acting for the camera – apart from the particular requirements of *House of Cards* – that has evolved over the years that might be helpful to young actors?

IR: It sounds very basic, but the first thing you have to learn is which camera is actually photographing you, if there is more than one. A helpful little red light comes on. It is important to make friends with the camera and still more with the camera operator. It is sometimes helpful to know what lens he is using, i.e. is it a close-up or a long-shot? This can affect the way you perform. And you *must* be truthful, and let your soul show through your eyes.

CZ: Has there ever been a battle of personalities between you and another actor or a director? Do you in general tend to find directors helpful? How do you tend to resolve a situation where there is friction?

IR: I've never had a bad time with an actor, other than the usual temperamental things, and you can nearly always trust. There was one director who must remain nameless, who was a man with a tremendous ego, and totally unjustified conceit, *totally* unjustified. We were doing a film in Ireland and he behaved so badly. He behaved like the world's worst sergeant major – a sergeant major with a posh accent if you can imagine such a thing. So martinetish, and dictatorial, and I don't work that way. I think that, with your director, as with the rest of the cast, it's a question of sharing, of an input of effort, not sort of standing in line with your heels together like some squaddy on a parade ground, being shouted at and told your number. That's not the way an actor responds to a director.

CZ: Have there been times when you've felt that your creative juices weren't flowing? What do you do in that situation? Do you use improvisation as a means of getting through a problem in acting?

IR: There have been many times when I've felt the juices not flowing and what I do about it depends on the cause. Sometimes it's because I am out of sympathy with a director – we don't see eye to eye about anything, or he is of no help to me. In this situation, after trying very hard to co-operate – I usually think out what I want to do, agree with everything he says, and do it my way all the same. It is amazing how many directors just don't notice that you have, in fact, defied their instructions. Sometimes it is because the script is poor, usually because it's been accepted because one's been out of work for a long time and needs both the occupation and the money. I try reworking the script, if I'm allowed to, and if I'm not I just do it loud and fast and hope not too many people see the film. I don't think I've ever found improvisation helpful because, in the end, it's the lines you have to say.

CZ: Do you ever use rushes as a tool?

IR: I never watch rushes. They would either depress me or imbue me with false confidence, and either would be bad for me or for the rest of the film.

CZ: How do you go about giving life to characters when there is very little backstory? For example, *M. Butterfly* or *Dark City* or any other film in which you've played a supporting role.

IR: It all depends on the script. There exist very small parts which are jewel-like in their construction, where you know all about the character from what he has to say and it would be pointless to make any kind of subplot for oneself. General Burgoyne in *The Devil's Disciple* and Sir Robert Morton in *The Winslow Boy* are such examples; they are known in the trade as 'actor proof'. There are other scripts where the characters are so cardboard that it is essential to make up some kind of background, which will not be known to the audience, but will help the actor to breathe some life into the part.

CZ: What do you think it is about the British character that doesn't make heroes out of their actors, where actors – no matter what their status – are fond of calling themselves 'jobbing actors', as opposed to America where stardom is such a big and much-wished-for thing?

IR: Most English actors *are* jobbing actors, that is to say they are ready to take on anything and are not ashamed of playing small parts. This is partly to do with money – even established actors can have long periods of inactivity, when they rapidly run out of funds – it being a sad truism that the better and more interesting the work, the poorer it is paid, so that if you want to play, for example, *Medea*, you have to do it for tuppence and you do, because it's a part you want to play. The jobs that pay the most are usually the pits as far as artistic satisfaction is concerned, but we do them so we can afford to do the good work. This is known in the trade as FU money, meaning that we will be able to turn down the next truly ghastly part that comes along, and finance ourselves through the next bit of artistic satisfaction. English 'stars' are not paid as much as their American counterparts but I was interested to learn that our supporting actors are much better paid, which I think is a good thing. I think on the whole we're quite humble, recognizing how much is due to luck, at least when starting out.

I, for one, find the amount of money paid to American film stars quite grotesque. It means there is correspondingly less money for everything else involved in a film, or it means that the film costs so much to make that it is almost impossible to make a profit. If you make a nice cheap little film, nobody's going to be ruined if it's not a huge success and therefore the film gets made. It seems to me that many of the trappings of American stardom are out of all proportion to the talent involved – my Winnebago has to be bigger than yours – I want a personal gym hitched on to my trailer – I can only eat Peruvian broccoli so please ship it in for me – if any lowly actor gets into my eye line, he's to be fired – the last one's true, by the way. What is all that to do with acting? There are many honourable exceptions, of course, Paul Newman and Richard Dreyfuss spring to mind.

CZ: Judi Dench remarked that there was something quintessentially British about Peggy Ashcroft. Do you think there is something about British acting that makes it different from other styles of performance?

IR: I think, on the whole, English acting tends to be understated and depends heavily on nuance and irony, which is why Chekhov has always been so popular here – much more popular than in Russia, by the way. Of course there are many styles and they are constantly changing. There has been a heavy upsurge of raw realism lately which has produced some remarkable actors, most of them with heavy regional accents and therefore probably not all that versatile, and I don't think they can be deemed typical. Back to irony. If one has to make comparisons I would say that to the British, Americans in general seem to suffer from a serious irony deficiency, which is strange given that the Russians and Jews are wonderfully ironic – I should know, I'm married to that mixture – and that they form a large part of the US population. So perhaps, going back to the last question, that's why we can't quite believe our own publicity and the stars can.

CZ: Is there anything about yourself as an actor about which you would say 'If only I could have been more . . . if only I could have had this or that quality'? In other words, is there something you see as a problem area for you as an actor?

IR: I think very often I come over as cold, and I would like to be able to get more of the common touch.

CZ: Do you have any great heroes? Whom do you feel you've learned a lot from in your life as an actor?

IR: Alec Guinness is one of my heroes, and he it was who first taught me about acting for the camera, and how to simplify things, because I tend to overelaborate . . . Shakespeare, of course, the God of my idolatry . . . Sir John Gielgud, the greatest exponent of Shakespeare and the classics in general . . . Ralph Richardson as an object lesson of how to go over the top convincingly – interestingly enough, he was capable of really appalling performances, especially in his youth, but he seemed to have had no fear and I admired him for that . . . Paul Scofield, an actor who is never less than mesmerizing.

12

BIBLIOGRAPHICAL NOTES

Peter Krämer

The following bibliography brings together a wide range of writings on acting. It draws on the references given in the preceding chapters, and it also goes beyond them by listing numerous additional publications, both in areas that are covered in this book and in areas that we have not been able to deal with. Since there is a lot of overlap between the study of film acting and work on film stars, many publications on stardom have been included, although they may not always deal explicitly with acting. The bibliography, then, is meant to give a more detailed picture of the research traditions from which this book has emerged, and also to indicate ongoing research in other related areas.

In these introductory notes, I want briefly to indicate what these traditions and related lines of enquiry are and to provide lists of relevant works from the bibliography for certain topics. There have been at least two previous attempts (by Bisplinghoff in 1980 and Braudy in 1976) to list publications on film acting and to offer suggestions for the future development of the field. There have also been several recent collections of essays by Butler, Gledhill, and Zucker, which, together with Naremore's study, provide important points of departure for future research on film acting and film stars, by reprinting classic theoretical texts, by surveying historical developments in cinema and related media, and by presenting current theoretical reflections and close textual analyses. I have incorporated some of the references and suggestions contained in the above studies into this bibliographical essay. In line with the overall emphasis of our book, most of the following references relate to the United States.

As the chapters in this book have demonstrated, the study of theatre acting provides a wealth of information, ideas, and insights for the study of film acting, and as the recent debate between Barker, John Russell Brown, and Schechner indicates, it also raises important questions about teaching. There are several important strands in the research on acting in the theatre which are worth delineating here. To begin with, there are wide-ranging histories of acting by, for example, Boynton, Downer, Fischer-Lichte, Kohansky, Wilson, and Young. Between them, these studies provide an overview of long-term historical developments, in the United States and in Europe, concerning the changing sets of ideas about acting prevalent at various points in time as well as the changing realities of acting. Film acting clearly is part of this long history of theatrical ideas and practices. More specifically, the fundamental separation of the performer from the audience as well as the high levels of physical restraint characteristic of mainstream film acting would seem to fit the underlying logic of the history of theatre acting which has long been moving towards a less overtly physical and presentational style.

The immediate context for an investigation of the emergence of film acting is provided by studies of nineteenth-century and early twentieth-century theatrical acting. These include general studies of the craft and profession of acting by Gilman, Hanrers, McArthur, and Taylor, as well as more specific studies, for example on casting practices and types of roles ('lines of business') by Burge and on acting schools and theories by McTeague. A number of books deal specifically with women performing in the theatre, with their public image, their roles and working conditions, their fame and power. These books include studies by Auster, Cima, Davis (on English actresses), Dudden, and Johnson. While there is some work on the twentieth century here, most of it concerns the nineteenth century.

Early performances on film at the turn of the century, and the beginnings of the debate about the nature and quality of film performances (which Yampolsky's essay deals with in the Russian context), have to be seen against the background of theatrical ideas and practices. Early theorists of the cinema in the 1920s and 1930s such as Kuleshov, Pudovkin, Eisenstein, Balazs, and Arnheim (whose key works are included in the bibliography) were interested primarily in defining the specificity of film acting in opposition to the theatre. They highlighted and promoted aspects of film acting (such as its magnification in close shots and its subjection to the operations of film editing) which had no equivalent on the stage. Quite unlike these early theorists, recent historians of silent cinema have emphasized the continuities between theatre and cinema.

As far as the study of film acting is concerned, the silent period (in particular the 1910s) is perhaps the most thoroughly investigated era in film history. The most important works include those by Brewster and Jacobs, deCordova, Graham, Kaufman, Kerr, Musser, Pearson, Staiger and Studlar, as well as chapters in Bowser's historical survey of American cinema between 1907 and 1915. These studies are concerned with the similarities and differences between theatrical acting and staging and their filmic equivalents, the emergence of film acting as a new profession and the rise of the star phenomenon in the cinema, the criteria developed for 'good' film acting in the 1910s, as well as the close textual analysis of a wide range of film performances. While most of this work deals with the United States, in-depth studies of other national cinemas also include sections on acting, for example Abel's book on early French cinema and Tsivian's work on Russian cinema of the 1910s. And while most of the work on acting in the cinema in the early decades of this century is concerned with dramatic performance, studies by Jenkins and Raider as well as the edited collection by Karnick and Jenkins outline the impact of musical and comic performance in the theatre on film acting. The vast literature on stage and film comedy and musicals, which is not included in the bibliography, is potentially quite relevant for developing an understanding of forms of performance which are not primarily aimed at the embodiment of fictional characters. Studies of the film performances and critical reception of Charles Chaplin by, for example, Kamin and Maland as well as Studlar's essay on Douglas Fairbanks, indicate the directions which such research may take.

The preceding chapters have suggested that, from the 1920s onwards, the single most important and consistent influence on American film acting was the ideas and practices of Constantin Stanislavsky. The bibliography includes some of the English translations of his writings and also studies of his influence in America by Blum, Carnicke, Munk, and Senelick. The particular adaptation of Stanislavsky's ideas by the Actors Studio and, more specifically, in the work and writings of Lee Strasberg and Elia Kazan (some of which are included in the bibliography) is the subject of studies by, for example, Braudy, Garfield, Hethmon, Hirsch, Vineberg, and Wexman. Between them, these studies deal with the organization and operations of the Actors Studio, the sets of ideas and exercises which made up its 'Method', the resulting stage and film performances and the cultural context within which the Method was developed and practised. This work is complemented by a vast amount of writing on some of the key performers associated with the Method, especially Marlon Brando and James Dean; however, these publications have not been included in the bibliography.

Compared with the attention Method acting has received in academic circles, the studio era of the 1930s and 1940s is definitely an underdeveloped field of research. Yet there are a few books, for example by Affron, Hirsch, and Patrick, which examine the film performances of a wide range of actors from across this century, including the studio era. There are also studies of the star system by Kindem and Walker, and of individual actors by, for example, Gaines, Garton, Gerlach, McGilligan, McKerrow, Rollyson, and Vaughn. While these studies tend to examine actors' star images as much as, or even more than, their acting and career management, they make contributions to our understanding of how actors practised their craft.

Going outside the field of academic publishing, we can find two types of books which, as several of the preceding chapters have demonstrated, are very useful sources for the study of the work of film actors. On the one hand, there are numerous acting manuals aiming to teach aspiring actors about their chosen profession, outlining basic ideas about the nature of acting and offering concrete advice on how to do it. On the other hand, star and director biographies and autobiographies, which undoubtedly are the single most popular genre of film-related writing, also provide insights into actors' work, although acting is rarely discussed explicitly in these publications. A more direct engagement with the ideas and practices of actors is provided by collections of texts written by, and of interviews conducted with, performers. The list of collections includes those edited by Cardullo *et al.*, Cole and Chinoy, Funke and Booth, Kalter, Matthews, Sonenberg, Stevens, Tomlinson, Vilga, and Zucker. While the focus of most of these collections is on recent decades, some of them range across the nineteenth and twentieth centuries, and in particular they provide a lot of material for a reconsideration of the studio era.

To situate actors' statements about their work during the studio era, it is useful to look at the comprehensive studies of the studio system by Bordwell, Staiger and Thompson, and by Schatz. While not considering acting in great detail, these studies outline the professional roles and hierarchies shaping the work of all studio employees including actors, and the norms, rules, and procedures underpinning their work, in particular the crucial roles of the script and the producer. A more focused examination of the working conditions for actors as well as their contractual relations with production companies from the 1930s to the 1950s is provided by studies on particular actors by Hagopian, Schatz, Sklar and the chapter on star contracts in Gaines's book. The vast literature on the Academy Awards, which has not been included in the bibliography, offers insights into other important aspects of an actor's professional life, especially the mechanisms for critical evaluation and peer approval. A further important strand of research into the operations of the film industry, are studies of Hollywood unions and labour relations (with specific references to blacklisting procedures) by Clark, May, Nelson, Nielsen and Mailes, and Prindle. A parallel study of unions in radio and television is offered by Harvey.

By considering Hollywood's workforce as a whole, the close relationship between acting and other professions comes into focus. The study by Bruzzi as well as that of Gaines and Herzog on costumes and costume designers are a case in point. For the contemporary period, there are several studies, for example by Cohen, Curry, Gamson, Hines and Vaughan, Prindle, Seger and Whetmore, and Stone, which deal with the activities of actors' agents, managers, and publicists as well as the role of casting directors and film directors. Furthermore, in parts of his book, Goldman presents the scriptwriter's perspective on contemporary actors, while in-depth studies of individual films by Bach, Salamon, and Sayles explore the complex involvement of actors in contemporary film production, ranging from casting and deal making right through to the marketing of the finished product.

While they are less fully developed than the work on Hollywood, studies by Crisp, Gundle, Macnab, Mitchell, and Street provide a useful starting point for the investigation of the position of actors within the production systems of the French, Italian, and British film industries, and they also discuss the work of individual stars in detail. In addition, Vincendeau has published a series of case studies on the careers and star images of various French actors, which are complemented by Rosen's essay on Isabelle Adjani. For a consideration of acting arising from a very different cultural tradition, the essays by Mishra *et al.* and Rai on Indian cinema are useful reference points.

As the above comments and the majority of chapters in this book make clear, a lot of the work on acting focuses on the most privileged group within the acting profession, namely the stars. This makes it particularly important to take note of studies such as the ones by Twamey, Loukides and Fuller, dealing with the work of supporting actors, and those by Base and Burkhart and Stuart, which examine the casting decisions that became turning points in the careers of actors. Furthermore, there are statistical analyses of the employment situation for actors, as well as psychological and sociological profiles of various groups within the profession, ranging from aspiring actors and drama students to stars, by Cantor and Peters, Golden, Jarvie, Levy, Peters and Cantor, and Taft. These diverse studies examine the totality of the acting profession with respect, for example, to the motivations and ambitions as well as the social background of its members.

Some of these studies address the ways in which an actor's gender, ethnicity, and nationality may influence their work. Novak extends these concerns into the contemporary period by outlining the huge differences in the opportunities and salaries for men and women, while Segrave and Martin provide an encyclopaedic survey of the careers of American and European actresses in the post-war period. The susceptibility of female Hollywood stars to scandal is examined in an essay by McLean, who, in another essay, also deals with the suppression of ethnicity in the image of Rita Hayworth.

The situation of African-American performers is discussed by Cripps, Leff, Manchel, and Regester, in terms both of working conditions and of the kinds of roles that were available to African-Americans. The stereotypes with which these actors were confronted can be traced back to nineteenth-century blackface performance, as examined by Bean *et al.* Similarly, Kirihara explores the relationship between existing stereotypes of Asians and the performances of Sessue Hayakawa in the silent period. The role of 'camp' performances, or of 'camp' readings of performances, is the subject of studies by Robertson, Shingler, and White. Such studies are important for the future integration of the primarily 'practical' concerns of our book (emphasizing actors' concrete objectives and skills) with the critical issues (to do with power relations and representation) at the centre of recent cultural theory. Similarly, work by Butler on television acting and by Ruby on performance in documentary, as well as Higson's essay on acting in independent cinema (in particular the influence of Brechtian ideas), all combine an interest in what actors do with the critical concerns of media theory.

There is also a considerable theoretical literature on stardom and on performance. This literature operates at a high level of generality and abstraction, exploring the very nature of stardom and performance and offering typologies of the various forms that stardom and performance may take. Some of this literature is primarily concerned with investigating the complex meanings of key terms and concepts used in more empirically oriented studies. Other texts seek to offer a coherent explanation for the emergence and function of stardom in modern societies, and also for the role of performance in textual systems. In doing so, they often go well beyond the confines of cinema, addressing the phenomena of celebrity and performance in a range of media. Such theoretical concerns characterize the work of, for example, Alberoni, Jeffrey A. Brown, Cawelti, Dyer, King, Morin, Quinn, Roach, Grahame F. Thompson, John O. Thompson, and Weiss.

Theoretical work of this kind is complemented by studies based on extensive empirical research, for example by Braudy, Fowles, Gamson, Goertzel *et al.*, Marshall, Rein *et al.* and Schickel, into the biographies, personalities, career trajectories, performances, and public images of large samples of celebrities of one kind or another (both within the sphere of entertainment and in other spheres of public life). The most wide-ranging and complex of these studies of public personalities in modern societies is the one by Sennett. If such work seems far removed from the immediate concerns of our book, it is nevertheless connected to them because, as Sennett shows, by practising their craft, actors have historically fulfilled an important function for their audiences, serving as models and guides for new forms of behaviour and new ways of being. At the same time, it is undoubtedly the case that, in academia and in society at large, the acting profession has attracted so much attention precisely because some of its members have become celebrities, and not because of a widespread interest in the craft of acting itself. There are good reasons, then, for linking the study of acting to the study of celebrity.

BIBLIOGRAPHY

Abel, Richard, *The Ciné Goes to Town: French Cinema, 1896–1914*, Berkeley, University of California Press, 1998 (revised edition).

Affron, Charles, *Star Acting: Gish, Garbo, Davies*, New York, Dutton, 1977.

Alberoni, Francesco, 'The Powerless "Elite": Theory and Sociological Research on the Phenomenon of the Stars', *Sociology of Mass Communications*, ed. Denis McQuail, London, Penguin, 1972.

Arnheim, Rudolf, *Film as Art*, Berkeley, University of California Press, 1957.

Auster, Albert, *Actresses and Suffragists: Women in the American Theatre, 1890–1990*, New York, Praeger, 1984.

Bach, Steven, *Final Cut: Dreams and Disaster in the Making of Heaven's Gate*, London, Faber & Faber, 1986.

Balazs, Bela, *Theory of the Film*, New York, Dover, 1970.

Barker, Clive, 'What Training – for What Theatre?', *New Theatre Quarterly*, May 1995, vol. 11, no. 42.

Base, Ron, *Starring Roles: How Movie Stardom Is Won and Lost*, London, Little Brown, 1994.

Bean, Annemarie, Hatch, James V., and McNamara, Brooks (eds) *Inside the Minstrel Mask: Readings in Nineteenth-Century Blackface Minstrelsy*, Hanover, Wesleyan University Press, 1996.

Bisplinghoff, Gretchen, 'On Acting: A Selected Bibliography', *Cinema Journal*, 1980, vol. 20, no. 1.

Blum, Richard, 'The Method: From Stanislavsky to Hollywood – The Transition of Acting Theory in America from Stage to Screen (1900–1976)', PhD thesis, University of Southern California, 1976.

Blum, Richard A., *Working Actors: The Craft of Television, Film and Stage Performance*, Boston, Focal Press, 1989.

Bordwell, David, Staiger, Janet, and Thompson, Kristin, *The Classical Hollywood Cinema: Film Style and Mode of Production to 1960*, London, Routledge & Kegan Paul, 1985.

Bowser, Eileen, *The Transformation of Cinema, 1907–1915*, New York, Scribner, 1990.

Boynton, Sandy, 'The History of American Acting: A Detour', *Yale Theatre*, 1977, vol. 8, no. 2–3.

Braudy, Leo, 'Film Acting: Some Critical Problems and Proposals', *Quarterly Review of Film Studies*, February 1976, vol. 1, no. 1.

Braudy, Leo, '"No Body's Perfect": Method Acting and 50s Culture', *Michigan Quarterly Review*, Winter 1996, vol. 35, no. 1.

Braudy, Leo, *The Frenzy of Renown: Fame and Its History*, New York, Oxford University Press, 1997 (2nd edn).

Brewster, Ben, and Jacobs, Lea, *Theatre to Cinema: Stage Pictorialism and the Early Feature Film*, Oxford, Oxford University Press, 1997.

Brouwer, Alexandra, and Wright, Thomas, *Working in Hollywood*, New York, Avon, 1990.

Brown, Jeffrey A., '"They Can Imagine Anything They Want . . . ": Identification, Desire and the Celebrity Text', *Discourse*, 1997, vol. 19, no. 3.

Brown, John Russell, 'Performance, Theatre Training, and Research', *New Theatre Quarterly*, August 1996, vol. 12, no. 47.

Bruzzi, Stella, *Undressing Cinema: Clothing and Identity in the Movies*, London, Routledge, 1997.

Burge, James C., *Lines of Business: Casting Practice and Policy in the American Theatre, 1752–1899*, New York, Peter Lang, 1986.

Burkhart, Jeff and Stuart, Bruce, *Hollywood's First Choice: How the Greatest Casting Decisions Were Made*, New York, Crown, 1994.

Butler, Jeremy G., '"I'm not a doctor, but I play one on TV": Characters, Actors and Acting in Television Soap Opera', *Cinema Journal*, Summer 1991, vol. 30.

Butler, Jeremy G. (ed.) *Star Texts: Image and Performance in Film and Television*, Detroit, Wayne State University Press, 1991.

Cantor, Muriel G., and Peters, Anne K., 'The Employment and Unemployment of Screen Actors in the United States', *Economic Policy for the Arts*, ed. William S. Hendon, James C. Shanahan, and Alice J. MacDonald, Cambridge, MA, Abt Books, 1980.

Cardullo, Bert, Geduld, Harry, Gottesman, Ronald, and Woods, Leigh (eds) *Playing to the Camera: Film Actors Discuss Their Craft*, New Haven, Yale University Press, 1998.

Carnicke, Sharon M., *Stanislavsky in Focus*, London, Harwood Academic Press, 1998.

Cawelti, John G., 'Performance and Popular Culture', *Cinema Journal*, Fall 1980, vol. 20, no. 1.

Chenoweth, Stuart, 'A Study of the Adaptation of Acting Technique from Stage to Film, Radio and Television in the United States 1900–1951', PhD thesis, Northwestern University, 1957.

Cima, Gay Gibson, *Performing Women: Female Characters, Male Playwrights and the Modern Stage*, Ithaca, Cornell University Press, 1994.

Ciment, Michel (ed.) *Kazan on Kazan*, New York, Viking, 1974.

Clark, Danae, 'Acting in Hollywood's Best Interest: Representations of Actors' Labor during the National Recovery Administration', *Journal of Film and Video*, Winter 1990, vol. 42, no. 4.

Clark, Danae, *Negotiating Hollywood: The Cultural Politics of Actors' Labor*, Minneapolis, University of Minnesota Press, 1995.

Cohen, Robert, *Acting Professionally: Raw Facts about Careers in Acting*, New York, Harper & Row, 1983 (3rd edn).

Cole, Toby, and Chinoy, Helen Krich (eds) *Actors on Acting*, New York, Crown, 1970.

Cripps, Thomas, *Slow Fade to Black: The Negro in American Film, 1900–1942*, New York, Oxford University Press, 1977.

Cripps, Thomas, *Making Movies Black: The Hollywood Message Movie from World War II to the Civil Rights Era*, New York, Oxford University Press, 1993.

Crisp, Colin, *The Classic French Cinema, 1930–1960*, Bloomington, Indiana University Press, 1993.

Curry, Renee R., 'To Star Is to Mean: The Casting of John Waters' *Hairspray*', *Cultural Power/Cultural Literacy*, ed. Bonnie Braendlin, Tallahassee, Florida State University Press, 1991.

Davis, Tracy C., *Actresses as Working Women: Their Social Identity in Victorian Culture*, London, Routledge, 1991.

deCordova, Richard, *Picture Personalities: The Emergence of the Star System in America*, Urbana, University of Illinois Press, 1990.

Downer, Alan S., 'Nature to Advantage Dressed: Eighteenth Century Acting", *PMLA*, 1943, vol. 58.

Downer, Alan S., 'Players and Painted Stage: Nineteenth Century Acting', *PMLA*, June 1946, vol. 61.

Downer, Alan S., 'Early American Professional Acting', *Theatre Survey*, November 1971, no. 12.

Dudden, Faye E., *Women in the American Theatre: Actresses and Audiences, 1790–1870*, New Haven, Yale University Press, 1994.

Dunagan, Clyde Kelly, 'A Methodology of Film Acting Analysis and an Application to the Performance of Clint Eastwood', PhD thesis, Northwestern University, 1985.

Dyer, Richard, *Stars*, London, British Film Institute, 1997 (2nd edn).

Dyer, Richard, *Heavenly Bodies: Film Stars and Society*, London, Macmillan/BFI, 1987.

Eisenstein, Sergei, *Film Form/The Film Sense*, New York, Meridian, 1957.

Fischer-Lichte, Erika, 'Theatre and the Civilizing Process: An Approach to the History of Acting', *Interpreting the Theatrical Past: Essays in the Historiography of Performance*, ed. Bruce McConachie and Thomas Postlewait, Iowa City, University of Iowa Press, 1989.

Fowles, Jib, *Starstruck: Celebrity Performers and the American Public*, Washington DC, Smithsonian Institution Press, 1992.

Funke, Lewis, and Booth, John E. (eds) *Actors Talk about Acting*, New York, Random House, 1961.

Gaines, Jane M., 'The Popular Icon as Commodity and Sign: The Circulation of Betty Grable, 1941–45', PhD thesis, Northwestern University, 1982.

Gaines, Jane M., *Contested Culture: The Image, the Voice, and the Law*, London, British Film Institute, 1992.

Gaines, Jane M., and Herzog, Charlotte (eds) *Fabrications: Costume and the Female Body*, New York, Routledge, 1990.

Gamson, Joshua, *Claims to Fame: Celebrity in Contemporary America*, Berkeley, University of California Press, 1994.

Garfield, David, *A Player's Place: The Story of the Actors Studio*, New York, Macmillan, 1980.

Garton, Joseph, 'The Film Acting of John Barrymore', PhD thesis, New York University, 1978.

Gerlach, Michael, 'The Acting of Paul Muni', PhD thesis, University of Michigan, 1971.

Gilman, Richard, 'The Actor as Celebrity', *Humanities in Review*, 1982, no. 1.

Gledhill, Christine (ed.) *Stardom: Industry of Desire*, London, Routledge, 1991.

Goertzel, Mildred George, Goertzel, Victor, and Goertzel, Ted George, *Three Hundred Eminent Personalities: A Psychosocial Analysis of the Famous*, San Francisco, Jossey-Bass, 1978.

Golden, Alfred C., 'Personality Traits of Drama School Students', *Quarterly Journal of Speech*, 1940, vol. 26.

Goldman, William, *Adventures in the Screentrade: A Personal View of Hollywood and Screenwriting*, London, Macdonald, 1984.

Graham, Cooper C., 'Unmasking Feelings: The Portrayal of Emotions in the Biograph Studio Films of 1908–1910', *Library of Congress Performing Arts Annual 1988*, ed. Iris Newsome, Washington, Library of Congress, 1989.

Gundle, Stephen, 'Sophia Loren, Italian Icon', *Historical Journal of Film, Radio and Television*, 1995, vol. 15, no. 3.

Gundle, Stephen, 'Fame, Fashion and Style: The Italian Star System', *Introduction to Italian Cultural Studies*, ed. David Forgacs and Robert Lumley, Oxford, Oxford University Press, 1996.

Hagopian, Kevin, 'Declarations of Independence: A History of Cagney Productions', *The Velvet Light Trap*, 1986, no. 22.

Hanrers, John, *'It Was Play or Starve': Acting in the Nineteenth Century American Popular Theatre*, Bowling Green, Bowling Green State University Popular Press, 1993.

Harvey, Rita Morley, *Those Wonderful, Terrible Years: George Heller and the American Federation of Television and Radio Artists*, Carbondale, South Illinois University Press, 1996.

Hethmon, Robert H. (ed.) *Strasberg at the Actors Studio*, New York, Theatre Communications Group, 1991.

Higson, Andrew, 'Film Acting and Independent Cinema', *Screen*, May–August 1986, vol. 27, no. 3–4.

Hines, Terrance, and Vaughan, Suzanne, *An Actor Succeeds: Career Management for the Actor*, Hollywood, Samuel French, 1990.

Hirsch, Foster, *A Method to Their Madness: The History of the Actors Studio*, London, DaCapo, 1986.

Hirsch, Foster, *Acting Hollywood Style*, New York, Harry N. Adams, 1991.

Jarvie, Ian C., 'Stars and Ethnicity: Hollywood and the United States, 1932–51', *Unspeakable Images: Ethnicity and the American Cinema*, ed. Lester D. Friedman, Champagne, University of Illinois Press, 1990.

Jenkins, Henry, *What Made Pistachio Nuts? Early Sound Comedy and the Vaudeville Aesthetic*, New York, Columbia University Press, 1992.

Johnson, Claudia D., *American Actress: Perspectives on the Nineteenth Century*, Nelson Hall, 1984.

Kalter, Joanmarie, *Actors on Acting: Performing in Theatre and Film Today*, New York, Sterling, 1979.

Kamin, Dan, *Charlie Chaplin's One-Man Show*, Metuchen, Scarecrow, 1984.

Karnick, Kristine Brunovska, and Jenkins, Henry (eds) *Classical Hollywood Comedy*, New York, Routledge, 1995.

Kaufman, J.B., 'Fascinating Youth: The Story of the Paramount Pictures School', *Film History*, 1990, vol. 4.

Kerr, Catherine E., 'Incorporating the Star: The Intersection of Business and Aesthetic Strategies in Early American Film', *Business History Review*, Autumn 1990, vol. 64.

Kindem, Gorham, 'Hollywood's Movie Star System during the Studio Era', *Film Reader*, 1985.

King, Barry, 'The Hollywood Star System', PhD thesis, University of London, 1984.

King, Barry, 'Articulating Stardom', *Screen*, September–October 1985, vol. 26, no. 5.

King, Barry, 'Screen Acting – Reflections on the Day', *Screen*, May–August 1986, vol. 27, no. 3–4.

King, Barry, 'Stardom as an Occupation', *The Hollywood Film Industry: A Reader*, ed. Paul Kerr, London, Routledge, 1986.

King, Barry, 'The Star and the Commodity: Notes towards a Performance Theory of Stardom', *Cultural Studies*, 1987, vol. 1 no. 2.

Kirihara, Donald, 'The Accepted Idea Displaced: Stereotype and Sessue Hayakawa', *The Birth of Whiteness: Race and the Emergence of U.S. Cinema*, ed. Daniel Bernardi, New Brunswick, Rutgers University Press, 1997.

Kohansky, Mendel, *The Disreputable Profession: The Actor in Society*, Westport, Conn, Greenwood, 1984.

Kuleshov, Lev, *Kuleshov on Film*, ed. Ron Levaco, Berkeley, University of California Press, 1974.

Leff, Leonard J., 'The Search for Hattie McDaniel', *New Orleans Review*, 1983, vol. 10, no. 2–3.

Levy, Emanuel, 'The Choice of Acting as a Profession', *The Sociology of Art*, ed. J. Blau and A. Foster, New York, Cap and Gown, 1984.

Levy, Emanuel, 'The Democratic Elite: America's Movie Stars', *Qualitative Sociology*, Spring 1989, vol. 12, no. 1.

Levy, Emanuel, 'Social Attributes of American Movie Stardom', *Media, Culture and Society*, April 1990, vol. 12, no. 2.

Loukides, Paul, and Fuller, Linda K. (eds), *Beyond the Stars: Stock Characters in American Popular Film*, Bowling Green, Bowling Green University Popular Press, 1990.

McArthur, Benjamin, *Actors and American Culture, 1880–1920*, Philadelphia, Temple University Press, 1984.

McGilligan, Patrick, *Cagney: The Actor as Auteur*, San Diego, Barnes, 1982 (rev. edn).

McKerrow, Margaret, 'A Descriptive Study of the Acting of Alla Nazimova', PhD thesis, University of Michigan, 1974.

McLean, Adrienne L., '"I'm a Cansino": Transformation, Ethnicity and Authenticity in the Construction of Rita Hayworth, American Love Goddess', *Journal of Film and Video*, 1992/93, vol. 44, no. 3–4.

McLean, Adrienne L., 'The Cinderella Princess and the Instrument of Evil: Surveying the Limits of Female Transgression in Two Postwar Hollywood Scandals', *Cinema Journal*, Spring 1995, vol. 34, no. 3.

Macnab, Geoffrey, *J. Arthur Rank and the British Film Industry*, London, Routledge, 1993.

McTeague, James, *Before Stanislavsky: American Professional Acting Schools and Acting Theory, 1875–1925*, Metuchen, Scarecrow, 1993.

Maland, Charles J., *Chaplin and American Culture: The Evolution of a Star Image*, Princeton, Princeton University Press, 1989.

Manchel, Frank, 'The Man Who Made the Stars Shine Brighter: An Interview with Woody Strode', *Black Scholar*, Spring 1995, vol. 25, no. 2.

Marshall, P. David, *Celebrity and Power: Fame and Contemporary Culture*, Minneapolis, University of Minnesota Press, 1997.

Matthews, Brander (ed.) *Papers on Acting*, New York, Hill & Wang, 1958.

May, Lary, 'Movie Star Politics: The Screen Actors' Guild, Cultural Conversion and the Hollywood Red Scare', *Recasting America: Culture and Politics in the Age of Cold War*, ed. Lary May, Chicago, University of Chicago Press, 1989.

Mishra, Vijay, Jeffery, Peter, and Shoesmith, Brian, 'The Actor as Parallel Text in Bombay Cinema', *Quarterly Review of Film and Video*, October 1989, vol. 11.

Mitchell, Tony, 'The Construction and Reception of Anna Magnani in Italy and the English-Speaking World, 1945–1988', *Film Criticism*, Fall 1989, vol. 14, no. 1.

Morin, Edgar, *The Stars*, New York, Grove, 1960.

Munk, Erika (ed.) *Stanislavski and America*, New York, Hill & Wang, 1966.

Musser, Charles, 'The Changing Status of the Actor', *Before Hollywood: Turn-of-the-Century American Film*, ed. John L. Fell, New York, Hudson Hills, 1987.

Naremore, James, *Acting in the Cinema*, Berkeley, University of California Press, 1988.

Nelson, Michael, 'Towards a Worker's History of the U.S. Film Industry', *The Critical Communications Review. Volume I: Labor, the Working Class and the Media*, ed. Vincent Mosco and Janet Wasko, Norwood, Ablex, 1983.

Nielsen, Mike and Gene Mailes, *Hollywood's Other Blacklist: Union Struggles in the Studio System*, London, British Film Institute, 1995.

Novak, Deborah, 'What Every Actress Knows', *Women and Performance*, 1993, vol. 6, no. 2.

Patrick, Dennis, 'Male Spectatorship and Hollywood Star Acting', PhD thesis, Ohio State University, 1990.

Pearson, Roberta, *Eloquent Gestures: The Transformation of Performance Style in the Griffith Biograph Films*, Berkeley, University of California Press, 1992.

Peters, Anne K., 'Aspiring Hollywood Actresses: A Sociological Perspective', *Varieties of Work Experience*, ed. Phyllis L. Steward and Muriel G. Cantor, New York, Wiley, 1974.

Peters, Anne K., and Cantor, Muriel G., 'Screen Acting as Work', *Individuals in Media Organizations: Creativity and Constraint*, ed. J. Ettema and C. Whitney, Beverly Hills, Sage, 1982.

Prindle, David F., *The Politics of Glamour: Ideology and Democracy in the Screen Actors' Guild*, Madison, University of Wisconsin Press, 1988.

Prindle, David F., *Risky Business: The Political Economy of Hollywood*, Boulder, Col., Westview Press, 1993.

Pudovkin, V.I., *Film Technique and Film Acting*, New York, Grove, 1970.

Quinn, Michael L., 'Celebrity and the Semiotics of Acting', *New Theatre Quarterly*, May 1990, vol. 6, no. 22.

Rai, Amit, 'An American Raj in Filmistan: Images of Elvis in Indian Films', *Screen*, Spring 1994, vol. 35, no. 1.

Raider, Roberta Ann, 'A Descriptive Study of the Acting of Marie Dressler', PhD thesis, University of Michigan, 1970.

Regester, Charlene, 'African-American Extras in Hollywood during the 1920s and 1930s', *Film History*, 1997, vol. 9, no. 1.

Rein, Irving J., Kotler, Philip, and Stoller, Martin R., *High Visibility*, New York, Dodd Mead, 1987.

Roach, Joseph, *The Player's Passion: Studies in the Science of Acting*, Newark, University of Delaware Press, 1985.

Robertson, Pamela, *Guilty Pleasures: Feminist Camp from Mae West to Madonna*, Durham, Duke University Press, 1996.

Rollyson, Carl E. Jr, *Marilyn Monroe: A Life of the Actress*, London, DaCapo, 1993.

Rosen, Miriam, 'Isabelle Adjani: The Actress as Political Activist', *Cineaste*, 1990, vol. 17, no. 4.

Ruby, Jay, 'The Ethics of Imagemaking: Or "They're Going to Put Me in the Movies. They're Going to Make a Big Star Out of Me"', *New Challenges for Documentary*, ed. Alan Rosenthal, Berkeley, University of California Press, 1988.

Salamon, Julie, *The Devil's Candy: The Bonfire of the Vanities Goes to Hollywood*, London, Picador, 1993.

Sayles, John, *Thinking in Pictures: The Making of the Movie Matewan*, Boston, Houghton Mifflin, 1987.

Schatz, Thomas, '"A Triumph of Bitchery": Warner Bros, Bette Davis and *Jezebel*', *Wide Angle*, 1988, vol. 10, no. 1.

Schatz, Thomas, *The Genius of the System: Hollywood Filmmaking in the Studio Era*, New York, Pantheon, 1989.

Schechner, Richard, 'Transforming Theatre Departments', *The Drama Review*, Summer 1995, vol. 39, no. 2.

Schickel, Richard, *Common Fame: The Culture of Celebrity*, London, Pavilion Books, 1985.

Seger, L., and Whetmore, E.J., *From Script to Screen*, New York, Owl Books, 1994.

Segrave, Kerry, and Martin, Linda, *Postfeminist Hollywood Actress: Biographies and Filmographies of Stars Born after 1939*, Jefferson, McFarland, 1990.

Segrave, Kerry, and Martin, Linda, *The Continental Actress: European Film Stars of the Postwar Era*, Jefferson, McFarland, 1991.

Senelick, Laurence (ed.) *Wandering Stars: Papers on Russian Emigré Theatre from 1900–1940*, Iowa City, University of Iowa Press, 1992.

Sennett, Richard, *The Fall of Public Man*, New York, Knopf, 1977.

Shingler, Martin, 'Masquerade or Drag? Bette Davis and the Ambiguities of Gender', *Screen*, Autumn 1995, vol. 36, no. 3.

Sklar, Robert S., *City Boys: Cagney, Bogart and Garfield*, Princeton, Princeton University Press, 1992.

Sonenberg, Janet, *The Actor Speaks*, New York, Crown, 1995.

Staiger, Janet, 'The Eyes Are Really the Focus: Photoplay Acting and Film Form and Style', *Wide Angle*, 1985, vol. 6, no. 4.

Staiger, Janet, 'Seeing Stars', *The Velvet Light Trap*, Summer 1983, no. 20.

Stanislavsky, Constantin, *An Actor Prepares*, New York, Theatre Arts Books, 1939.

Stanislavsky, Constantin, *Building a Character*, London, Reinhardt & Evans, 1950.

Stanislavsky, Constantin, *Stanislavsky on the Art of the Stage*, London, Faber & Faber, 1950.

Stanislavsky, Constantin, *Creating a Role*, London, Geoffrey Bles, 1963.

Stanislavsky, Constantin, *An Actor's Handbook*, London, Methuen Drama, 1990.

Stevens, Jon (ed.) *Actors Turned Directors*, Los Angeles, Silman-James, 1997.

Stone, Whitney, *Stars and Star Handlers: The Business of Show*, Santa Monica, Roundtable, 1985.

Strasberg, Lee, *A Dream of Passion: The Development of the Method*, Boston, Little Brown, 1987.

Street, Sarah, *British National Cinema*, London, Routledge, 1997.

Studlar, Gaylyn, 'Douglas Fairbanks: Thief of the Ballets Russes', *Bodies of the Text: Dance as Theory, Literature as Dance*, ed. Ellen W. Goellner and Jacqueline Shea Murphy, New Brunswick, Rutgers University Press, 1995.

Studlar, Gaylyn, *This Mad Masquerade: Stardom and Masculinity in the Jazz Age*, New York, Columbia University Press, 1996.

Taft, Ronald, 'A Psychological Assessment of Professional Actors and Related Professions', *Genetic Psychology Monographs*, 1961, vol. 64.

Taylor, George, *Players and Performances in the Victorian Theatre*, Manchester, Manchester University Press, 1989.

Thompson, Grahame F., 'Approaches to "Performance": An Analysis of Terms', *Screen*, September–October 1985, vol. 26, no. 5.

Thompson, John O., 'Screen Acting and the Commutation Test', *Screen*, Summer 1978, vol. 19, no. 2.

Thompson, John O., 'Beyond Commutation: A Reconsideration of Screen Acting', *Screen*, September–October 1985, vol. 26, no. 5.

Tomlinson, Doug (ed.) *Actors on Acting for the Screen: Roles and Collaborations*, New York, Garland, 1994.

Tsivian, Yuri, 'Early Russian Cinema: Some Observations', *Inside the Film Factory: New Approaches to Russian and Soviet Cinema*, ed. Richard Taylor and Ian Christie, London, Routledge, 1991.

Twamey, Alfred E., *The Versatiles: A Study of Supporting Character Actors and Actresses in the American Motion Picture, 1930–1955*, South Brunswick, A.S. Barnes, 1969.

Vaughn, Steven, *Ronald Reagan in Hollywood: Movies and Politics*, Cambridge, Cambridge University Press, 1994.

Vilga, Edward, *Acting Now: Conversations on Craft and Career*, New Brunswick, Rutgers University Press, 1997.

Vincendeau, Ginette, 'Community, Nostalgia and the Spectacle of Masculinity', *Screen*, November–December 1985, vol. 26, no. 6.

Vincendeau, Ginette, 'The Old and the New: Brigitte Bardot in 1950s France', *Paragraph*, March 1992, vol. 15, no. 1.

Vincendeau, Ginette, 'Gérard Depardieu: The Axiom of Contemporary French Cinema', *Screen*, Winter 1993, vol. 34, no. 4.

Vineberg, Steve, *Method Actors: Three Generations of an American Acting Style*, New York, Macmillan, 1991.

Walker, Alexander, *Stardom: The Hollywood Phenomenon*, London, Michael Joseph, 1970.

Weiss, Allen S., 'Acting, Identity and Scenarisation', *Art & Text*, Spring 1989, no. 34.

Wexman, Virginia Wright, *Creating the Couple: Love, Marriage and Hollywood Performance*, Princeton, Princeton University Press, 1993.

White, Patricia, 'Supporting Character: The Queer Career of Agnes Moorehead', *Out in Culture: Gay, Lesbian and Queer Essays on Popular Culture*, ed. Corey K. Creekmur and Alexander Doty, Durham, Duke University Press, 1995.

Willett, John (ed.) *Brecht on Theatre*, New York, Hill & Wang, 1976.

Wilson, Garf B., *A History of American Acting*, Bloomington, Indiana University Press, 1966.

Yampolsky, Mikhail, 'Kuleshov's Experiments and the New Anthropology of the Actor', *Inside the Film Factory: New Approaches to Russian and Soviet Cinema*, ed. Richard Taylor and Ian Christie, London, Routledge, 1991.

Young, William C., *Famous Actors and Actresses of the American Stage: Documents of American Theatre History*, New York, R.R. Bowker, 1975.

Zucker, Carole (ed.), *Making Visible the Invisible: An Anthology of Original Essays on Film Acting*, Metuchen, Scarecrow, 1990.

Zucker, Carole, *Figures of Light: Actors and Directors Illuminate the Art of Film Acting*, New York, Plenum, 1995.

Journals

Special issues of journals on film stars and/or film acting:

Cinema Journal, Fall 1980, vol. 20, no. 1.

Journal of Film and Video, Winter 1990, vol. 42, no. 4.

Postscript, Winter 1993.

Screen, September–October 1986, vol. 26, no. 5.

The Velvet Light Trap, Winter 1972/73, no. 7.

Wide Angle, 1984, vol. 6, no. 4.

INDEX

Academy Awards 47, 56, 59, 104;
    literature on 168
accents 100, 128
acting 24, 115; *see also* Method acting;
    screen acting; stage acting
acting manuals 27n, 35, 167
acting styles 31–2
action 80, 84, 114
actor 2; Stanislavsky and 80–1, 82;
    literature on 169
Actors' Laboratory 34, 40
Actors Studio 75, 77, 78, 79–80, 82,
    84
actress 3; feminism and 7
ADR (Automatic Dialog Replacement)
    136n
affective memory 83, 84
African-American actors, literature on
    169
Age of Reason, acting in 13
Albertson, Lillian 34, 35, 40, 41–2,
    42–3
All About Eve, Davis in 56
American Academy of Dramatic Art
    34
American acting 14; compared to
    British 16, 152–3, 162–4
Andrews, Dana 7
appearance *see* physical appearance
art nouveau 22
Arvidson, L. 28n, 29n
L'Assommoir (Zola) 15
Atlantic City, Sarandon in 89, 95–8
attitudes to acting 93–4
audience: distance from 77; size of actor

from point of view of 37; speaking
    directly to 161
auditions 139
auditory signifiers 66
authorship 2; *see also* director
awareness of other actors 114–15, 117

Bach, S. 8
Barr, Tony 78, 109
Barrymore, John 64
Bean, A. 169
behaviourism 153
Bigger than Life 71
Biograph Company 14, 15, 22, 23
biographies 168
Blake, Larry 133
Bleak Moments 138
Bouchier, Chili 20
Bouciault, Dion 16, 17
Brando, Marlon 155–6
Brecht, Bertolt 4
Bringing Up Baby 32
British acting, compared to American
    16, 152–3, 163–4
Broadway 33
Brook, Peter 156
Brown, Gilmor 34, 35
Bruzzi, S. 168
Bull Durham 131, 133; Sarandon in 91,
    98–101
Burns, Lillian 34, 37, 39, 40

Cabin in the Cotton, Davis in 48–9
Caine, Michael 78
camera 5, 113, 148–9, 162; altering

actor's work 76, 78; and close-ups 38, 77
'camp' performances, literature on 169
Carnovsky, Morris 40, 41, 42
case histories 141, 144, 156
casting 7, 8; Leigh and 139
character development 39–43, 108–9; Leigh and 140–50; Shaver and 107, 108–9
characterization 93, 98; of Norman Maine (*A Star is Born*) 62–4, 66–8; Richardson and 157–9, 163
Chekhov, Michael 107
choices 106, 122
close-ups 77–8, 103, 159
communion with other actors 114–15, 117
concentration 41–2, 153, 158
Cook, Ron, on Leigh 141–2, 142–3, 149
The Cook, the Thief, his Wife and her Lover 149
The Craft, Shaver in 107, 117, 119–21
creative freedom 108–9, 113
Cronyn, Hume 36, 37, 38–9, 39–40
crux scenica 13
Cukor, George 64, 68

dance 20–2, 49
Dangerous, Davis in 53–6
Darwin, Charles 14
Davies, Andrew 157, 158, 161
Davis, Bette 36, 37, 39, 46–57
Dead Man Walking, Sarandon in 102–4
Delsarte, François 11, 24n
dialogue 94, 98, 100–1, 103; and sound mixing 132, 133, 134
dialogue coaches 33, 34
Dillon, Josephine 35, 37, 38, 42
director 2, 8, 108; in Method acting 76–7, 78, 80; relationship with actors 162
Dmytryk, Edward 78
drama schools 33, 34; *see also* training for actors
Drink 15
Driving Miss Daisy 127–8

A Drunkard's Reformation 14–15, 16
A Dry White Season 91

editing 5, 76, 117
Ellis, John 71
emotions 42–3, 68, 84, 85–6, 114; in Method acting 153
Enlightenment actors 13
Enright, Florence 34
ensemble principle 144, 146, 156
expression: Davis and 49–50, 55; magnification of 37–8; range of 37; *see also* facial expression; gesture
extratextual factors in interpretation 69–72
eyes 101, 122, 159, 161; Davis' use of 50, 52, 55

facial expression 10, 14, 66, 67; in close-ups 77–8; Sarandon and 96, 103; *see also* eyes
Fatal Memories, Shaver in 107, 110, 114, 115
feminism 7, 106–7
film acting *see* screen acting
Film Studies 12
Fincher, David 127
focal depth 23
frame, voice in 113–14
framing 109–10
Freeman, Morgan 127–31
French film industry, literature on 169
The Fugitive 134–5
Fuller, Loïe 21–2

Garson, Greer 39
gesture 12, 13, 14, 66, 99, 104; dance and 21; music and 18–20; in silent film acting 11–12, 17–18, 22–3; Sarandon and 96, 97
Goldman, W. 168
Graham, Cooper C. 24n, 25n
Graham, Martha 49
Griffith, D. W. 16, 25n
Group Theatre 84
Guest, Ivor 20–1
Guinness, Alec 78, 159, 164

Guy, Alice 20

Hall, Peter 161
Hanlon-Lee acrobatic pantomime
   troupe 21
Hardwick, Cedric 76
Hicks, Seymour 14
High Hopes 138
Higham, Charles 49
Hirshenson, J. 8
'histrionic code' 11
Hoffman, Dustin 79, 130
Hollywood studio era: acting in 31–45;
   literature on 168
honesty 84, 162
Hopper, Hedda 70
Hornby, Richard 75
House of Cards 159–62
Howard, Leslie 50

ideology 4
imagination 42, 109
improvisation, Leigh and 139–50
interaction with other actors 129–30,
   144
internal dialogue 38
interpretation 40, 63–4; *see also*
   characterization
intertextuality 62, 65–8, 72
Irving, Henry 16

Jackson, Anne 79
January Man, The 91
Jenkins, J. 8
Jennings, Wade 72
jobbing actors 163
'Jocko' plays 21, 56n
Johnson, Arthur 14, 16
Jones, Tommy Lee 134–5

Kazan, Elia 79–80
key lines, identification of 130
Kirihara, D. 169
Knebel, Maria 81
Kuleshov, Lev 76, 85

Lambert, Gavin 50
language 153

Leaming, Barbara 49, 53
Leigh, Mike 3, 149–51; *Secrets and Lies*
   138–49
Life is Sweet 138
Light Sleeper 91
lighting 102
listening to other actors 93, 155
locations 147
logic 82–3, 84
Lorenzo's Oil, Sarandon in 92, 93, 94
Loughton, Phyllis 34

MacKaye, Steele 16, 17
McLean, A. L. 169
Malle, Louis 95
Mankiewicz, Joseph 56
Marat/Sade 156
March, Fredric 64–5; as Norman
   Maine (*A Star is Born*) 59, 60, 62,
   63, 66, 67, 68, 69–70; star image of
   69–70
Martin, L. 169
masking 134
Mason, James 65; as Norman Maine
   (*A Star is Born*) 59, 61, 62, 63–4,
   66, 67, 68, 71–2; star image of
   70–2
massaging the voice 137n
medium, actors' awareness of 127–31
melodrama 19, 25n
mental pictures 41–2, 43
Method acting 3, 16, 43; British actors
   and 153, 154, 155; literature on
   167; Strasberg and 75–6, 78–9,
   81–6
microphones 113, 132
Millward, Jessie 15
mime dramas 21
Mirren, Helen 153, 154
mise-en-scène 2
Modern Acting: A Manual (Rosenstein)
   35, 38, 42
moods 42
Motion Picture Patents Company 23
motivations of characters 64–5, 72, 81,
   140
movement 55–6, 99–100, 104,
   109–10; Davis and 49, 50, 55;

under restraint 55–6; Sarandon and 96, 97; *see also* gesture
Mulvey, Laura 3
music 17, 18–20

Naked 138
Naremore, James 73n, 75
naturalism 5, 12, 24, 26n, 31, 84–5, 85–6
Neville, Henry 16, 17, 22
New Drama 25n
A Night at the Opera 32
Novak, D. 169

Of Human Bondage, Davis in 47, 48, 49–50, 52, 53
Olivier, Laurence 78
Oscars *see* Academy Awards
Ouspenskaya, Maria 34, 35
overacting 53, 57
Ozu, Yasujiro 139

Page, Geraldine 83
Pasadena Playhouse 34, 35
Pearson, Roberta 5, 15, 25n
performance 5, 10, 62, 65–8; creating 31–45; styles of 32
physical appearance 6–7; Davis 52–3; and definition of character 101–2; Sarandon 94–5
physicalization 109–10
play, Stanislavsky and the 81
playing off other actors 129
Poltergeist 114
Pope, Dick, working with Leigh 148–9
post-production, impact on performance 133–5
Postlewaite, T. 26n
posture 66, 67
power 7–8
Prejean, Helen 102, 103
preparation 38–9, 154
Preston, Robert 76
Pretty Baby 89
private moments 83, 84
production, and transition to sound 32–5

production dialogue 132, 133
profession, acting as 7–8
Pudovkin, V. 84, 85

Quinn, Anthony 77

Ray, Satayjit 139
Reade, Charles 18
realism 11, 12, 22, 52, 164; Leigh and 150
recording, matching sound perspective 132–3
rehearsals: lack of 38, 39; Leigh and 140–1, 143, 144, 146, 149
remakes 5
Remick, Lee 77
Renoir, Jean 139
research: on screen acting 166–70; on stage acting 165–6
researchers, use of 141
Richardson, Ian 154–64
Richardson, Natasha 153
Richardson, Ralph 164
Rosenstein, Sophie 34, 35, 38, 42
Rushbrook, Claire, working with Leigh 143–4, 147, 149
Rydstrom, Gary 134

Salamon, J. 8
Sarandon, Susan 88, 133; career development 88–95; performances 95–104
Saving Private Ryan 134
School of Dramatic Art 34
scientific training 34
Scofield, Paul 164
Scott, Ridley 102
screen acting 76–7; compared to stage acting 32, 33, 35–9, 77–8, 153; research on 166–70
screen actors, stage experience for 33, 35, 36–7
scripts 39–40, 93–4; actors' relationship with 2–3, 62–3, 65–8, 162–3; of *Bull Durham* 98, 100; interpretation of 63–4; in method acting 85; neglect of 2; Sarandon and 93–4; starting point of performance

40, 43; voice and 127, 129, 130, 136
Se7en 128–30
Secrets and Lies 138–49
Segrave, K. 169
self-confidence 158, 159
semiological/psychoanalytic position 3–4
Sennett, R. 170
sexist stereotype, resistance to 106–7, 117–21, 123
Shaver, Helen 106–25
Shaw, Fiona 153
The Shawshank Redemption 130–1
Shelton, Ron 98, 100, 101
shooting out of sequence 38, 39, 77
silent film: acting on 10–30; literature on 166–7
silent thinking 38
Skinner, Otis 33
sound 5, 132–3; transition to 32–5, 38
soundscape, awareness of 131
soundtrack 126, 131; place of voice in 133–5
speech patterns 66, 67, 113–14
speech training 34
Spice World: The Movie 149
stage acting: compared to screen acting 32, 33, 35–9, 77–8, 153; early 13; study of 4–5, 165–6
stage actors, moving to screen 23–4, 33
stance 13, 16, 17
Stanislavsky, C.S. 3, 80–1, 82, 107, 109, 154; and action 114, 115; and speech 113–14; studies of 167
Stanley, Kim 76
star images 4, 31, 92; Frederic March 69–70; James Mason 70–2
A Star is Born, characterization of Norman Maine 59, 61–8
stardom 163–4; Davis and 53–4; literature on 169, 170
Strasberg, Lee 75–86
Streep, Meryl 92, 94
studio era 5–6, 31–45; research on 168

subtext 18, 140, 154
supporting sound 134–5

Tandy, Jessica 41
Taylor, George 13
technology 5, 76
television performances, Richardson and 157–62
textual analysis 4, 81, 82, 85
theatre, influence on early screen acting 11, 12, 17–24
Thelma & Louise, Sarandon in 92, 93–4, 101–2
Toporkov, Vasily 81
Toy Story 134
training for actors: early twentieth century 16, 23; for screen actors 33–5, 36, 43, 85, 154, 155
Trescony, Al 39
truth 84, 162
Tsikhotsky, Sam 82
Tucker, Patrick 109, 110, 113

USA: English actors in 14; nineteenth-century actors 14

Vardac, Nicholas, *Stage to Screen* 11, 12
variety-house ballet 20–2
'verisimilar code' 11
Victorian theatre: gesture in 11, 12; music in 17
Vincendeau, G. 169
visual effects 102
voice 100, 104, 122, 126; actors' awareness of 127–31; of Davis 52; recording of 131–5, 136; training 154; volume of 96, 113–14, 129–30

Warner, Charles 15–16
Way Down East 19
White Palace 91–2, 93
Widmark, Richard 76
Witches of Eastwick, The 90
writing 153
Wyler, William 56